REAL NUMBERS
Analyzing Income Properties
for a Profitable Investment

REAL NUMBERS
ANALYZING INCOME PROPERTIES
FOR A PROFITABLE INVESTMENT

Joseph T. Sinclair

BUSINESS ONE IRWIN
Homewood, Illinois 60430

Project editor: Jane Lightell
Production manager: Ann Cassady
Designer: Mercedes Santos
Compositor: BookMasters, Inc.
Typeface: 11/13 Times Roman
Printer: Book Press

Library of Congress Cataloging-in-Publication Data

Sinclair, Joseph T.
   Real numbers : analyzing income properties for a profitable investment / Joseph T. Sinclair.
      p.   cm.
   ISBN 1-55623-817-7
   1. Real estate investment—Evaluation.   2. Investment analysis.
I. Title.
HD1382.5.S48   1993
332.63'24—dc20   92–33393

Printed in the United States of America
1 2 3 4 5 6 7 8 9 0BP0 9 8 7 6 5 4 3

To Lani and Brook

ACKNOWLEDGMENTS

A book is written only with assistance from many people. I would like to express my thanks to Joseph P. O'Leary, a former magazine editor and currently a real estate attorney in Evergreen, Colorado, for his editing of a major portion of the manuscript.

The technical review is as important as the editing. It entails submitting appropriate portions of one's manuscript to appropriate experts. And I would like to give my thanks to my colleagues in the real estate business who were kind enough to review select chapters for me. I should say that mentioning them here does not indicate that they either agree with or approve of everything I have presented in this book. Their advice has been invaluable, but I take full responsibility for making the final decisions on the information included and excluded and on how that information is stated. Any errors or misrepresentations should be attributed directly to me.

Robert M. Kagan, currently a residential developer in Northern California, fellow member of the adjunct faculty at Golden Gate University, San Francisco, former Vice President (real estate joint ventures) of Cal Fed Enterprises (a subsidiary of California Federal Bank), former Vice President of Bank of America (real estate joint ventures), generously spent his time providing a technical review of a major portion of the manuscript and additionally spent time discussing many important issues with me personally. Thanks. The following people provided me with technical reviews of specific chapters: Rebecca A. Broyles CCIM, commercial investment broker, Pearl Corporation, Kansas City, Missouri, fellow Certified Commercial Investment Member of the Commercial Investment Real Estate Institute; Robert O. Stevens MAI, commercial appraiser, Grand Junction, Colorado; Kenneth E. Lehrer PhD, real estate consultant and commercial review appraiser, Houston, adjunct faculty member at the University of Houston Graduate School of Business

Administration (real estate), former chairman of the board for several Louisiana savings & loans associations as agent for the Federal Home Loan Bank Board; William C. Witting CRE, real estate consultant and developer, Mt. Vernon, Washington; William D. Flora CPA, real estate and tax accountant, Coopers & Lybrand, San Francisco, fellow alumnus of the University of Michigan Law School; Robert Rosenberg CCIM, commercial investment broker, Investnet, Sacramento; Jerry Warrington, financial institution consultant, President of Financial International Corp., Durango, Colorado, former Senior Vice President and head of commercial lending at Mid Kansas Federal Savings & Loan, Wichita; James H. Cantrell CPM, property and asset manager, Cantrell Harris & Associates, San Francisco, fellow member of the adjunct faculty at Golden Gate University; and Robert Natale JD PhD, Atlanta, Georgia, consultant on commercial loan CMOs (collateralized mortgage obligations), former President Aetna Mortgage Bankers, author of *Property Specific Commercial Mortgage Underwriting*. Thanks.

My agent, Laurie Harper of Sabastian Agency, the preeminent literary agency in the San Francisco Bay Area, was very helpful from the beginning to the end of the long process of writing and publishing this book. Thanks.

There are many other people who also assisted in less direct ways than the people mentioned. My thanks to them too.

And finally, a very big thanks to my spouse Lani and my four-year-old daughter Brook for their support and indulgence during the many hours I labored over the manuscript.

Joseph T. Sinclair

CONTENTS

INTRODUCTION

This is not a book on how to make a million dollars in real estate, part time, in just three days, while working two jobs and taking care of your convalescent grandmother, for no money down, and using other people's money. Whose money? I'm not saying it can't be done. It must be possible, because so many people write books about it. It's just that this book is not about that.

This book is about real estate investment analysis. It teaches you the skills needed to calculate how a property will perform. It doesn't matter whether you are investing in a duplex or in a regional shopping mall, or whether you are highly leveraged or purchasing for cash. It also doesn't matter whether you are an occasional purchaser of small properties or an acquisitions officer buying downtown office buildings for a major pension fund. The same analysis furnishes you with useful numbers. And after the real estate excesses of the 1980s, making accurate calculations regarding real estate performance is more important than ever.

Investment analysis predicts the future. For millenniums, man has attempted to predict the future with varying degrees of success. If you're right, you're a hero (sometimes); and if you're wrong, you're a bum (almost always). You perpetually face the Monday morning quarterbacks who are always right. On the one hand, you can't beat them. On the other hand, they never play in any games. If you want to play, you have to make some assumptions, take some risks, do some research, and take action.

How you make assumptions and how you organize them to make sense for the future are important. For instance, let's say you want to avoid making assumptions altogether on an apartment investment. You base your investment decision on how the property performed last year under another owner and under another property manager. No speculation for you, just a good conservative approach, right? But wait. How will each of the following commonplace factors affect your investment? Consider them each separately, not cumulatively:

1. Expenses are inflating faster than income.
2. A major apartment project is currently being worked through the planning department that will increase the number of apartment units in the area by 35 percent in two years.
3. The population is declining.
4. The region has periodic droughts that invariably kill all the landscaping on the average of one year in five.
5. The property was previously managed by an aggressive and competent property manager. You're going to have your old college buddy, Fred, do it.
6. The units have not been rehabilitated in 15 years.
7. The property is in the "Oil Belt," and the price of oil is headed down.
8. The city has decreed that all rental housing shall be asbestos free within four years.
9. The city's five-year moratorium on the development of new units will be over in three months.
10. HUD is making severe cuts in its rent subsidy program.
11. Single-family home prices are declining.

These factors show you that even in taking a "conservative" approach, you are overlooking events that could impact the value of the property. Before you invest in any property, you should do three things:

1. You must make a broad range of assumptions about the economic environment and the property.
2. You must do some research to test and modify those assumptions.
3. You must organize your calculations so that you can make sense out of the first two.

Fortunately, the third is easy to do. Once mastered, the calculations become routine. With the use of computers, you can make the calculations easily and quickly. Nonetheless, like anything else, you will struggle through the learning process until you practice enough to become skillful.

There's not much in this book about the first two elements of predicting: making assumptions and researching them. But in doing the calculations, you will become more aware of your assumptions and become more sensitive to their effect on the "bottom line" of your calculations. Any attempt of mine to cover assumptions and research adequately would take another book or perhaps two; all I can do is alert you to some common problems.

Thus, this book will stick primarily to the calculations. Calculations are not infallible. But they're useful. They're easy and quick to do with a computer. They make you question your assumptions and motivate you to do supporting research. They give you a basis of comparison between alternative real estate investments. And that's the best you can do.

This book offers you a special format. The numbered chapters 1–27 correspond to line entries in a financial forecast format that is commonly used among real estate professionals. The forecast is the summary of four financial analysis statements:

1. Income and expense.
2. Taxable income.
3. Cash flow.
4. Sales proceeds.

For instance, on line 1 of the forecast, you will find the label Potential Rental Income. Thus, Chapter 1 is entitled Potential Rental Income.

Many of the concepts in the real estate financial reports interrelate, and treating each separately strains the learning process occasionally. Nonetheless, by treating each separately in separate chapters, this book can provide a quick reference for you. You learn best by doing; and when you're doing analysis, a quick reference can be valuable. With that in mind, you will see that this book covers more than just understanding real estate financial reports. It includes learning to create reports, thoroughly and accurately, for yourself or for your employer or clients. But keep in mind that the remainder of the Introduction is an integral part of the book, and you cannot afford to skip over it if you are to understand the book fully.

You are about to experience some exciting education. You will never be intimidated again by anyone in the real estate profession. (And you will be well situated to intimidate others, if that's your wish.) You will learn to accurately calculate real estate financial reports that are useful in making decisions. At the least, you will be confident that you're working with the real numbers.

Pro Forma Real Estate Financial Reports

Income and Expense Statement

Potential Rental Income
−Vacancy and Credit Loss
=Effective Rental Income
+Other Income
=Gross Operating Income
−Operating Expenses
=**Net Operating Income**

Taxable Income Analysis

Net Operating Income
−Interest Expense
−Cost Recovery
−Nonoperating Expenses
=**Taxable Income**

Cash Flow Analysis

Net Operating Income
−Debt Service
−Nonoperating Outlays
−Capital Additions
−Reserves
+Reserves to Additions
=**Cash Flow before Tax**
−Tax Liability
=**Cash Flow after Tax**

Sale Proceeds Analysis

Sale Price
+Reserve Fund
−Loan Balances
−Cost of Sale
=**Sale Proceeds before Tax**
−Tax Liability on Sale
=**Sale Proceeds after Tax**

**Forecast (Combined Multiyear Pro Forma
Real Estate Financial Reports)**

  1   Potential Rental Income

  2 −Vacancy and Credit Loss

  3   Effective Rental Income

  4 +Other Income

  5   Gross Operating Income

  6 −Operating Expenses

  7   **Net Operating Income**

  8 −Interest Expense

  9 −Cost Recovery

10 −Nonoperating Expenses

11   **Taxable Income**

12   Net Operating Income

13 −Debt Service

14 −Nonoperating Outlays

15 −Capital Additions

16 −Reserves

17 +Reserves to Additions

18   **Cash Flow before Tax**

19 −Tax Liability

20   **Cash Flow after Tax**

21   Sale Price

22 +Reserve Fund

23 −Loan Balances

24 −Cost of Sale

25   **Sale Proceeds before Tax**

26 −Tax Liability on Sale

27   **Sale Proceeds after Tax**

Chapters 1–27 correspond to lines 1–27.

POINTS OF VIEW

Numbers are abstract; they are self-evidently correct or incorrect; you can test them mathematically to determine their correctness. Right? Don't be fooled. Numbers have a point of view. To understand real estate numbers, first you have to understand how different points of view affect the numbers. Then you have to determine what point of view is going to be useful to you.

Here are some possible points of view:

1. **Historical**   What happened last year? This is normally considered to be the point of view of the owner, the property manager, or the accountant.
2. **Taxation**   How will the property be taxed? The Internal Revenue Service (IRS) takes this point of view. Because the IRS takes this point of view, the owner or potential owner will be interested in it too.
3. **Seller**   How will the property perform? This is a subjective point of view. The seller estimates this optimistically. The reason is that the better the performance, the higher the price.
4. **Buyer and lender**   How will the property perform? This is another subjective point of view. The buyer and lender are going to be the new investors in this property. They estimate this conservatively.
5. **Real estate professional**   How will the property perform? This is an objective estimate of how the property will perform. At least it's objective until the real estate professional becomes an advocate of either the seller, buyer, or lender.

Four Financial Reports

To understand these points of view better, you first need to understand four concepts that often appear together in such a way in real estate forecasts that they seem to be one or two concepts. Each concept taken by itself is easy to understand. Scrambled together, they can be confusing. These are the concepts:

1. **Income & expense statement** An *objective* analysis that provides the calculation of net operating income (NOI):

   Potential Rental Income
   −Vacancy & Credit Loss
   Effective Rental Income
   +Other Income
   Gross Operating Income
   −Operating Expenses
   Net Operating Income

2. **Income tax analysis** A *subjective* analysis that estimates taxable income:

   Net Operating Income
   −Interest Expense
   −Cost Recovery
   −Nonoperating Expenses
   Taxable Income

3. **Cash flow analysis** A *subjective* analysis that furnishes the forecast of the actual cash going into or out of an investor's pocket:

   Net Operating Income
   −Debt Service
   −Nonoperating Outlays
   −Capital Additions
   −Reserves
   +Reserves to Additions
   Cash Flow before Tax
   −Tax Liability
   Cash Flow after Tax

4. **Sale proceeds analysis** A *subjective* analysis that predicts the cash flow going into or out of an investor's pocket resulting from the sale of the property:

   Sale Price
   +Reserve Fund
   −Loan Balances
   −Cost of Sale
   Sale Proceeds before Tax
   −Tax Liability on Sale
   Sale Proceeds after Tax

To make things a little more confusing, the cash flow and the sale proceeds each come in two types: "before tax" and "after tax."

To understand how these concepts fit together more graphically, look at the forecast format on page xxv and note that the income and expense concept includes lines 1 through 7 in the forecast. The taxable income concept includes lines 7 through 11. Note that the taxable income analysis includes net operating income from the income & expense statement. The cash flow idea is covered by lines 12 through 20. Keep in mind that the cash flow analysis incorporates net operating income from the income & expense statement and also determines tax liability by using taxable income from the taxable income analysis. And finally, the concept of sale proceeds includes lines 21 through 27.

Income & Expense Statement

Your first concern is with the income & expense statement. The essence of this idea is that expenses subtracted from income equals net operating income (NOI). For income properties, NOI is a direct determinate of the value of the property (see Chapter 39). The higher the NOI, the higher the value of the property. Thus, the seller desires to maximize income and minimize expenses in any estimate. The buyer desires to do the opposite. The property manager and the accountant want to report the numbers exactly as they happened in the last year. A real estate professional (commercial investment broker, commercial appraiser, asset manager, developer, etc.) desires to make an accurate estimate. Once an accurate estimate has been made, an advocacy point of view on behalf of a client may be adopted, if appropriate.

Another way to understand the various points of view is to look at the variety of income & expense statements:

1. **Owner's statement** This is the income and expense statement prepared by the property manager or an accountant. It is a historical record of what actually happened in the operation of the property. It is unlikely to be arranged in the proper format or to be scrutinized for adherence to investment real estate criteria. It is essentially raw data.

2. **Reconstructed statement**   This is an owner's statement that has been adjusted to adhere to investment real estate criteria. It is adjusted historical data.

3. **Income & expense statement**   This is a pro forma estimate for the property of the next year's income and expenses. It considers only the operation of the property and does not include the effects of ownership. In other words, it is an objective statement that should be the same for any owner. It is estimated using both past performance data from the property and current market data.

4. **Seller's pro forma**   This is a pro forma income and expense statement that been shaded toward the optimistic to enhance the seller's negotiating position.

5. **Buyer's pro forma**   This is a pro forma income & expense statement that has been shaded toward the conservative to enhance the buyer's negotiating position.

This book is addressed to real estate professionals (but see The Book's Point of View). Since real estate professionals have a professional duty to make an accurate forecast, the goal of this book is to show you how to carry through a process of financial analysis that yields objective information on the property being considered. It is the contention of this book that your first obligation as a real estate professional is to create an objective pro forma income & expense statement (paragraph 3 immediately above). With that in mind, when this book refers to the income & expense statement, it is an objective statement. The income & expense statement is a profit and loss statement *for the property*, not the owner. If the property is operated according to the standards of professional property management, the property should perform the same regardless of ownership. The income and expenses are objective. They will be the same for each owner. In one sense, the income & expense statement is idealistic because it doesn't take into consideration different styles of ownership and operation. In another sense, it is also practical because you must have an objective standard on which to evaluate the future performance of the property and compare it to other properties.

Owner

The historical point of view is yesterday's news. To determine what happened, a property manager or an accountant analyzes the books and creates an operating statement that summarizes how the property performed financially. Historical financial data is ultimately the realm of the accountant. As a real estate professional, you should tread in this realm with caution. Although there may be a reasonable purpose for you to adjust historical financial data to meet investment real estate criteria and create a reconstructed statement, such an adjustment should be made in accord with the owner's accountant.

Future

Although accountants focus on yesterday, sellers, buyers, and real estate professionals focus on tomorrow. Buyers are interested in the IRS point of view too, so they can estimate the affect of taxation on tomorrow's investment performance. Lenders must estimate how the property will perform in the next year because they will be an investor. Real estate professionals serve sellers, buyers, and lenders. Real estate professionals are expected to become involved in this estimation of a property's future income and expenses.

Thus, investment real estate financial analysis focuses on what will happen tomorrow. Specifically, in our culture, the year is the most predominate time frame for estimating investment performance. Therefore, the next year becomes the initial time unit for the evaluation of real estate investment performance. Historical data often plays an important role in estimating what will happen in the next year, but it is unlikely that last year's income and expenses will be the same as next year's income and expenses.

Accountants also do forecasting, so this is not the exclusive realm of real estate professionals and investors. Estimating an income & expense statement requires much market data, however, and real estate professionals may be better able to obtain and use real estate market information. If you are to become involved in the process of calculating income & expense statements, you need to learn to obtain the data and do the calculations properly and according to investment real estate criteria. This book will assist you in such learning. And if you are an experienced real estate analyst, you will find this book a useful reference for resolving analysis problems that arise from time to time.

Real Estate Professional

What is a real estate professional? A real estate professional is person, duly trained, who has a relationship to a real estate asset. It could be a real estate broker, mortgage broker, appraiser, real estate consultant, income property loan officer, asset manager, professional investor, or anyone concerned with the performance of the property as an investment. There is a certain logic that specifically refines the point of view of the real estate professional.

A real estate professional's first responsibility is to objectivity. Even when taking an advocacy point of view, he or she should know the facts first. Otherwise, the professional and the client are being deluded. Thus, the first task of a real estate professional is to estimate the future performance of the property as objectively as possible. An appraiser has an ethical responsibility to be objective unless disclosing to the world that he or she is being otherwise.

As an asset manager, real estate consultant, or mortgage broker, you have a responsibility to your client to be objective. The development of a subsequent advocacy position is permissible at your client's request. Caution must be used, however, if presenting an advocacy position. Your credibility is on the line, and there is also a danger of misrepresentation. To protect your good reputation and to minimize your liability, you should always disclose that you are representing your client's point of view and that nonclients should develop their own information and data concerning the property. Thus, realistically, you are in a position similar to that of an appraiser.

As a real estate broker, you usually have a legal and ethical obligation to represent sellers regardless of whether you are working with the buyer or seller. It is not uncommon, however, to legally represent a buyer based on a "buyer's broker" agreement. In either case, you have an ethical obligation to provide your client with objective estimates first. A subsequent advocacy position requested by your client is permissible and even expected for the purposes of marketing a property or negotiating a transaction. You will be wise, however, to avoid an advocacy position so extreme that it constitutes blatant misrepresentation. And brokers representing sellers should always include disclaimers on pro forma forecasts.

Your estimates regarding the future performance of income real estate cannot be absolutely accurate because you are predicting the future. But any shading to create an advocacy position must be done subsequent to the creation of an objective income & expense statement. By shading the line entries as you make the calculations, you will lose control of the process. The results can be disastrous, embarrassing, or self-defeating. Once you have an objective analysis, however, you can go back and shade it appropriately. There is nothing unethical about shading. In real estate analysis, there is always a range of values. In representing a client, you are simply at the end of the range that best represents your client. It's only when you provide information outside a reasonable range of values that it is unfair dealing, misrepresentation, or fraud; and you may lose your creditability or jeopardize your client's creditability.

Seller

The seller estimates the future performance of the property to provide sales information for prospective buyers, to provide operational information for prospective lenders, and to establish a price for the property. In either case, sellers are invariably optimistic in making such estimates. This becomes an advocacy point of view. As such, it is hardly objective. It is usually shaded in favor of the highest believable performance to enhance the seller's negotiating position.

Buyer

The buyer wants to enhance negotiation too. The buyer is more skeptical and conservative regarding the future performance of the property. The buyer's estimates of performance are likely to be lower than the seller's. Although this position is often justified by prudence, it is done to enhance the buyer's negotiating position as well. It is seldom any more objective than the estimate of the seller.

Internal Revenue Service

The IRS point of view is not determined by the income & expense statement. The taxable income analysis represents the IRS point of view. The taxable income analysis incorporates subjective information. Different owners use different-size loans and get different interest rates resulting in different-size interest deductions. They can choose different cost recovery periods for depreciation. And they have different subjective expenses (nonoperating expenses) that are tax deductible. The income tax analysis is an estimate of what the IRS point of view will be based on this subjective criteria (i.e., how much the taxable income will be?).

Accountants and tax attorneys calculate tax liability. There is no reason for you to duplicate their efforts. Yet tax liability does have an effect on the performance of a real estate investment. You cannot ignore it completely. For many clients, the tax liability must be estimated. The estimation can be done drawing on your tax knowledge with additional input from your client's tax adviser. No one, however, should ever be led to believe that this estimate of tax liability is the same as filing a tax return or is necessarily any more accurate than any other assumption about the future.

Investor

There is another place for subjective analysis, and that's the cash flow analysis. The cash flow analysis tells just one thing: how much cash is going into the investor's pocket from the real estate investment (positive cash flow) or how much cash is flowing out of the investor's pocket into the real estate investment to keep it alive (negative cash flow). Let's look at one reason why the income & expense statement does not do this. Suppose you have an income property producing a NOI of $200,000 annually. Suppose the owner has borrowed to invest in the property and has annual loan payments (debt service) of $160,000. Regardless of the debt service, the NOI is still $200,000 per year. But the cash flowing into the owner's pocket is only $40,000 per year. The cash flow reflects what's left of the NOI after the loan payments are made. The sale proceeds analysis is similar to the cash flow analysis. It's a customized analysis reflecting the investment choices of the investor (e.g., the loan balance of the loan, if any, is subtracted from the sale price). It, too, can be calculated both before tax and after tax.

The annual cash flow comes in two varieties: "before tax" and "after tax." The tax liability based on the taxable income from the taxable income analysis is used for determining the after-tax cash flow.

It is noteworthy that the starting point for the taxable income analysis and the cash flow analysis is NOI. Likewise, the starting point for the sale proceeds analysis is the sale price, which is usually directly determined by a cap rate applied to the NOI. Thus, all the custom calculations—subjective calculations—are based on the objective determination of NOI.

EXAMPLES

To assist you in comprehending how these ideas (income & expense statement, taxable income analysis, cash flow analysis, and sale proceeds analysis) work using common investment properties, the appendices contains these analyses:

1. Appendix I: Maplewood Apartments, a 100-unit apartment project.
2. Appendix II: Ridgeline Tower, a 60,000 square foot, five-story office building.
3. Appendix III: Crossroads Plaza, a 60,000 square-foot neighborhood shopping center.
4. Appendix IV: Fourplex, a four-unit apartment building.

These properties are fictitious but are based on actual real estate projects. These analyses will be referred to throughout the book. The examples are not necessarily "typical" of their genre. Rather, they are presented to illustrate a variety of calculations in a realistic setting. For instance, for Maplewood Apartments, refrigerators are presented as an example of a capital replacement. Carpeting, which would be treated identically in a typical property, is virtually ignored in the Maplewood Apartments by presenting the fact that all carpeting was recently replaced and will be assumed to last the duration of the holding period. To have included a schedule of carpeting replacement would have been unnecessarily redundant for learning purposes. These examples do not represent typical rates of return either. The yields of investment real estate vary widely from place to place, from property to property, and from time to time.

The examples are based on a world in which rents, expenses, and property values are increasing at a normal rate of inflation, and occupancy is 95 percent. When the real estate market is stable and supply and demand are in balance, the examples will seem reasonable. Certainly, there are times everywhere when the real estate market is unstable, and the assumptions made for the forecast examples will seem utterly unrealistic. But examples must be chosen, and optimistic examples have been selected to be more utilitarian learning devices. The book covers analysis thoroughly, but you must make your own assumptions based on your market research. Each real estate market is unique, and there are always local markets that are not in synchronization with regional or national real estate and economic cycles.

The Property

Exactly what is the "truth" about a property? In essence, it is perceiving an income property without a specific owner. Objectivity requires that only those expenses that all owners will experience shall be included in the calculations. Only the income that can reasonably be expected in the market environment shall be included, and it shall be primarily rental income. A vacancy factor accurately reflecting the current market shall be used. And there is an assumption that the property shall be competently managed. Rather than being tied to a specific owner's competency, whims, eccentricities, good fortune, or bad fortune, the objective income & expense statement is a year's projection of average competent performance. Therein lies the value of the property: the ability to produce a certain amount of income with average competent management within existing market conditions.

Once this essential reality about the property is established, the succeeding real estate financial reports customize the performance of the property for a specific investor. These distinctions, once understood, make it easier to calculate an intelligent forecast. But it takes experience to assimilate these subtleties.

THE BOOK'S POINT OF VIEW

It is the assumption of this book that you, the reader, are a real estate professional. Because real estate professionals represent parties to real estate transactions, they have a fiduciary obligation as agents to represent the best interests of their clients. For the purposes of this book, if you were a commercial investment broker, asset manager, or another real estate professional representing a prospective investor, your best interests would be identical to your investor's best interests under the obligation of fiduciary duty. *Therefore, this book is addressed to both real estate professionals and the investors they represent.* It is addressed to both as if they were one in the same.

Analysis is usually done in anticipation of a transaction. For a seller, it is done in anticipation of marketing the property. For a buyer, it is done to evaluate a property for purchase. An appraiser usually evaluates a property before a lender makes a loan or before a buyer completes a purchase transaction. Occasionally, an analysis is done as an asset management chore. A lender or asset manager may evaluate a property as part of a portfolio management procedure. When this type of evaluation is done, it is always with an eye to the future: Should the asset be disposed of or retained?

For these reasons, the underlying assumption in this book is that the property is being analyzed for purchase. Thus, *the point of view of this book is that of a real estate professional or investor evaluating a property for potential acquisition.*

THE QUEST FOR ACCURACY

What are you trying to do here? You are not trying to make sense out of last year's performance. That is the job of the accountant. As a real estate professional, it is customarily part of your job to predict the future. Predicting the future means estimating next year's performance.

Quite naturally, you will look to the past to determine the future. Last year's expenses may be a good starting point from which to estimate expenses for the next year. Last year's rents are a guideline for predicting the next year's. There may be a trend in the vacancy rate upon which you can rely for estimating next year's vacancy losses. But buyers don't buy based on how the property performed last year. They buy based on a sensible estimate of how the property will perform in the next year and perhaps in the years beyond.

Unfortunately, there are some real pitfalls in predicting the future. Ask any soothsayer. For that matter, ask any investor, lender, or developer. In fact, it is impossible to predict the future accurately on an ongoing basis. The thesis of this book is that a forecast correctly calculated, based on assumptions intelligently conceived, is the most reliable you can make. This is a *pro forma* forecast. It estimates the future performance *according to a customarily prescribed form.* But keep in mind that the fatal flaw of any pro forma forecast is that predicting the future is a risky business at best.

The alternative to creating a pro forma forecast is making no assumptions at all. It is clear that there is no such thing as making no assumptions about the future. Since assumptions are always made, why not subject them to rigorous analysis and then organize them? It doesn't guarantee accuracy, but it's the best you can do. That's what pro formas are all about. That's what investing in real estate is all about. That's how value is determined. In this book, when income & expense statements, taxable income analyses, cash flow analyses, and sale proceeds analyses are discussed, the focus is estimating performance for the next year. Forecasts (projections) estimate performance over multiyear periods.

Numbers

Although accuracy is important in doing forecasts, precision is not. If your numbers are a little different than the book's, the validity of your forecasts or the book's forecasts is not necessarily conflicting or in error. Calculators and computer programs act differently in different situations. They may round up, or they may round down. They may use numbers calculated to nine decimal places. Or they may take the integer. And people do the same. The result is that forecasts done by different people, even using the same numbers and assumptions, seldom match exactly. This is not cause to be concerned when you keep in mind that you are attempting to predict the future.

In doing forecasts, the easiest method for people to use in handling numbers is to take the integer. This means that you never read to the right of the decimal point. You truncate at the decimal point. You read and use only the numbers to the left of the decimal point (i.e., whole numbers). In other words, you don't waste time and energy rounding up, rounding down, or using fractions. For example, it is seldom productive to keep track of the cents when calculating dollars. Only the dollars are of interest. What is the following number?

$1,091.67

If you take the integer rather than rounding, it is

$1,091

There are, of course, exceptions to the practice of taking the integer, and your common sense will assist you to make the appropriate exceptions.

A similar practice to taking the integer is simply reading the decimals when you are using numbers that are appropriate to be expressed in decimals. That means that you don't round. For instance, what is the following rate of return to one decimal place?

11.38 percent

If you simply read the decimal rather than rounding, it is:

11.3 percent

Taking the integer or reading the decimal is accurate and appropriate for the type of real estate analysis calculations covered in this book. But in many circumstances, you will have little control over what computers and calculators do. Don't let it worry you. Don't be distressed by small differences.

You may notice specifically in this book that the numbers in Chapters 28–31 (forecast examples) were calculated using an HP-12C financial calculator, taking the integer and reading the decimal. In contrast, the corresponding forecasts in Appendices I–IV were calculated using JavelinPlus, a spreadsheet-like computer program. There are some insignificant differences in the numbers.

Tax

The income taxation of real estate is well beyond the scope of this book, and there are many excellent books that treat the income taxation of real estate thoroughly. The tax treatment in this book is simple and straightforward, but superficial. Tax does have an impact on real estate analysis, and it must be included in any comprehensive real estate analysis. The tax calculations in this book, however, should be taken as examples of how tax calculations are incorporated into the analysis, not as examples of a definitive application of the Tax Code to real estate investments. You can refine your tax calculations as much as suits your needs, and you will get a good idea from this book how to incorporate such refined tax calculations into the analysis in a meaningful way.

Regardless of how refined you make your tax calculations, you must keep in mind that you are not filing a tax return. You are only estimating the future impact of income tax on the real estate investment. The quest for precision in tax calculations can quickly reach the point of diminishing returns. And, no matter how precise you make your calculations, Congress may change the Tax Code.

Classic tax principles are generally applied throughout the book wherever appropriate. An attempt has been made to limit the coverage of newer tax principles to Chapter 32 with the thought that only Chapter 32 will become outdated as the Tax Code changes.

What Year?

If you are doing an after-tax forecast that is important to tax planning, the calendar year (or tax year, if the investor is not on a calendar year) is important. A five-year projection will include the remainder of the calendar year (or tax year) after the closing and the next five calendar years (or tax years).

Many forecasts ignore calendar years (or tax years). If you close the purchase transaction on October 1, the first year of the forecast is assumed to run from October 1 to September 30 of the next year. Even though the first year and subsequent years of the investment are not calendar years (or tax years), they are treated as if they were. The forecasts in this book are done on such a basis. (See Appendices I–IV.)

PART 1

INCOME & EXPENSE STATEMENT

Two essential characteristics compose the idea of the income & expense statement. First, it is a pro forma statement; that is, it is an estimate of the income and expenses for the next year reported in the customary form. Second, it is a statement of how the property will operate, not how the investor will fare.

Although any number of years can be projected with multiple income & expense statements, the first year following the acquisition is the most crucial. The first year is often used as the basis to predict the income and expenses of succeeding years. It is the year in which a prediction is most likely to be accurate because it's the near future. Although last year's income and expenses are relevant to predict the future, parties to a transaction do not use such figures to make decisions without making adjustments first. Therefore, the income and expenses anticipated for the next year are covered in this part of the book and are used in making decisions.

Keep in mind that last year's income & expense statement is the realm of the accountant, not the real estate professional or real estate investor. It is an established accounting record and a summation. You will want to be careful not to adjust or reorganize last year's income & expense statement without assistance from an accountant, particularly when making representations to potential buyers or clients.

Above all, the income & expense statement is objective. No adjustments are made for the ownership or potential ownership of the property. In fact, a reasonable and prudent owner is assumed. The income & expense statement is an estimate of how the property will perform. The effect of ownership on the property (i.e., the owner's tax situation and means of financing) is considered in the subsequent analyses (chapters 8–27) but not here. Net operating income (NOI) is the bottom line of the income & expense statement. Because the NOI is the result of an objective estimate, the NOI is useful in property valuation.

Here is the form for the pro forma income & expense statement and the corresponding chapters:

Chapters

1 Potential Rental Income
2 −Vacancy & Credit Loss
3 Effective Rental Income
4 +Other Income
5 Gross Operating Income
6 −Operating Expenses
7 **Net Operating Income**

CHAPTER 1

POTENTIAL RENTAL INCOME

Potential Rental Income
−Vacancy & Credit Loss
  Effective Rental Income
+Other Income
  Gross Operating Income
−Operating Expenses
  Net Operating Income

MARKET DATA

Potential rental income starts the quest for reliable information. This data comes from the market. A good property manager continually tests the rents of a property against the market. If its rents are lower than the market, they are raised to market. If they are higher than the market, they may have to be lowered to keep tenants. Thus, potential rental income in a well-managed property is always determined by market.

Much of the data that you need to establish rents can be found locally. Call owners, leasing agents, property managers, brokers, and appraisers. Many markets have market surveys that can be purchased. Some markets have publications that include useful statistics. In other markets, newspapers sometimes do market surveys and publish them.

APARTMENTS

Take a new apartment project as a example. The Lakeview Apartments offer 100 units. Twenty of the units have one bedroom. Twenty of the units have three bedrooms. The remaining units have two bedrooms.

Taking careful notes, you talk to nine property managers in the area managing similar projects. You conclude from your research that the one-bedroom units will rent for $400 per month, the two-bedrooms units for $500 per month, and the three-bedroom units for $600 per month. What is the potential rental income?

The formula you will use is easy. The goal is to determine the potential annual income from the units. So, you take the number of units and multiply by the monthly rent and finally multiply by 12.

Number	Units	Monthly Rent	Total Monthly	Total Annual
20	1 BR	$400	$ 8,000	$ 96,000
60	2 BR	500	30,000	360,000
20	3 BR	600	12,000	144,000
100	Total		$50,000	$600,000

These rent calculations assume that the project is 100 percent rented, 100 percent of the time. There are two factors here, the number of units and time. Assuming all the units are rented all the time, Lakeview Apartments has the potential to produce rental income of $600,000 per year.

Is this possible? It may be possible, but it's unlikely. Even in a full apartment project, tenants come and go. Apartments have to be cleaned between tenants. Thus, some vacancy is likely even in a very good rental market. There is a place where you can adjust for such vacancy in the income & expense statement, but here only the 100 percent potential of the project is expressed.

RENT–UP

Naturally, it will take time to rent these new apartment units. Suppose your research indicates that the project has been renting apartments for two months already at the rate of 10 apartments per month as was predicted by an absorption study. At this rate, it will take another eight months to rent the entire project to its maximum. What adjustment must you make in potential rental income for the loss of income?

There is no adjustment to be made. Potential rental income always shows the potential of the property; that is, it shows 100 percent of the units rented 100 percent of the time. Since there is no adjustment to be made to potential rental income for the loss of rent during the rent-up period, there has to be an adjustment somewhere. Where it's made depends on the situation.

For instance, if the seller (developer) gives the buyer a full-income guarantee (guarantees the full potential rental income for a period regardless of vacancy), the adjustment for rent-up is made outside the pro forma. In effect, the adjustment is the guarantee itself. Without a guarantee, however, the adjustment can be made in nonoperating expenses and nonoperating outlays. The adjustment comes from the absorption schedule:

Month	Rent Collected	Potential Rent	Rent Loss
1	$ 5,000	$ 50,000	($ 45,000)
2	10,000	50,000	(40,000)
3	15,000	50,000	(35,000)
4	20,000	50,000	(30,000)
5	25,000	50,000	(25,000)
6	30,000	50,000	(20,000)
7	35,000	50,000	(15,000)
8	40,000	50,000	(10,000)
9	45,000	50,000	(5,000)
10	47,500	50,000	(2,500)
Total	$272,500	$500,000	($227,500)

The absorption schedule shows a rent loss of $227,500 for the first year of operation. In the tenth month, the property stabilizes at 5 percent vacancy.

CURRENT RENTS

Suppose that Lakeview Apartments is a one-year-old complex instead of new and is currently rented with normal occupancy at $370 for a one-bedroom unit, $485 for a two-bedroom unit, and $575 for a three-bedroom unit. Assume market rents are the same as shown in the first schedule above. This situation indicates the project is "rented under the market": it could be getting higher rents. Assuming there's nothing wrong with the property, the current owner is not managing Lakeview Apartments effectively. Which rents do you use for potential rental income?

You must assume that the next owner of the property is going to be an effective property manager and is going to raise the rents to market. Thus, potential rental income is determined by the market, not the owner. Market rents have nothing to do with who owns the property. Market rents are decided by supply and demand.

If the rents that the property is getting are below market, this raises a concern that the property may have a problem that causes the rents to be lower. Certainly, you will want to investigate. For example, were you to discover that Lakeview Apartments has an underdesigned air conditioning and heating system that is a source of constant irritation to the tenants, that might explain the lower rents. In such a case, the current rents of the project, which seem to be below market, may actually be at market. Because of the defective design, the units are not equivalent to other similar apartments that do have adequate air conditioning and heating, and Lakeview Apartments cannot get equivalent rents. Thus, you are justified in adjusting your research data; and you are justified in using the current rents as being the market rents. Without such a specific justified reason for adjusting market rents, however, it is the market that dictates the rents. The current rents of the property are just one piece of evidence of market rents and must be considered along with other evidence.

TIMING

Unfortunately, real estate is a messy business. Although they may be easy, calculations are seldom simple. The timing of rents is a good example. Suppose that Lakeview Apartments is five years old and one-bedroom units are rented for $390, two-bedroom units for $490, and three-bedroom units for $590. The current market rents are as stated in the first rent schedule above ($400, $500, and $600). As vacant units are rented, the rents are raised to market rent. The rent schedule we used for Lakeview Apartments as a new project won't work here. Why? Because all the units were not rented for the same amount at the same time. Only the ones becoming vacant now are rented at the current market rents.

There are many different possibilities. The apartments could be rented on a year's lease or on a six-month lease. Perhaps there are no leases, only month-to-month tenancies with a few months notice required for rent increases. Each lease or tenancy will have started in a different month. Periodically, the rents for new tenants are adjusted to market, so the same units rented in different months throughout the year may have different rents.

Remember that your goal is to estimate income for the next year, the next 12 months. The best way to accurately estimate rents is to analyze each unit individually. If the rent for the unit is below market, you must determine the earliest time it can be raised to market. If rents are going up, or down, you must determine how many adjustments are to be made in the rent for the unit before the end of the next 12 months. Once that is determined, the estimated income for the unit can be charted and totaled. Once the estimated rent for each unit is totaled, the total rent for the project can be calculated. And that is the potential rental income.

That's a lot of work, and normal standards of accuracy may not require such a thorough examination. It may be reasonable to analyze groups of units (e.g., all units rented in April). That would make your analysis easier. Whatever strategy you can devise to streamline the analysis—and still maintain accuracy—will lessen your work load. If rents are adjusted for all units at the same time, the analysis is easiest.

For instance, assume that at Lakeview Apartments all the rents are increased simultaneously twice each year on April 1 and October 1 and that every tenant is on a month-to-month tenancy. Your first year pro forma starts July 1 and ends June 30 the next year. The current rents stated above are in effect on July 1. Accordingly, they will go up October 1 and in the following year on April 1. Assume a $10 per unit increase in October and a $10 per unit increase the following April. The rent schedule will be as follows:

Number	Units	Monthly Rent		Periodic Rent
20	1 BR	$390	× 3	$ 23,400
		400	× 6	48,000
		410	× 3	24,600
60	2 BR	490	× 3	88,200
		500	× 6	180,000
		510	× 3	91,800
20	3 BR	590	× 3	35,400
		600	× 6	72,000
		610	× 3	36,600
100		Annual total		$600,000

The potential rental income for the pro forma year is $600,000 as is shown in the preceding chart. Every situation is different. Every chart is going to look different. Some may be simple. Some may be complicated. But accuracy requires more than just a superficial look. (See Chapter 28 for a more detailed analysis of apartments.)

INCENTIVES

In competitive markets, particularly ones where vacancy is high, incentives (concessions or abatements) may be given to tenants to move in—or to stay in—an apartment project. These incentives may come in various forms. However they are accounted for by the property manager, they must reduce potential rental income if not made as part of a start-up promotion.

For example, suppose tenants at Lakeview Apartments who sign a one-year lease are given a free trip to Hawaii if they stay and pay rent for the full year. If the property manager buys a packaged Hawaiian trip for $625, the rent for the year for each unit for which the trip is awarded is decreased by $625.

When an apartment project is being leased for the first time, however, after initial construction or after a thorough rehabilitation, there is usually a budget for promotional (start-up) expenses. This is a nonoperating expense. If this Hawaiian trip is a legitimate promotional expense used to fill the apartment project quickly at market rents, then this expense is properly categorized as a one-time nonoperating promotional expense. If, however, the trip incentive is used to lure tenants into units at rents above market, the cost of the trip must somehow be shown to decrease the income of the property rather than to be shown as a promotional expense.

When the rent is not above market and the trip incentive is written off as a normal operating expense, it is a wash, and the net operating income (NOI) stays the same. Perhaps there is no distortion. But if the next year the prior year's rent is the same (or adjusted higher for inflation) and the incentive is not projected as an expense, the forecast may be misleading. The rent for the next year may not be realized without the incentive continuing through that year. The best practice is to avoid distortion in future projections by decreasing potential rental income by the amount of the incentive.

Of course, if the incentive is "free rent" instead of a Hawaiian trip, the principle is the same. It must decrease the income of the property or be a one-time promotional expense associated with a lease-up program.

OFFICES

When an office building is new, a rent schedule is made to guide the leasing. First, the building must be properly measured to determine the leasable space. The Building Owners and Managers Association (BOMA) has a guide that sets the standard methodology for doing this. It is the *Standard Method for Measuring Floor Area in Office Buildings.* It includes three types of measurements: (1) usable area, (2) rentable area, and (3) construction area. You are interested in the "rentable area," which includes a pro rata portion of the common areas of the building for each suite. When doing office rent research, make sure that you know whether the information you obtain on the rent per square foot (SF) per year is for usable area or rentable area. Normally, it will be for rentable area.

The rent schedule will show the different rents for different parts of the building (e.g., higher rent for the side of the building with the good view) and for different-size suites (e.g., tenants in smaller suites usually pay a higher rent per SF). For instance, you determine that there are four levels of rent for a 100,000-square-foot office building. You assume that 60 percent of the building will be leased to tenants taking large spaces with 40 percent of the building being leased to tenants taking small spaces. The 25 percent of space with a prime view will be spread evenly between large and small tenants:

Tenants	Size (SF)	Rent/SF/Year	Rent
Large/with view	15,000	$13.75	$ 206,250
Large/without view	45,000	13.00	585,000
Small/with view	10,000	14.75	147,500
Small/without view	30,000	14.00	420,000
Total	100,000		$1,358,750

This is a simple way of looking at a new office building, but you can make it as complex as the market demands.

As with new apartment units, you will have to make some assumptions regarding the length of time it will take the building to become fully leased. Then you can determine the rent loss due to the lease-up of the building. But the potential rental income shows all the rent as if the building were 100 percent leased. The loss due to absorption is shown as a nonoperating expense (adjustment) and a nonoperating outlay.

For an office building that is leased, the timing considerations require that you analyze *every lease* and chart every lease in a rent schedule. That is the only accurate way of determining the potential rental income for future years. For anticipated vacancies due to the expiration of lease terms, assumptions must be made regarding when such space will be re-leased and on what terms. (This is treated in more detail in Chapter 29.)

RENT CONCESSIONS

Free rent may be a legitimate promotional expense when it is used in moderation and used only to fill up a new office building quickly at market rents. As a promotional expense, it is a nonoperating expense and a nonoperating outlay. This promotional technique is prone to abuse, however, and must be evaluated carefully.

When a substantial amount of free rent is granted, and it is used by the tenant at the beginning of the lease, it usually distorts the financial performance of the property in later years. For instance, suppose the following five-year rent schedule is established, but the tenant is given the first year's tenancy free:

Year	Rent	
1	$230,000	(rent concession = $230,000)
2	250,000	
3	270,000	
4	290,000	
5	310,000	

The tenant, of course, is going to compare the total cost of the lease to competing leasing opportunities in the market. In doing so, the tenant will average the yearly rent, do a discounted cash flow analysis of the lease cash flows, calculate the total rent to be paid, or use some other calculation device that rationalizes the schedule of rent actually paid. Such a rationalization is required for comparative purposes.

The owner is going to show the rent concession as a promotional expense in the first year. After that, the owner shows a normally performing property. The free rent of the first year will not be shown to decrease the rent levels of the later years and will not be shown to decrease the NOIs of the later years. With the value of the property determined by the NOI (see Chapter 39), the value of the property after the first year will not be shown to be affected by the free rent. Yet the tenant made the decision to lease based on an evaluation of the overall lease. It is clear that if market rents stay level, the space cannot be leased again at the rent specified in the lease.

When analyzing a property, you must get accurate information on rent concessions and then adjust the rent downward for the term of the lease using a method that makes sense. What method makes sense? Use the method the tenants are using. Unfortunately, the tenants may be using a variety of methods. Additionally, other office building owners may be granting varying amounts of free rent in widely varying configurations. The distortions caused by these practices may make it difficult or impossible to determine what market rent is.

Potentially, the most accurate method of redistributing free rent over the term of the lease is using discounted cash flow analysis. It is doubtful, however, that most tenants are sophisticated enough to use such a method. A simpler technique is probably more appropriate. If the rent were flat for the five-year lease term, simply reducing the rent 20 percent to compensate for the one year of free rent is probably what manyprospective tenants would do. For rents increasing each year, a pro rata arithmetic calculation that accomplishes the same effect might be appropriate:

Year		Adjusted Rent	
1	$ 230,000 − 17.037% =	$ 190,815	
2	250,000 − 17.037% =	207,407	
3	270,000 − 17.037% =	224,000	
4	290,000 − 17.037% =	240,593	
5	310,000 − 17.037% =	257,185	
Total	$1,350,000	$1,120,000	Total adjusted rent

In the preceding calculations, the annual rents are reduced by the percentage of the total attributable to the rent conceded. This book does not offer a definitive way to make this adjustment calculation. Nonetheless, the adjustment must be made. If there is a standard way to make such adjustments in the market, use that method. If not, use a method that approximates what most prospective tenants are using. Your method should reflect what is actually happening in the market.

SHOPPING CENTERS

Anchor tenants draw customers into a shopping center. For instance, in a neighborhood shopping center, it is often a supermarket that draws the customers. In an enclosed mall, the department stores draw the customers. The anchor tenant takes the attitude that its presence creates potential customers for other retail businesses. The owner of the shopping center takes the attitude that the shopping center creates a better place to locate a retail business. As a result, the nonanchor tenants pay a premium rent while the anchor tenants enjoy a low rent. In other words, the nonanchor tenants, in effect, subsidize the anchor tenants.

A complicating factor is the practice of percentage rents. Because shopping centers boost a tenant's business so that it is substantially greater than in freestanding building, the owners of shopping centers want to share in that boom. On the other hand, if that boom doesn't materialize, the tenant doesn't want to pay for it. Thus, a common arrangement is for the tenant to pay a percentage of its gross sales as rent. There is usually a minimum rent (base rent) too. The tenant pays the base rent or the percentage rent, whichever is higher.

There is another complicating factor. Some types of tenants do better than others in a shopping center. It is difficult for an owner to treat them all the same. Thus, through years of national experience, certain leasing practices have evolved. Sometimes it is not practical to ascertain such customary practices through local research. National statistics must be consulted. For instance, national statistics may tell you that the mean rent for family shoe stores in neighborhood shopping centers is $7.83/SF/year with a percentage rent of 5 percent and that the mean sales per square foot per year is $129. The same statistics may tell you that for jewelry stores the mean rent is $14.43/SF/year with a percentage rent of 6 percent and that the mean sales per square foot is $227. To anticipate what the potential rent will be in a new shopping center, you must make assumptions as to the types of tenants and the levels of rent they will pay as well as assumptions regarding the other factors, such as absorption, already discussed in this chapter.

The tenant mix is important for shopping centers. If the right combination of tenants is brought together into the shopping center, it may attract more customers and do better than if it is filled with tenants haphazardly. Thus, a shopping center owner may wait for the right tenant to come along rather than lease the remaining space to just any tenant desiring to lease it. So it is sometimes difficult to predict the absorption. Here is a potential rent schedule for a new shopping center:

Store	Sales $/GLA*	SF	% Rent	% Rent /SF	Base Rent /SF	Year 1 Rent
Supermarket	$369	40,000	1½%	$ 5.54	$ 5.93	$237,200
Drug store	283	10,000	2½%	7.08	7.29	72,900
Hardware	156	10,000	5%	7.80	8.05	80,500
Restaurant	219	5,000	5%	10.95	11.35	56,750
Gift shop	178	2,500	6%	10.68	11.91	29,775
Dry cleaners	181	1,500	7%	12.67	13.95	20,925
Liquor store	198	3,000	6%	11.88	12.26	36,780
Total		72,000				$534,830

*GLA = gross leasable area

Notice that base rents are often set so that tenants are unlikely to pay percentage until sometime in the future. When tenants are paying percentage rent, the base rent (minimum rent) and the overages (percentage rent in excess of base rent) are often presented separately to facilitate capitalizing them at different capitalization rates.

Rent incentives or concessions also exist in shopping center leasing. Treat them in a similar manner to rent concessions for other types of income real estate.

OTHER RENT

All rent should be included in potential rental income. (The exceptions are discussed in Chapter 4.) If the project you are analyzing offers parking and charges rent for it, the parking rent goes in the rent schedule for potential rental income. Any fees charged for the use of the physical facilities of the property are rent. Rent for storage, parking, community rooms, common areas, and the like should be scheduled under potential rental income.

REIMBURSED EXPENSES

Pass-through charges to tenants that are reimbursements for utilities, common area maintenance, and services do not fall into the potential rental income category. They are placed in the other income category.

DEPOSITS

The character of a deposit is determined by the agreement with the tenant. In normal situations, the deposit is not rent. It is a deposit to ensure that all rent is paid and that the unit is left by the tenant in an undamaged and clean condition when vacated. If the rent is paid and the unit is vacated in good condition, the deposit is returned to the tenant. Different states have different requirements regarding the handling of and accounting for deposits. For the purposes of financial analysis, the deposit should not be treated as rent unless there is an agreement with the tenant that it is nonrefundable.

When the deposit is refundable, the only portion not refunded is that portion used to cover an item that the parties agreed would be covered out of the deposit. If a portion of a deposit is applied to unpaid rent, such a portion does not constitute extra rent. It is simply the payment of the normal rent even though it comes out of the deposit rather than immediately out of the tenant's pocket. If a portion of a deposit is used to pay for a specific cleaning cost, that portion is extra rent and the cleaning cost is an operating expense; but if they are accounted for separately by the property manager outside the income & expense statement, they are a wash, and you can ignore them.

When a tenant agrees that a portion of a deposit or the entire deposit is nonrefundable, such an amount is additional rent. There is no intention by the parties that it is to be refunded. This is common when a nonrefundable "deposit" is collected to cover the cleaning expense incurred at the end of the tenancy. The cost of the cleaning may be more or less than the deposit collected. The deposit is rent, and the cost of cleaning is an operating expense.

It's only when the portion of a deposit intended to cover a specific expense is included, but the expense isn't, or when the specific expense intended to be covered by the portion of the deposit is included, but that portion of the deposit isn't, that a distortion is created. Your careful review of the property manager's operating statement should catch such distortions if they exist.

LEASE CLAUSES

It is not feasible in this book to cover every possible lease clause that may have an economic effect on the performance of the property as an investment. For nonresidential properties, you must carefully read all the leases. For every building, different leases are negotiated at different times, perhaps by different parties, and have different provisions even for identical issues. Only a careful reading of each lease will reveal all the effects that the leases will have on the performance of the property. Sometimes it takes only a word or two in a standard lease clause to make a large change and impact. For instance, in the phrase "utilities will be paid by the owner," change "owner" to "tenant" and you will have a difference that may have a significant impact. Sometimes the parties negotiating the lease make an ordinary provision hopelessly complicated. You must reduce the complication into figures that can be used in your analysis. Reading the leases is essential to the accuracy of your analysis.

For residential leases, the deviations from the norm are small in most cases. You will want to spot-check the leases for uniformity, but reading all the leases for a residential property is seldom warranted.

ABSORPTION

An absorption study is part of a marketability study or feasibility analysis (see Chapter 43). If such an analysis has been done, refer to the report to support the absorption figures you use. If you do an informal absorption study yourself to predict absorption, refer to your research to support your absorption figures. Absorption estimates are required for new projects, rehabs, and turnaround situations.

SUMMARY

Rental income can be as simple or as complicated as the leases and the situation require. Only through careful analysis and reference to market data can you develop an estimate of potential rental income that is likely to be accurate. For specific applications of rental income analysis, see Chapter 28 for apartments, Chapter 29 for offices, and Chapter 30 for shopping centers.

CHAPTER 2

VACANCY & CREDIT LOSS

Potential Rental Income
−**Vacancy & Credit Loss**
Effective Rental Income
+Other Income
Gross Operating Income
−Operating Expenses
Net Operating Income

Vacancy & credit loss is usually calculated by a "vacancy rate." The rate is derived from dividing the vacancy & credit loss amount by the potential rental income and rounding to the nearest whole percent.

VACANCY

There are several ways to estimate a vacancy rate. First, you can look at how the property has performed in the past. If the vacancy rate has been stable, you can use it to estimate future vacancy.

Second, you can derive a vacancy rate from the market. You can conduct your own market survey by contacting owners and property managers to get a picture of what the current market vacancy rate is. This method is effective because you can limit your survey to properties similar to one you are analyzing.

Third, you can purchase vacancy rate statistics. Many cities have services that compile rent and vacancy statistics and sell the resulting printed surveys. These services vary in quality, and you will want to make sure that the statistics are compiled accurately.

CREDIT LOSS

When a tenant occupies a property without paying rent, it is a credit loss. A well-managed property will have minimal credit losses, perhaps close to zero. Even with professional management, however, there are unavoidable situations that allow a tenant to occupy the premises for a period without paying rent. Two of the best defenses are security deposits that are substantial enough to cover unpaid rent for a reasonable period and quick action to eject a nonpaying tenant from the building. These two strategies are easy to state but sometimes more difficult to put into effect.

Credit loss information may be more difficult to pin down than vacancy information. You can get it the same way you get information on vacancy, but sometimes it's not included in the vacancy rate. When you gather information on vacancy rates, you will want to know whether credit loss is included.

Urban properties may experience higher credit losses than rural properties. Urban tenants are more likely to resort to the court system to perpetuate free occupancy. Such litigation often results in a credit loss even when the landlord wins the case.

CALCULATING A VACANCY RATE

In Maplewood Apartments (Appendix I), there are 36,500 unit-days (100 units × 365 days). If tenants have their rent prorated daily when they move in and when they move out, the property manager will have a record of the number of days that rent was not paid for each unit. Suppose the records show that rent was not paid for a total of 2,190 unit-days. That's a 6 percent vacancy and credit loss (2,190 ÷ 36,500 = 6%). If you can get a further breakdown on how many of the 2,190 unit-days are due to vacancy and how many due to credit loss, you will have greater insight into the operation of the property.

You apply the 6 percent vacancy rate to the potential rental income (6% × $1,014,069 = $60,846) and subtract the vacancy & credit loss amount ($1,014,096 − $60,846 = $953,250).

One way to refine this calculation is to determine the vacancy & credit loss of the different size apartment units separately. In many markets, different-size units will have different vacancy rates. Because the rent for each size is different, you can get a more accurate computation of the vacancy rate. Similarly, you can use a unit-dollars calculation for each category of unit (instead of a unit-days calculation) and determine the vacancy & credit loss more precisely too.

CERTAIN AMOUNT

Although it is not a normal practice, you can treat vacancy & credit loss as a certain amount rather than as an amount calculated by a vacancy percentage. For instance, an analysis of the leases for a property may indicate different amounts of lost income due to vacancy & credit loss for different years in the future. There may be no consistent percentage vacancy, so the specific amounts for each year are used.

RATE CHANGE

When you use a vacancy rate, you normally assume the same rate will prevail for the length of the projection. Sometimes, however, the market information is to the contrary. For example, if there is a large new office project that will create an oversupply of office space, the vacancy rate for your office building may be likely to rise over the next few years. Therefore, you may decide to increase the vacancy rate a little each year for the duration of the forecast.

SHOPPING CENTERS

The vacancy rates for shopping centers may be misleading. They are often expressed as a percentage of the *nonanchor* potential rental income. It is assumed that the anchor tenant is a credit tenant on a long-term lease.

AN ARBITRARY STANDARD

There is a tendency for "sophisticated" analysts to use 95 percent occupancy as the optimal performance for an apartment project, office building, or supermarket. Such a percentage is arbitrary. Each type of property and each specific property has an optimal occupancy rate depending on its situation. For instance, an apartment project might experience occupancy higher than 100 percent. Old tenants move out and are charged rent to the end of the month. But as soon as they move out, the new tenants move in, before the end of the month, and start paying rent immediately. When leasing practices are accommodating and apartments are in short supply, this is not unusual. If you use 0 percent as the vacancy rate, however, your projections may lose credibility. Most buyers will refuse to use anything less than a 5 percent vacancy rate. Nonetheless, if you can justify that apartment vacancy rates have been less than 5 percent for a long historical period and nothing in the market indicates a change, you may be able to make a solid case for using a lower vacancy rate.

Another example is an office building that is only 90 percent occupied. It has been 90 percent occupied for a few years, and the market has been stable. There is no current growth in the market. The 90 percent occupancy may indicate the optimal performance of the property, and a 10 percent vacancy rate is an accurate assessment of future performance. Usually, when a property has a vacancy rate higher than 5 percent, the owner (seller) will go to extremes to prove that the vacancy rate will come down to 5 percent within a reasonable time. For a seller to act otherwise is tantamount to admitting that there is something wrong with the property. But the property may be perfectly sound, operating at its optimum under the circumstances, and if so, it may be an excellent investment assuming the net operating income (NOI) is calculated using the 10 percent vacancy rate.

The underlying premise for investors using the 5 percent arbitrary standard for vacancy is that they will not acquire property in any market that has a vacancy rate higher than 5 percent. This can lead to bypassing good investments in depressed markets. For those who forget the premise, it can lead to making investments in performing properties in depressed markets. Such properties may not be able to sustain their superior performance.

Do not assume that 5 percent vacancy is the optimal performance for all properties under all circumstances. It is simply an arbitrary and convenient standard. A more compelling standard is the market vacancy.

MARKET VACANCY

The vacancy rate in the market is derived from market research. The vacancy rate for the property you are considering is revealing when compared to the market vacancy rate. If the property's vacancy rate is higher, it may signal problems with the property. Or it may indicate substandard property management. If the property's vacancy rate is lower, it may indicate there are some above-average attributes of the property. Or it may indicate superior property management. For either situation, further investigation is warranted. If you do your forecast based on the assumption that the property is going to have a higher or lower vacancy rate than the market vacancy rate, you must support such a forecast with solid reasons. In other words, a market standard is more productive in making good investments than an arbitrary standard.

Because there is a generally accepted arbitrary standard of 5 percent vacancy for "investment-grade" properties, much time and effort are typically wasted attempting to somehow conform attractive properties to this standard. The time is better spent on the more difficult task of determining the long-term optimal performance of the property in the circumstances of the property's environment and creating a forecast based on such performance.

SUMMARY

A vacancy rate is an important adjustment to the potential rental income. Compare the historical vacancy rates for the property and for the market to determine an intelligent prediction for your pro forma income & expense statement and for your multiyear forecast.

CHAPTER 3

EFFECTIVE RENTAL INCOME

Potential Rental Income
−Vacancy & Credit Loss
Effective Rental Income
+Other Income
Gross Operating Income
−Operating Expenses
Net Operating Income

This calculation and category entry exists to show the total real estate income from the property alone (i.e., the rent) excluding nonrental income. All the rental income that is attributed to the property is included in potential rental income. A vacancy and credit loss factor is estimated and applied. The resulting adjusted income is effective rental income.

Effective rental income does not include rent that is not associated with similar types of property. For instance, if a garden apartment project included a substantial ministorage facility on the premises, rent from the storage facility should not be included in potential rental income and consequently not in the effective rental income. The storage facility is best analyzed separately. Even if included, the rent for the storage facility should be in the other income category. And all nonrental income should be excluded from potential rental income. Consequently, nonrental income is not included in effective rental income.

Why have a category of effective rental income? It allows you to compare your property directly to other identical properties (e.g., garden apartments to garden apartments) to learn how your property is performing. This is often done on a "per-square-foot" basis. In this case, the apartment rent is the common denominator. All garden apartments collect apartment rent. Not all collect ministorage rent. If you were to include the ministorage rent (in the above example), you would render comparisons the invalid. Because there is a sense that nonrental income may not be as endurable as rental income, nonrental income is also excluded from effective rental income. The property will always generate rent so long as it is operated. But will the activities that provide nonrental income always exist? Or will they be eliminated or replaced sometime in the future? Are such activities essential to the operation of the real estate? Many investors perceive the rental income as the essential income of the property that should be separated in the mind's eye from income that is not so essential. (Other income is discussed in detail in Chapter 4.)

Effective rental income can be the divisor for either the gross income multiplier or for the operating ratio (see Chapter 40). It is, of course, optional to include effective rental income in this analytical scheme. It is only a subtotal. Nonetheless, it can be a useful subtotal.

CHAPTER 4

OTHER INCOME

Potential Rental Income
−Vacancy & Credit Loss
Effective Rental Income
+**Other Income**
Gross Operating Income
−Operating Expenses
Net Operating Income

DEFINITION BY EXAMPLE

Maplewood Apartments (100 units) provides laundry facilities to tenants. Laundry rooms equipped with coin-operated washers and dryers are located in convenient locations around the apartment complex. A laundry management company supplies the equipment, maintains it, and collects the money. Of the gross receipts, 50 percent goes to the property owner. The property owner provides no intensive management to obtain this income, which is incidental to operating the property. Enter it in the other income category.

Generally, other income is not rental income. It is income that requires no intensive management and is incidental to operating the property.

If Maplewood Apartments provides 200 parking spaces to tenants for an additional rent of $35 per month per space, is this other income? This rent is not the same as renting apartment units. Nevertheless, it is the rental of surface space. Therefore, categorize it as potential rental income, rather than other income, and include it in the rent schedule.

Now suppose there is a small convenience store on the premises staffed by a manager-clerk and part-time clerks. Is this income other income? In this case, the business is management intensive. The property manager cannot run it. It takes a retail manager to conduct its trade activities. Therefore, it is not appropriate to include it with the real estate. Why? Because real estate investors make real estate investments. Convenience store businesses experience higher risk and require specialized management. A real estate investor is not likely to be interested. A different kind of investor invests in retail enterprises. Therefore, the real estate investment and the convenience store investment are incompatible.

Have the seller separate the convenience store from the real estate and keep the convenience store, or sell it separately to someone else. Show the convenience store real estate (space) as being rented to the retail business owner, and include the rent in the potential rental income.

Occasionally, a potential purchaser for Maplewood Apartments will desire to purchase the convenience store business along with the real estate. Nonetheless, treat the retail business separately. For the purpose of estimating its value, capitalize its net operating income at a capitalization rate (cap rate) appropriate to such retail businesses. Such a cap rate is likely to be significantly different (usually much higher) than the real estate cap rate. You can see that the retail business really must be evaluated by a retail business appraiser or consultant, not a real estate professional.

Some cases do not provide easy categorization. What about executive suites? Executive suites are individual offices resulting from the subdivision of office space. Typically, the landlord rents the offices to different tenants and provides a smorgasbord of clerical services and office equipment usage (e.g., receptionist, secretary, fax machine, copy machine) for a price that's in addition to the rent. It looks like a real estate operation. But do not be deceived: it's a management-intensive operation that is profitable only with specialized management. Like the convenience store, treat it separately.

The classic case is a hotel. Clearly, a hotel is a complex, management-intensive business that has little to do with real estate. If a real estate investor purchases a hotel, it is inevitably because the hotel is leased (long term) to an experienced hotel operator with prime credit. In other words, it's a one-tenant property. It's unlikely a normal real estate investor would take on the responsibility of managing a hotel.

Thus, the other income category is for income that is incidental to the operation of the real estate and not derived from a management-intensive business. It is also for rental income that you desire to treat separately from the potential rental income (see the following extra parking example). Carefully evaluate every source of other income. If income does not pass these tests, treat it separately from the real estate analysis. Beware when other income is more than a nominal amount.

REIMBURSED EXPENSES

Sometimes the owner passes along specific operating expenses to the tenants. When this is done, enter the reimbursement of such expenses in other income. It is common in shopping center leasing, for instance, to have the tenants each pay a pro rata share of the shopping center's common area maintenance (e.g., parking lot, landscaping—often referred to as CAMs). This reimbursement of CAMs can be treated as other income, and CAM is but one item on a list of reimbursable expenses. If you are a specialist in shopping centers, you might even relabel other income to be "Expense Reimbursements" or something similar.

When expenses are completely reimbursed by the tenants, it is sometimes tempting to leave them off the pro forma; that is, don't enter them as either operating expenses or other income. After all, if the tenant pays them, why include them? But leaving them off the pro forma is a poor practice. It gives an incomplete picture of the property and prevents fruitful comparisons with published operational statistics.

BEFORE OR AFTER?

Notice that you add other income to potential rental income after the vacancy & credit loss rate is applied:

Standard Income & Expense Statement
   Potential rental income
   −Vacancy & credit loss
   Effective rental income
   +**Other income**
   Gross operating income
   −Operating expenses
   Net operating income

Other income is added to potential rental income after the vacancy & credit loss rate is applied because such a placement allows effective rental income to give an accurate picture of exactly how much the vacancy affects the rent. Other income could distort such a picture. This format also matches the format of published property management statistics. But there is another reason, too.

Suppose Maplewood Apartments has 300 parking spaces, about 50 percent more than required for a 100-unit apartment project. And suppose the project is located downtown near numerous office buildings. Office workers rent the extra parking spaces for $75 each per month. If you include this extra income in the potential rental income, it distorts the amount of income that an apartment investment is expected to earn. This situation is really like two properties combined, an apartment project and a downtown parking lot. The extra parking income is best entered into other income. If it is entered in other income, however, it is not desirable to subject it to the vacancy & credit loss factor of the apartments project, because the vacancy & credit loss factor for apartments may be different. For instance, the extra parking for office workers could have 5 percent vacancy while the apartment units had 30 percent vacancy, or vice versa.

The placement of the other income category, however, is one over which knowledgeable real estate professionals disagree. Some real estate professionals would have the vacancy & credit loss rate (it is a percentage) applied to potential rental income plus other income. This is appropriate in many cases. For instance, in the laundry example above, the laundry income goes up and down with increases and decreases in occupancy. With more tenants, the laundry makes more money. Likewise, in a shopping center, higher occupancy will generate more expense reimbursements. Consequently, you can argue that other income should be subject to vacancy (when the vacancy & credit loss is a percentage):

Alternative Income & Expense Statement

Potential rental income
+**Other income**
Effective rental income
−Vacancy & credit loss
Gross operating income
−Operating expenses
Net operating income

Perhaps there should be two other income categories, one subject to the vacancy & credit loss percentage factor and one that is not. Experts can argue over this dilemma for hours.

It's important to recognize the dilemma and to alert the readers of the pro forma how you are handling the problem. You can use two different pro forma formats to handle different property situations. One will show other income entered before vacancy & credit loss, and another will show it entered afterward. Or you can have one format and use footnotes for exceptional cases. The important thing is that the reader be informed of potential distortions to income caused by your choice of format.

INTEREST

A reserve fund may earn interest (in an interest-bearing account). Do not include such interest income in other income. Interest income is not included in the calculation of net operating income. Reserve accounts are discretionary, and interest income produced by them is not considered part of the real estate investment (see Chapter 16).

CHAPTER 5

GROSS OPERATING INCOME

Potential Rental Income
−Vacancy & Credit Loss
Effective Rental Income
+Other Income
Gross Operating Income
−Operating Expenses
Net Operating Income

Gross operating income is the sum of all income available to operate the property. If assumptions about market rent, vacancy, and other income are accurate, gross operating income is the total amount of income the property can be expected to generate.

Like effective rental income, gross operating income is a subtotal, and it is optional to include it. Even though it's a subtotal, it is also the bottom-line figure for income, before operating expenses are subtracted. It tells you exactly what income is available to pay the operating expenses and to provide a operational profit. When gross operating income is used to make a comparison between similar types of properties, the comparison is usually made on a "per-square-foot" basis.

Gross operating income is also the divisor for the operating ratio, although potential rental income or effective rental income is sometimes used instead. When operating expenses are expressed as a percentage of income, they are normally a percentage of gross operating income. If operating expenses are calculated as a percentage of potential rental income, they do not increase or decrease with changes in vacancy and other income. But there is a sense that operating expenses may be lower when occupancy is lower. Thus, a percentage estimate for operating expenses is often estimated as a percentage of gross operating income.

Yet not everyone makes calculations the same way. Some may use potential rental income or effective rental income as the divisor for the operating ratio. The Institute of Real Estate Management uses *gross possible income* (potential rental income + other income) as the divisor for the operating ratio, although that is undoubtedly for the convenience of expressing statistics rather than for the purpose of specifically expressing an operating ratio. Keep in mind that gross operating income is the same as effective rental income if other income is zero.

CHAPTER 6

OPERATING EXPENSES

Potential Rental Income
−Vacancy & Credit Loss
Effective Rental Income
+Other Income
Gross Operating Income
−**Operating Expenses**
Net Operating Income

The operating expenses are the mundane expenses incurred in operating the property according to professional standards. These expenses must be objective in the sense that they are the ones that any owner will incur. Subjective expenses (i.e., expenses unique to a particular owner) should not be included here. Subjective expenses go in the nonoperating expense category.

Professional practices are established by property managers trained by the Institute of Real Estate Management (IREM), Building and Owners Management Association (BOMA), International Council of Shopping Centers (ICSC), and similar organizations. These property management organizations also publish books, periodicals, and statistics that establish guidelines and standards for professional management. Operating expenses do not include anything that any property manager happens to record as an expense. Operating expenses must be scrutinized to determine their objectivity. That does not necessarily mean that you have to audit last year's operating statement. It does mean that you should look over the operating statement carefully for expense items that may not belong.

If the owner of a 12-unit apartment building sends the on-site manager to a one-week property management seminar at a cost of $2,500 including tuition and travel expenses, that may not be a reasonable expense. However, if the owner of a 120-unit apartment project does the same, it may be a reasonable expense. But, if the owner of the 120-unit apartment projects incurs an annual expense of $11,000 to pay the tuition and college expenses for the on-site manager's enrollment in a local university's MBA program, it may not be a reasonable expense. This would be particularly true if the on-site manager happens to be the owner's niece.

In all of these cases, the expense is likely to be legitimate for income tax purposes. So, tax deductibility is not the proper test. The test is whether the expense is reasonably necessary to operate the property according to professional property management practices. This is determined by a broad range of factors. For instance, suppose there is a 40-unit apartment building in a Nevada mining town about 75 miles north of Las Vegas. It houses miners. The only other buildings in town are a convenience store, a gas station, a bar, and a laundromat, as well as a few other multiunit residential buildings. A property manager from Las Vegas visits the site and meets with the on-site manager quarterly. Is it reasonable to include the travel expenses from Las Vegas to the site in the operating expenses? Because there is unlikely to be a selection of professional property managers in the mining town, it makes sense that one from the nearest city will be hired, and the travel expenses are reasonable.

Suppose the 40-unit apartment building were located in Modesto, California, which is about a three-hour drive east from downtown San Francisco. The property manager flies from Nashville, Tennessee, to the San Francisco airport, visits the property, meets with the on-site manager, and spends two nights in a San Francisco hotel in transit during these expensive quarterly trips. Are these travel expenses reasonable to attribute to the operation of the property? Modesto is a city of about 200,000 people. There are plenty of professional property managers available there. It does not seem reasonable that this property needs a property manager from Nashville. But if it were a 400-unit apartment project in Modesto, the expense might be reasonable because large apartment projects are considered to be in the national market. It is not unusual for large properties in the national market to be managed from afar. For a 400-unit apartment project, a property manager from someplace as far away as Nashville would not be unusual. Therefore, the travel expenses from Nashville would be reasonable.

So reasonableness is a better test of objectivity for operating expenses than tax deductibility. What is reasonable is determined by the type and size of property, the location, the market, and the customary professional property management practices and standards. An objective expense is one that any owner and property manager would incur in the reasonable operation of the property to maximize both short-term and long-term net operating income (NOI).

It is also helpful to understand what is not included in operating expenses. Interest is not included as an expense. Not all owners finance their real estate purchase, so some will not pay interest. Therefore, it is not an objective expense. Depreciation is not included as an operating expense. There is enough flexibility in the tax laws to provide a choice of useful lives to calculate depreciation. One owner may choose one, and another may choose another. Additionally, it is possible to acquire a property by exchanging. When that is done, the owner's tax basis in the old property is a factor in calculating his or her basis in the new property. Thus, the basis in the same property may be different for different owners. The basis determines the depreciable amount. Because depreciation is likely to be different for different owners, it is not an objective expense.

Acquisition costs vary from investor to investor. One may find properties on his or her own effort. Another may have the expense of an acquisitions staff. Additionally, acquisition costs are extraordinary one-time expenses that do not recur from year to year. So acquisitions costs are not operating expenses.

Capital additions are not operating expenses, either. These are additions to improvements or the acquisition of personal property items that have useful lives in excess of one year. They are allowed as tax deductions only if the costs are amortized (i.e., depreciated). Because they are extraordinary expenses and often occur unpredictable, they distort the operation of the property in the year that they occur. Therefore, they are not appropriate to include in operating expenses.

Any expense that is not an operating expense and is not specifically otherwise categorized is properly categorized as a nonoperating expense. It may have a place in the analysis of the real estate investment and it may be tax deductible, but it does not belong in the category of operating expenses.

Operating expenses are those recurring annual expenses necessary to the operation of the property as a viable business. The Commercial Investment Real Institute lists the following expenses on its widely used form, the Annual Property Operating Data (APOD):

Real estate taxes

Personal property taxes

Property insurance

Off-site management

Payroll—on-site personnel

Expenses/benefits (for personnel)

Taxes/worker's compensation (for personnel)

Repairs and maintenance

Utilities

Accounting and legal

Real estate leasing commissions

Advertising/licenses/permits

Supplies, miscellaneous

Contract services

Operating expenses will be paid on the property annually with few exceptions. For instance, some insurance coverage may be paid for three years. If it is paid in three installments, it's a normal situation. If it's paid in one installment, the income & expense statements for the three years must artificially show the one installment as being paid in three installments. Be cautious with expenses covering more than one year. They may be capital improvements that do not belong on the income & expense statement.

The APOD form is a generic form designed to be useful for a broad range of properties. It is meant as a disclosure form, not a comparative form. There are no instructions that accompany it and no customary practices in assigning expenses to each category.

In contrast, the later chapters of this book on income and expenses for apartments, offices, and shopping centers present specific categories of operating expenses established by annual surveys of property management organizations. For those categories, the customary practices are thoroughly defined. Those forms are used for comparing properties to the statistics established by the surveys.

The APOD form is useful, however, in exploring the role that operating expenses play in creating an objective income & expense statement. The following categories are presented to you as if you were evaluating last year's operating statement with the purpose of creating a pro forma income & expense statement, or as if you were thoroughly analyzing a pro forma income & expense statement created by someone else.

REAL ESTATE TAXES

This tax is the "property tax" due annually (or semiannually in many places). Don't confuse real estate taxes paid to the county with other taxation (e.g., income tax, payroll withholding tax). Every property is taxed locally by the county based on mil levies for the county, school districts, improvement districts, and the like. If you want to know what the property tax is for a property, inquire at the county tax assessor's office.

Next year's taxes usually cannot be ascertained until the end of this year when all the mil levies are finally determined. The mil levies are applied to the assessed valuation of the property. Each property in a county is reappraised periodically. If your property was recently reappraised at a substantially higher valuation and the mil levies increase substantially, the property tax on your property might increase a surprising amount from one year to the next. A sale can have the same effect as a reappraisal.

PERSONAL PROPERTY TAXES

Some municipalities levy a tax on personal property used in business. If your property is located in such a municipality and it includes personal property, you should include the payment of this tax in your income & expense statement.

PROPERTY INSURANCE

This includes both casualty protection and liability. When the premium is paid in one installment for three years, the APOD should show one-third of the premium as being paid for the year. For undeveloped land, only liability insurance is likely to be obtained.

Casualty insurance is keyed to the value of the property, its fire protection rating, and other environmental factors. Liability insurance may be keyed more closely to other factors such as the amount of liability protection desired by the owner.

Insurance premiums usually do not vary much from one year to another. Occasionally, however, an insurance cost crisis will cause them to take a big jump from one year to the next. Fortunately, when this happens, all properties are affected, not just yours.

OFF-SITE MANAGEMENT

This is the property management fee paid to a professional property manager or management firm. The property manager supervises the on-site personnel and otherwise manages the property. A substantial portion of the management task is keeping the books and operating records for the property. The property management fee is often a percentage of gross operating income. In some property management arrangements, this fee covers on-site personnel too, and the property manager is responsible for all the normal personnel expenses and taxes for on-site employees.

Asset management is a nonoperating expense and should not be included as an operating expense. When the property manager is also providing asset management services, the asset management services should be billed separately from the property management services and should not be included as an operating expense. Asset management expenses should be placed in the nonoperating expenses category and the nonoperating outlays category.

PAYROLL—ON-SITE PERSONNEL

People who work on the premises regularly should be employees of the owner. The owner may be held responsible for withholding taxes, worker's compensation premiums, and the like, regardless of the agreed upon legal status relationship with such people. Therefore, the payments to these people should be set up as an employee payroll. When a tenant is given a reduced rent or free rent as partial or full payment for services to the owner (usually in an apartment building), that amount of rent should be considered payroll.

EXPENSES—BENEFITS

These are payments made for employee benefits or other expenditures made on behalf of on-site personnel (employees).

TAXES/WORKER'S COMPENSATION

These are withholding payments for federal and state income tax, Social Security, worker's compensation premiums, and the like.

REPAIRS AND MAINTENANCE

Repairs listed on income & expense statements cannot be capital improvements. Repairs that are temporary or of nominal cost are appropriate here. Major repairs should be evaluated to determine whether they are really capital improvements instead of repairs or maintenance. If a repair includes a major replacement (e.g., a roof), it may be a capital improvement. Capital improvements are not included in operating expenses.

Many owners indulge in aggressive accounting in order to write off capital improvements as repairs or maintenance for income tax purposes. For instance, if there are multiple buildings in a project, one roof may be replaced each year as a repair item instead of all the roofs being replaced at once. Such practices may pass the scrutiny of the IRS. But you should not let them distort the income & expense statement for the purpose of real estate analysis. The test as to whether a repair or maintenance expenditure is a capital improvement is not a tax test. It is simply a test of common sense and customary practice. (See Chapter 15 for a more extensive review of the distinction between repairs and capital improvements.)

UTILITIES

When utilities are metered to each tenant, they are usually paid by each tenant. In such cases, the tenants' utility expenses are not included as an operating expense. However, when a tenant moves out and is not immediately replaced, the owner may have to cover utility expenses for that space or unit for the period of vacancy. In that case, the utility expense is properly entered as an operating expense.

When the utilities are paid by the owner, whether metered separately or not, the costs are properly entered as operating expenses. The owner also normally pays for the utilities attributable to the common areas of the premises.

There may be an agreement between the owner and the tenants that utility expenses will be passed through to the tenants (i.e., paid by the owner and reimbursed by the tenants). In such a case, the expense and the income cancel each other. Nonetheless, you must put both the reimbursements in other income and the expenses in operating expenses. If you leave both of these out because they are a wash, you will distort the income & expense statement so that it cannot be accurately compared to the operating statistics of other similar properties.

ACCOUNTING AND LEGAL

These professional fees are operating expenses when the services performed are attributable to the normal operation of the property. Extraordinary accounting and legal fees should not be included. For instance, fees for legal services to clear the title to the property are extraordinary, whereas legal fees for legal representation in an eviction proceeding may be a routine part of the operation of the property and therefore a proper operating expense.

REAL ESTATE LEASING COMMISSIONS

Leasing commissions that are paid based on one year's tenancy or less are sometimes included on the APOD. This category is for residential income properties in competitive markets where it is commonplace for leasing agents to assist property managers in renting units. Such commissions are considered a necessary and routine promotional expense.

ADVERTISING/LICENSES/PERMITS

Licenses and permits may be required in some communities. The annual fees for them are operating expenses. Advertising can be a special case. Ordinarily, reasonable advertising expenses are categorized as operating expenses. But if advertising expenses are for a one-time promotional campaign (e.g., to lease a new building), they should be categorized as nonoperating expenses and nonoperating outlays.

Advertising is expensive. It is easy to underestimate the cost for the advertising that the property reasonably requires to operate normally. On the other hand, advertising can be a bottomless pit into which you pour funds with little effect on the performance of the property. It is easy to estimate this expense too high, expecting a benefit to the property that will not materialize. When advertising expenses are nominal or unusually large, they should be given extra scrutiny.

Advertising can give an analyst a license to create distortion in the income & expense statement. Advertising and promotional expenses are a good place bury rent concessions. For instance, suppose to get tenants for an apartment project, the property manager offers a trip to Hawaii (at a cost of $650) for signing a year's lease. The average monthly rent is $650. Is this an ongoing promotional expense? Is it an extraordinary promotional expense? Or is it a rent concession? The trip is roughly equal to one month's rent. Should this be an operating expense? Should this be a nonoperating expense? Should the rent be reduced by 1/12th?

The answer is determined by the circumstances of the property, the competing properties, and the market. If all the competing properties must make the same or similar incentive offers to get tenants, then it is probably a proper operating expense. If the property is alone in the marketing in making this offer, it is an extraordinary expense and should not be included in operating expenses. Under what circumstances should the rent be reduced rather than expressed as a nonoperating expense? That's perhaps more difficult to resolve. If the incentive is part of a promotion to quickly lease the apartment project because it's new or freshly renovated, then treatment as a nonoperating promotional expense may be justified. But if the incentive is simply to increase occupancy in a seasoned project that is not renting as well as desired, then the proper treatment is a 1/12th rent reduction.

Each situation is different. This book does not attempt to answer all questions raised by this issue. Rather, raising these questions will make you sensitive to the possibilities for distortion inherent in characterizing promotional programs one way or another.

SUPPLIES

There are numerous supplies required to keep a property functioning properly. Maintenance and repair supplies do not normally belong in this category. They are included in the maintenance and repairs operating expense.

MISCELLANEOUS

This is a necessary catchall. When this entry is a large amount, however, it bears further scrutiny.

CONTRACT SERVICES

This category is for the cost of the myriad of contractors whom property managers use from time to time, or regularly, in the operation the property. Any outside contractor who provides services or equipment for the necessary operation of the property should bill the owner on the contractor's own letterhead or billing statement. In other words, there should be no confusion about whether a person is an outside contractor or an employee.

OTHER CATEGORIES

There are many other potential categories for operating expenses. The ones expressed on the APOD form are arbitrary and merely intended to be a guide. In any format, behind each category there may be a subschedule of expenses that bears scrutiny. Keep in mind that there are certain expenses experienced in one locale but not another (e.g., snow removal in Minneapolis but not in Miami).

PERCENTAGE ESTIMATE OF EXPENSES

One way to estimate expenses is to refer to statistics and use a percentage of income. For instance, suppose you have a reliable statistic that indicates that apartments similar to yours in age, location, quality, and size will experience expenses that are about 39 percent of gross operating income. For a quick preliminary analysis, that percentage may be acceptably accurate. In your final analysis, however, you will want to refine the operating expenses category with a schedule of estimated expenses. Percentage estimates are rarely accurate enough for use in a competently prepared income & expense statement.

SUMMARY

The expenses included in the pro forma income & expense statement must be objective expenses. The test is not what is tax deductible, but rather what is reasonable. What are the reasonably expected expenses that any owner and property manager managing the property effectively will incur? Expenses that are not objective should be excluded along with capital expenditures and extraordinary, one-time expenses.

CHAPTER 7

NET OPERATING INCOME

Potential Rental Income
−Vacancy & Credit Loss
Effective Rental Income
+Other Income
Gross Operating Income
−Operating Expenses
Net Operating Income

You need a simple and direct method of evaluating the performance of an income property regardless of who the owner is. For such an evaluation, you do not need to look, nor should you look, any further than the property itself. Thus, inherent in the income & expense statement is the idea that it is an objective analysis of the property, a straightforward analysis unaltered by the details of the ownership. The bottom line for the income & expense statement is net operating income (NOI). It is the cornerstone of further real estate analysis.

In essence, the NOI is simply the rent less the operating expenses, a simple idea. Because it is productive to be more precise, however, the calculation of the NOI is complicated by subtracting vacancy and adding other income. But it remains a simple idea. It answers the question, "How is the *property* performing?" To answer the question "How is the *investment* performing?" requires information on the details of ownership. The NOI simply tells you how the property is performing.

Providing real estate for businesses or people to use is a business itself; that is, real estate is the business of providing residential and commercial building space. The NOI tells you how that business is doing regardless of who owns it. Nonetheless, the NOI doesn't tell you anything about how the real estate is doing as an investment. It doesn't take into consideration any of the details of ownership, such as the investor's debt service and tax bracket, that can help you analyze how the real estate is doing as an investment. Although the NOI is the goal of the income & expense statement, it is the beginning of further analysis that does consider the details of ownership and that does allow you to analyze the property as an investment.

For instance, suppose you are considering the purchase of property that will have an NOI of $173,000. To purchase this property, you must borrow $1,500,000 at 10 percent interest and pay monthly payments that will amortize the principal over 30 years. Another person might be able to buy the property for all cash, but you will need this loan to buy the property. You are not financially able to invest any more money in this property in addition to the down payment. This situation is a detail of your potential ownership and has little to do with the operation of the property. Your loan will be taken into account in the income tax analysis, the cash flow analysis, and the sale proceeds analysis, but not in the income & expense statement.

The NOI is used with the value of the property to calculate a rate of return. If the property above is valued at $1,922,222, the rate of return is 9 percent (173,000 ÷ 1,922,222 = 9%). This is the capitalization rate (cap rate). It is comparable to the yield of a bond when used to value property. Cap rates are found in the real estate market; that is, the market determines the value of real estate according to the amount of profit (NOI) the property produces. Thus, cap rates are used to appraise property. To value property, you obtain an appropriate cap rate through market research and apply it to the pro forma NOI (e.g., 173,000 ÷ 9% = 1,922,222). (See Chapter 39 for a more detailed explanation of cap rates.) Keep in mind that the NOI used for valuation is prospective. It is the anticipated NOI for the first year of an investor's ownership.

Once the NOI for the first year has been calculated, it is sometimes inflated over a holding period to create a forecast. So long as the vacancy rate is stable, and other income and operating expenses are inflating at the same rate as rental income, inflating the NOI by itself in a forecast is accurate. The NOI is also used as the numerator in the calculation of the debt coverage ratio. And it is used as the divisor in the net income multiplier (see Chapter 40).

Although the NOI is a resultant number—the bottom-line number of the income & expense statement—it is often used in other calculations as the starting number. Because the income tax analysis and the cash flow analysis both start with the NOI, the income & expense statement can be combined with either for a more comprehensive analysis. Usually, the income & expense statement is combined with the income tax analysis (see Appendix I and II). When there is no tax analysis, however, the income & expense statement can be conveniently combined with the cash flow analysis (see Appendix III). When the NOI is combined with another analysis, it becomes merely a *subtotal*. But it is a very important subtotal and should not be excluded in any analysis.

The NOI is not only an important number but it is also important that it be calculated accurately and objectively. If the market cap rate is 10 percent, every dollar of NOI creates $10 of value. Thus, when determining value, all miscalculations of the NOI are magnified by 1,000 percent. Both the income tax analysis and the cash flow analysis start with NOI. If the NOI is inaccurate, they will be inaccurate too. Because the sale price in the sale proceeds analysis is usually calculated using a cap rate divided into the next year's NOI, the sale price will be inaccurate, too, if the NOI is inaccurate.

PART 2

TAXABLE INCOME ANALYSIS

The income & expense statement is an objective analysis of the operation of the property assuming ownership by a reasonable and prudent owner. It has nothing to do with the actual ownership of the property and nothing to do with income tax considerations.

People pay income taxes; properties don't. Any consideration of the property in relation to the Tax Code and regulations requires an owner. It is the owner's tax bracket that determines the tax bracket in which the property's income will be taxed. It's the owner's choice of depreciation (cost recovery), when choices exist, that determines the amount of the depreciation expense. It's whether or not the owner borrowed money to purchase the property that determines whether interest is paid, and how much. Thus, the taxable income analysis is not only a different set of calculations from the income & expense statement but it is also subjective. It requires a specific owner. Or it requires a fictitious owner with specific subjective characteristics.

Don't confuse the income & expense statement with the taxable income analysis. They are two different ideas that serve different purposes. One evaluates how the property will operate objectively. The other examines the effect of the tax laws on the income or loss provided by the property to a specific tax-paying owner. Likewise, don't confuse the taxable income analysis with the cash flow analysis that shows the actual cash that flows into, or out of, a specific owner's pocket. The taxable income analysis does not show this because depreciation is a "paper" expense, and the payment of principal on a loan is not an expense for tax purposes. Thus, the actual cash flow, although subjective, is different from the taxable income analysis: it is a different idea.

Here is the taxable income analysis:

Chapters

7 Net Operating Income
8 −Interest Expense
9 −Cost Recovery
10 −Nonoperating Expenses
11 **Taxable Income**

TYPES OF DEDUCTIONS

Every dollar earned by the property is treated in one of five categories for tax purposes:

1. It is taxed.
2. It is deducted as an expense in the current year (i.e., operating expenses).
3. It is treated as an amortization expense deducted in the current year. (This treatment reduces the tax basis of the property.)
4. It is treated as an amortization expense deducted in the current year for an amortized expenditure that was not added to basis. The basis is not reduced, but the unamortized portion of the expense remaining at sale is a deduction from ordinary income upon the sale of the property.
5. It is deferred and deducted in the future.

Note: See chapters 9, 26, and 37 for a discussion of tax basis.

The interest line entry is the annual cost of financing. It is a major deductible expense (see Chapter 8). It fits into category 2. The cost recovery line entry is for depreciation. The price paid for the improvements on the property is part of the tax basis of the property. As the cost of the improvements is amortized over a cost recovery term and a portion is deducted each year, the basis is reduced (see Chapter 9). It fits into category 3. Keep in mind that capital expenditures are in the cash flow analysis. For the taxable income analysis, the capital expenditures are amortized and deducted in cost recovery.

An example of category 4 is the loan fee. It is not added to basis but is amortized over the term of the loan. A portion is deducted each year, and the unamortized amount remaining is a deduction upon the sale of the property. It doesn't quite fit either the interest or cost recovery categories, and it belongs in nonoperating expenses unless shown as a separate category (i.e., amortization of loan points).

Tax losses constitute "tax shelter." In certain cases, tax losses may be deferred until the sale of the property. Since the tax loss is created by tax deductible expenses in excess of income, the suspended losses represent expenses deferred into the future as in category 5.

The affect of income tax on the owner of the property is of interest to the IRS as well as the owner. The "bottom line" of the taxable income analysis is taxable income. The results of the taxable income analysis are needed to calculate the effect of tax liability on the owner's cash flow. Thus, in the calculation of cash flow after tax, the result of the taxable income analysis (i.e., taxable income) is used in the cash flow analysis to calculate tax liability.

Corporations and certain other business entities are considered taxpayers for the purposes of the tax law. But partnerships, limited partnerships, and some other business entities are not taxpayers. They pass their tax burdens or benefits through to their partners, limited partners, or other participants, who will be taxed.

CHAPTER 8

INTEREST

Net Operating Income
- **Interest Expense**
- Cost Recovery
- Nonoperating Expenses

Taxable Income

Potential investors for a property each seek financial arrangements that serve their goals. One investor may buy the property for cash. Another may get a loan for half of the purchase price. Yet another may manage to finance all of the purchase price. Some have excellent credit and get the lowest interest rate currently available. Others have marginal credit and have to pay a higher interest rate. It is easy to see why the calculation of the interest deduction belongs in a subjective, or custom, analysis. The interest calculation will not be the same for each potential investor.

When calculating the business expense of interest, you must be careful not to include principal. Principal is the capital or investment made in the loan by the lender. It is the loan amount. The repayment of principal is not tax deductible. Only interest is deductible for income tax purposes. Each type of loan has a different method of calculation.

INTEREST-ONLY LOAN

A good example of the interest-only loan is a loan of $1,000,000 at 10 percent interest for five years. Each year you pay 10 percent, or $100,000 in interest. At the end of five years, you repay the principal of $1,000,000. Keep in mind that interest is always expressed as an annual interest rate, but it could be payable monthly or quarterly. You simply divide to determine the periodic payment:

Annually—10% × $1,000,000 = 100,000
Quarterly—$100,000 ÷ 4 = 25,000
Monthly—$100,000 ÷ 12 = 8,333

The periodic loan payments are totally deductible because they are all interest. The principal remains the same until it is repaid at the end of the loan term.

PRINCIPAL PAYMENT LOAN

A $1,000,000 loan at 10 percent interest for five years with an annual principal payment of $50,000 will have a declining amount of interest paid each year. Here are the annual principal and interest payments (first two years):

First Year

10% × $1,000,000 =   100,000 interest
                   + 50,000 principal
                   150,000 total payment

Second Year

10% × $950,000 =   95,000 interest
                 + 50,000 principal
                 145,000 total payment

By the end of the fifth year, $200,000 has been paid in principal (for four years), and $800,000 is the balance of principal due (including the $50,000 principal payment for the fifth year). For the fifth year, the interest has declined to $80,000. Only the interest portion of the annual payment is deductible for computing income tax.

AMORTIZED LOAN

The calculations for an amortized loan are based on the principles of discounted cash flow analysis, and you need a financial calculator to make the calculations. Take a $1,000,000 loan at 10 percent interest payable monthly with the principal amortized over 25 years:

First Payment

$9,087   8,333 interest
                                   754 principal

Second Payment

$9,087   8,327 interest
                                   760 principal

Third Payment

$9,087   8,321 interest
                                   766 principal

Last Payment (300th)

$9,087   75 interest
                                 9,012 principal

At the end of the term of the loan (at the end of the 25th year), the principal has been reduced to zero. As you can see, the ratio of interest to principal changes with each loan payment because the interest is paid on only the balance of unpaid principal. Only the interest portion of the payment or payments for the year is deductible for computing income tax. Keep in mind that you must use a financial calculator, or a computer program, to make these calculations. The minimodel below is explained in Chapter 41. The minimodel is essentially a method of using your financial calculator more easily. First, you calculate the loan payment:

```
FV  =
PMT = (?)                   PMT = 9087
PV  = 1000000
I   = 10 ÷ 12
N   = 25 × 12
```

Financial calculators are able to amortize multiple loan payments with one set of keystrokes using the AMORT function. Thus, you can amortize one monthly payment and determine the interest paid for the month, the principal paid for the month, and the mortgage balance at the end of the month. Or you can amortize 12 monthly payments and determine the interest paid for the year, the principal paid for the year, and the mortgage balance at the end of the year.

ONE-PAYMENT LOAN

These loans can be tricky. You must determine whether the interest is simple or compound. Take a $1,000,000 loan at 10 percent interest with all principal and interest due and payable in five years. If the interest is simple,

> Interest = 10% × $1,000,000 = $100,000 × 5 = $500,000
> Principal = $1,000,000
> Total payment due in five years = $1,500,000

If the interest is compound, you will need a financial calculator to calculate the payment due in five years. You calculate what $1,000,000 will grow to in five years at 10 percent interest. But first you must determine the compounding period. (Use the minimodel below covered in Chapter 41.) If the interest compounds monthly,

> FV = (?)   FV = 1645309
> PMT =
> PV = 1000000
> I   = =0 ÷ 12
> N   = 5 × 12

> Principal and interest due at the end of five years $1,645,309
> Principal   − 1,000,000
> Interest   645,309

If the interest compounds annually,

> FV = (?)   FV = 1610510
> PMT =
> PV = = 1000000
> I   = 10
> N   = 5

Principal and interest due at the end of five years $1,610,510
Principal   − 1,000,000
Interest   610,510

These one-payment loans are also called "zero-coupon" loans, "lump-payment" loans, or "no-payment" loans.

ADJUSTABLE RATE MORTGAGES

These are usually amortized loans. Periodically, the interest rate changes, and the amortization payments have to be recalculated. Take an adjustable rate mortgage (ARM) of $1,000,000 amortized over 25 years with monthly payments and with the interest keyed to a published interest rate, adjustable each year. The loan starts with an interest rate of 10 percent:

First Year

Total payments = $9,087 × 12 = $109,044
Interest = $99,574
Principal = $9,470
Balance of principal due = $990,530

At the end of the first year, the interest rate goes to up 10.5 percent because it is keyed to a published interest rate, which has risen. The new amortization term is 24 years. The loan amount is $990,530. The new monthly payment is

Second Year

Total payments = $9,435 × 12 = $113,220
Interest = $103,549
Principal = $9,671
Balance of principal due = $980,859

And so it goes year after year. It's a lot of calculating to do.

NEGATIVE AMORTIZATION LOAN

A negative amortization is one for which the balance due grows larger after payment of the annual debt service. You can tell if a loan is a negative amortization loan. Simply figure what the simple interest loan payment is. If the actual loan payment is lower, it's a negative amortization loan. There are two kinds of negative amortization loans. One is intentional. It is designed to be that way for a certain period. It is the type of loan that allows an investor to make a lower payment in the early years of the holding period. The other is an adjustable rate loan with a fixed payment. The adjustment on the interest rate for the adjustable rate loan goes so high that the fixed payment is below a simple interest payment, creating an accumulation of interest rather than an amortization of principal.

The variations on these loans are too diverse to cover all the possible calculations. You will want to know if the unpaid interest becomes principal, thus earning interest. If not, the unpaid interest accumulates only as unpaid interest, and the principal remains the same while the balance due on the loan grows.

Here is a negative amortization loan of $1,000,000 at 10 percent with a monthly payment of $7,000 for five years with unpaid interest converted to principal. This loan requires a financial calculator to determine the figures:

Interest paid over five years = $7,000 × 60 = $420,000

Interest required for interest only loan = 10% × $1,000,000
= $100,000 × 5 = $500,000

Interest deficiency for interest only loan
= $500,000 − $420,000 = $80,000

Balance of loan due at the end of five years = $1,103,249

Additional interest due at the end of five years
= $1,103,249 − $1,000,000 = $103,249

Total interest to be deducted for income tax
= $7,000 × 12 = $84,000 each year

Total interest to be deducted for income tax in the last year
= $84,000 + $103,249 = $187,249

Compounding effect on interest deficiency
= $103,249 − $80,000 = $23,249 additional interest

These calculations assume, of course, that the loan is paid off at the end of the fifth year. Note that even though the unpaid interest is converted into principal, it is deductible for income tax purposes when paid.

Another situation that is similar to a negative amortization loan is a nonperforming loan. Although, presumably, the reduced payments made are unintentional and unanticipated, the effect is much the same. Borrowers and lenders sometimes use a version of the negative amortization loan idea to work out the financing on properties performing below original expectations.

PARTICIPATION LOAN

Participation in the profits of the property is usually a sweetener for the lender. The participation loan is often designed to help the lender keep up with inflation in times of high inflation. It is otherwise a normal amortized loan. For instance, a $1,000,000 loan at 10 percent amortized over 25 years has a monthly payment of $9,087. Suppose that the property has a net operating income (NOI) of $125,000. The property is valued at $1,400,000 at the time of the loan. Were the property to be sold at that time, the sale proceeds would amount to about $300,000. The participation part of the loan states that the lender shall get additional interest amounting to 10 percent of the NOI in excess of $125,000 and 10 percent of the sale proceeds in excess of $300,000. If the NOI were $155,000 in the fifth year, here's what the additional interest would be:

$$NOI = \$155,000 - \$125,000 = \$30,000 \text{ excess}$$

$$10\% \times \$30,000 = \$3,000 \text{ additional interest}$$

If the property were sold for $1,800,000 in the fifth year, here's what the additional interest from the sale would be:

$$\begin{aligned} \text{Sale price} &= \$1,800,000 - \$108,000 \text{ (6\% cost of sale)} \\ &= \$1,692,000 - \$941,637 \text{ (loan balance)} \\ &= \$750,363 \text{ sales proceeds} \end{aligned}$$

$$\$750,363 - \$300,000 = \$450,363 \text{ excess} \times 10\% = \$45,036$$

The participation payment on sale is included in the sale proceeds analysis. The participation is an addition to the interest for this amortized loan calculated in the usual way.

IRREGULAR PAYMENT LOAN

Now that financial calculators are widely used, it is much easier for buyers and sellers to calculate payments, interest, and loan balances on all types of unusual loans. Owner-carried custom loans that are tailored specifically to the needs of the buyer and seller are now practical. For instance, suppose the buyer and seller look at a normal amortized loan of $1,000,000 at 10 percent interest with monthly payments amortized over 25 years. The monthly payment is $9,087. They use that as a model to create a loan better suited to their specific needs. As a result, the seller carries a loan of $1,000,000 on the property. The monthly payment schedule is as follows:

Year	Loan Payment/Month
1	$ 8,000
2	8,000
3	8,000
4	10,000
5	10,000
6	10,000
7	12,000
8	12,000
9	12,000
10	14,000 + $900,000 loan balance

What is the interest rate on this lending arrangement? To calculate the interest rate for this loan, you must use the internal rate of return (IRR) function of a financial calculator. (See Chapter 42 for a detailed explanation of IRR calculations.) The interest rate is 11.23 percent. Once you have calculated the interest rate, you can accurately calculate the interest for each year. Just looking at this loan, you can tell that it has a negative amortization for the first three years. For income tax purposes, all payments paid in excess of the principal are interest payments. Now that everyone has the means (financial calculators and computers) of making intelligent calculations regarding these creative loans, expect them to become more popular.

LOAN DATA

For some loans, the only way to efficiently and conveniently ascertain the annual interest expense is to do a computer calculation of the periodic interest expense and incorporate it into your income & expense statement and forecast. This is particularly true of complex loan arrangements, irregular payment loans, and adjustable rate loans.

AMORTIZATION OF LOAN POINTS

The front-end loan fees charged by lenders for income property loans may have to be amortized over the life of the loan. The amortization of loan points is placed in nonoperating expenses as a tax deductible item, but it is not included in the interest category.

IMPUTED INTEREST

If a loan arrangement between a buyer and a seller secured by the property is at an interest rate less than the minimum rate defined by Congress and the Tax Code, part of the payment of principal will be imputed to be interest. For instance, if the current interest rate set by Congress is 8 percent and the seller is charging 6 percent interest on seller financing, a portion of the principal paid will be imputed to be interest (i.e., a larger enough portion to increase the interest to the rate set by the Tax Code). This is a complex part of the Tax Code designed to prevent abuses by sellers who carry back loans.

PREPAID INTEREST

Interest that is prepaid gets special treatment under the Tax Code. It is not necessarily deducted in the year paid and may have to be amortized.

INTERNAL REVENUE SERVICE

Remember that what you are doing by calculating the interest paid is to establish a legal deduction from income for income tax purposes. Under the Tax Code, interest is a permitted business expense. But the payment of principal is not. The calculation of interest is part of the taxable income analysis and has little to do with operation of the property. The Tax Code and IRS regulations govern the way interest is deductible. In addition to making the proper calculations regarding the financing, you must be sure that the interest deduction you have calculated is a permissible one. One sure way to keep interest deductions legal for cash basis taxpayers in most circumstances is not to deduct interest until it is actually paid if you are on a cash accounting basis. For accrual basis tax payers, the rules are different.

CHAPTER 9

COST RECOVERY

Net Operating Income
−Interest Expense
−**Cost Recovery**
−Nonoperating Expenses
Taxable Income

A property deteriorates slowly. It wears out. The tax statutes and the IRS recognize this and allow a deduction from income as an expense to reflect this deterioration. Since the property is used up slowly, the deduction each year is for only a portion of the cost of the property. Keep in mind that this is just an expense on paper for the owner of the property and does not come out of the owner's pocket each year. Why? Because it is, in effect, a prepaid expense. The owner paid for the depreciation when purchasing the property. It's included in the purchase price. This becomes clearer when depreciation is relabeled to be "cost recovery."

IMPROVEMENTS AND LAND

First, you must determine what is depreciable. Land is not depreciable. It has always been there. It will always be there. It does not get used up. Thus, the land must be separated from the improvements on the land. Depreciation is calculated on the cost of the improvements. The value of the property is the purchase price. The purchase price must be allocated between the land and the improvements on the land. There are a number of methods for doing this.

The property tax assessor (in the county where the property is located) puts a value on the land and a value on the improvements as part of the process of assessing property tax. You can look this up at the county assessor's office and use the same ratio to allocate the cost of the property between the land and the improvements. Suppose the tax assessor has determined the following assessment:

Land	$ 33,000
Improvements	$117,000

$117,000 + $ 33,000 = $150,000
$ 33,000 ÷ 150,000 = 0.22

You can see that the assessor has determined that the land value is 22 percent of the value of the property. To get that ratio, the assessor appraised the land and the improvements. If you purchase the property for $1,000,000, you can allocate $220,000 to the land. If you do, it will probably be acceptable to the IRS (even though the IRS has no association with the county tax assessor).

Another method of allocating the cost between land and improvements is to get an appraisal. The appraisal will include an allocation.

Often the buyer and seller will agree on the allocation of the purchase price between the land and improvements and put the agreement in the purchase contract. This may be a sound basis for determining the allocation for income tax purposes, but it is subject to abuse. The allocation can put a very low value on the land, giving the buyer more depreciation. Naturally, the IRS will look upon such an allocation with skepticism. So if the allocation is included in the purchase contract, be sure it is reasonable even if favorable to the buyer.

PERSONAL PROPERTY

After you make an allocation of value between the land and the improvements, you must make an allocation between the value of the real estate improvements and the personal property. Personal property is anything that is not permanently attached to the real estate. A good example is the refrigerators in apartments. Perhaps the best way to make this allocation is to have the personal property appraised as well as the real estate. But that is seldom done. In the case of the refrigerators, you might call an appliance dealer to get a retail price to use as a guideline.

Because the depreciation terms for personal property are shorter than those for real estate, the buyer may desire the highest possible allocation of value to personal property. Again, this allocation, if made by a buyer or seller, is often subject to abuse. But if the allocation is included in the purchase contract and is reasonable, it may be acceptable grounds for making the allocation for income tax purposes.

Suppose the property tax assessor has determined that the value of the personal property in the above property is $6,000. The allocation is $111,000 for real estate improvements and $6,000 for personal property. Applying that ratio (6,000 ÷ 150,000 = 0.04) to the above property purchased for $1,000,000, you calculate that the allocation for personal property is $40,000. Unfortunately, in the records available to the public, not all counties note the value of the personal property, and you may have to gain access to the tax assessor's appraisal file.

DEPRECIATION

Under prior tax statutes, depreciation of a real estate improvement required a useful life (how long will the property last?) and a residual value (even after it has worn down, what value will the property retain?). It is hard to argue with this idea because it reflects reality. Each property is different. But it was difficult to know for sure what the IRS would allow.

COST RECOVERY FOR IMPROVEMENTS

The Tax Code now provides a schedule of depreciation called *cost recovery*. The term of the depreciation is set. You may have your choice of different depreciation periods. There is no residual value. The cost recovery table containing the multiplication factors is the final answer. You simply make the calculation. There are separate cost recovery tables for different types of real estate improvements. You use the one that's appropriate for the property you are analyzing and make your calculations. For the commercial property above, the improvements (less personal property) were assessed at $111,000, which is 74 percent of the purchase price ($111,000 ÷ 150,000 = 0.74 × 1,000,000 = $740,000). Thus, the allocation of the purchase price to the improvements is $740,000 (see Chapter 32).

COST RECOVERY FOR PERSONAL PROPERTY

In the above property, $40,000 was allocated to personal property. There is a cost recovery table for each of the various types personal property (see Chapter 32).

CAPITAL ADDITIONS AND REPLACEMENTS

All capital expenditures are set up on a cost recovery schedule. They are added to basis. Each will have a beginning year and ending year that are likely to be different from the improvements or personal property existing at the time of purchase. See Maplewood Apartments in Appendix I for an example of a cost recovery schedule.

BASIS

Basis is a technical taxation term and is subject to the definitions and calculations of the Tax Code. Essentially, the tax basis of the property at purchase is the purchase price. As cost recovery is taken as an expense each year, the amount of the cost recovery is subtracted from the basis. The resulting amount is the "adjusted basis" of the property. Upon the sale, the adjusted basis of the property is subtracted from the sale price to calculate the capital gain. The more cost recovery taken, the larger the capital gain. Here are the adjustments to basis (starting basis):

Increases	*Decreases*
Capital expenditures	Cost recovery
Special expenditures	Partial sale
	Casualty losses

Note: Special expenditures are defined by the Tax Code for certain situations.

This is a complex area of the tax laws and is well beyond the scope of this book. Refer to books on income taxation of real estate for specific information.

RECAPTURE

Accelerated cost recovery, when allowed by the Tax Code, is subject to recapture rules (see Chapter 32). That is, at the sale of the property, the benefit of accelerated cost recovery is reclaimed by the Tax Code with the effect that the amount of accelerated cost recovery is not a permanent deduction but becomes taxable.

AMORTIZATION ITEMS

There are expenses that must be amortized over a certain period defined by the Tax Code. Loan points are a good example. They must be amortized over the term of the loan. Since loan points are not a cost recovery item amortized according to the cost recovery tables, the amortization of loan points does not belong in the cost recovery category. It should be scheduled in nonoperating expenses.

SUMMARY

Only capital expenditures added to basis and amortized according to the cost recovery tables belong in the cost recovery category in addition to the original improvements and personal property.

CHAPTER 10

NONOPERATING EXPENSES

Net Operating Income
−Interest Expense
−Cost Recovery
−**Nonoperating Expenses**
Taxable Income

Nonoperating expenses is a catchall category for tax-deductible expenses that are not properly included in operating expenses. Some expenses are subjective expenses. They are not necessary to the proper operation of the property. Because they are subjective, they are not included in the operating expenses. Nonetheless, they are incurred. And, if they are tax deductible, this is where you place them in the forecast.

Some expenses are one-time expenses that, were they to be included in the income & expense statement, would distort the NOI for the year.

A good example of a subjective expense was shown in Chapter 6. The owner pays $11,000 in tuition for an MBA program for the on-site manager of a 120-unit apartment building. This is probably excessive in any case, but because the on-site manager is the owner's niece, it is suspiciously excessive. Is it tax deductible? Probably. Is it an operating expense? No. It's too subjective. It is properly categorized as a nonoperating expense.

Some expenses are extraordinary expenditures that would distort the income and expense statement if included. These expenses may be reasonable expenses. Their "one-time" nature, however, does not reflect how the property normally operates. So they are not included in operating expenses. They are properly categorized as nonoperating expenses. For instance, the promotional expenses to initially get a building fully occupied are considered a one-time expense incurred during the lease-up phase of a new building.

To be included in the nonoperating expense category, an expense must be subjective or extraordinary, or both. It must be an extra expense that is not necessary for the *normal* management and operation of the property. And it must be tax deductible. It does not matter whether the owner incurred such an expense purposefully or inadvertently.

This category is not the same as nonoperating outlays in the cash flow analysis. There may be expenses that are properly placed in nonoperating expenses, but not in nonoperating outlays, and vice versa. For instance, the amortization of loan points is properly placed in nonoperating expenses. The Tax Code may require that a front-end loan fee (loan points) be amortized over the term of the loan. Therefore, an amortized portion of it can be deducted each year. But loan points for a loan obtained to purchase the property do not effect the cash flow and are not properly placed in nonoperating outlays.

AMORTIZATION OF LEASING EXPENSES

Leasing expenses are nonoperating outlays incurred as new tenants are found for nonresidential properties. But they are not deductible as they are incurred. They must be amortized over the life of the lease. The amortization amount is entered in nonoperating expenses. Such expenses include leasing commissions, lease buy-outs, and moving expenses.

GROUND LEASE RENT

Ground leases are similar to financing. Ground lease rent is deductible as an expense for tax purposes. But like interest, ground lease rent is not an operating expense. When a ground lease exists, it should be made a line entry to alert readers of the forecast that the land is not part of the property:

> Net operating income
> −Interest expense
> **−Ground lease rent**
> −Cost recovery
> −Nonoperating expenses
> Taxable income

The alternative is to treat ground lease rent as a nonoperating expense and put it on a schedule as backup data for nonoperating expenses.

PARTICIPATION PAYMENTS

If a loan includes a provision for participation payments based on an equity interest rather than as additional interest, such payments are categorized as a nonoperating expense or under a separate line entry, participation payments.

NON-REAL ESTATE EXPENSES

If an expense is not reasonably related to the operation of the property, it may not be tax deductible in the business of providing building space for commercial or residential use. In such a case, it should not be included in the taxable income analysis or the forecast.

SUMMARY

The nonoperating expense category is for all tax-deductible expenses that are not interest or cost recovery but are not categorized as operating expenses. For that reason, each must be treated and calculated individually. It may be a currently deductible expense, or it may be an amortization expense. When there is a variety of nonoperating expenses, a schedule is appropriate for this category. Nonoperating expenses are subjective or extraordinary expenses that would distort operating expenses if placed in that category.

CHAPTER 11

TAXABLE INCOME

Net Operating Income
- Interest Expense
- Cost Recovery
- Nonoperating Expenses
Taxable Income

Taxable income is the bottom line of the taxable income analysis. It is the amount of income generated by a property on which income tax must be paid. Chapter 19 covers the details of taxation and the calculations of tax. This line entry is merely a resultant number indicating how much taxable income exists.

It is quite possible that taxable income will be a negative number, particularly in the early years of an investment. A negative taxable income is simply an operating loss for tax purposes. It is "tax shelter" because in some circumstances it can be applied against other current taxable income you might have. If a tax loss reduces your other real estate income or your non-real estate income, a tax savings results. A tax savings is money that stays in your pocket instead of going into the government's pocket. Thus, a negative taxable income is not entirely undesirable.

What makes tax losses bearable? Most expenses are paid out of pocket, and an operating loss means money out of pocket. For tax purposes, however, a significant prepaid expense is allowed by the Tax Code each year, and this expense is not out of pocket for an investor. It is just a "paper" loss. The expense is cost recovery (depreciation). When you purchase the property, you pay for the improvements on the property. As those improvements are used up (wear out), the Tax Code allows you to recover part of the cost each year. Thus, cost recovery, which is painless, normally contributes to the tax loss, if any.

Of course, in the unfortunate circumstances that a profit is shown for tax purposes (i.e., a positive taxable income), you will have to pay income tax on such income. But if the property can pay the operating expenses, the interest, and the cost recovery and still make a profit, perhaps it is not such an unfortunate situation.

Because cost recovery is allowed by the Tax Code, the profit or loss for tax purposes is different than the profit or loss calculated on a cash flow basis. So taxable profit or loss must be calculated separately from other methods of determining profit or loss.

SUMMARY

The taxable income analysis begins with net operating income (NOI). The operating expenses subtracted from gross operating income to calculate NOI are tax deductible. In the taxable income analysis, additional expenses such as interest, cost recovery, and other nonoperating expenses are subtracted to calculate taxable income. If the resulting number is positive, it is taxed in the cash flow analysis to calculate the tax liability. If the resulting number is negative, it is a tax shelter. See Chapter 32 for specific details regarding taxable income and tax losses.

PART 3

CASH FLOW ANALYSIS

The income & expense statement shows how the property, not the investment, is performing. The income tax analysis shows you how the income from the property will be taxed. The cash flow analysis shows you how much money will flow into (or out of) your pocket. It is a subjective analysis that reflects a specific ownership. And it provides you with two "bottom lines." This analysis is a different idea than the other two. It shows how your investment, not the property, is performing.

Chapters

12   Net Operating Income
13   −Debt Service
14   −Nonoperating Expenses
15   −Capital Additions
16   −Reserves
17   +Reserves to Additions
18   **Cash Flow Before Tax**
19   −Tax Liability
20   **Cash Flow After Tax**

The first bottom line is the cash flow before tax. This figure shows the amount of money that the investor will receive from the investment before the effect of income taxation. Then the tax liability is subtracted from the cash flow before tax. The result is the ultimate bottom line, cash flow after tax. This tells the investor how the investment is performing, all things considered.

Note that "reserves to additions" is short for "reserves applied to pay for capital additions," a more descriptive phrase that is too long for the forecast format.

When financing proceeds during the holding period (not at the beginning of the holding period) produce a cash flow, another line entry (new financing) should be added to the cash flow analysis:

> Net operating income
> −Debt service
> −Nonoperating outlays
> −Capital additions
> −Reserves
> +Reserves to additions
> **+New financing**
> Cash flow before tax
> −Tax liability
> Cash flow after tax

The loan balance of any loan being paid off out of new financing should be entered in nonoperating outlays. But the interest portion, if any, should be entered in interest in the taxable income analysis.

Either cash flow before tax or cash flow after tax can be used to measure performance with net present value (NPV) or internal rate of return (IRR) analysis.

CHAPTER 12

NET OPERATING INCOME
(REEXAMINED)

Net Operating Income
-Debt Service
-Nonoperating Outlays
-Capital Additions
-Reserves
+Reserves to Additions
Cash Flow Before Tax
-Tax Liability
Cash Flow After Tax

The net operating income (NOI) is the profit produced by the property. It is the bottom line of the income & expense statement. It is not the profit produced by the investment. Only by gathering information on the details of ownership and entering them into a calculation scheme to determine the profits of the investment can you rationally evaluate the investment opportunity. For example, it is possible for the property to be profitable while the investment is unprofitable.

You must use the NOI to pay the debt service, the nonoperating expenses, and the capital additions as well as to save funds in a reserve account for future extraordinary expenditures. If the NOI is not adequate for such outlays, you must cover such items out of pocket. The NOI is the money that the operation of the property generates. It is the beginning amount for the cash flow analysis.

The NOI for this chapter is exactly the same as the NOI for Chapter 7. In the forecast format, the taxable income analysis normally immediately follows the income & expense statement in a continuum of calculations. Thus, in the cash flow analysis the NOI must be entered again, and it appears twice in the forecast format (see Appendices I and II). If tax calculations are not included, however, the cash flow analysis can immediately follow the income & expense statement in a continuum of calculations. Then, the NOI appears only once in the forecast (see Appendix III).

For the idea of income & expenses, the NOI is the bottom line. For the idea of cash flow, the NOI is the starting point. (Consult Chapter 7 for more details on the NOI.)

CHAPTER 13

DEBT SERVICE

Net Operating Income
- **Debt Service**
- Nonoperating Outlays
- Capital Additions
- Reserves
+ Reserves to Additions
  Cash Flow Before Tax
- Tax Liability
  Cash Flow After Tax

Each year owners pay the debt service on their real estate loans: principal plus interest. The debt service is simply all the interest and principal to be paid in a year—the sum of the loan payments.

DEBT COVERAGE RATIO

A lender is concerned that the property should be able to pay the debt service. Theoretically, lenders don't make loans to people but to properties. They look to the property to pay back the loan. Otherwise, the loan would have to be considered a type of personal loan. So the first concern is that the property—the NOI—be able to cover the loan payments.

But just covering the loan payments usually isn't quite enough. A lender likes to see a margin of safety; that is, a lender likes to see an NOI larger than the debt service. The question is, how much larger? The required debt coverage ratio tells you. Take a property with an NOI of $227,010. The lender is willing to make a loan at 10 percent with monthly payments amortized over 25 years. The lender requires a debt coverage ratio of 1.15. That means that the NOI has to be 1.15 times the debt service, or 115 percent of the debt service.

How do you figure the size of the loan available for this property? You divide the NOI by the debt coverage ratio. Then you must use a financial calculator. Here's the calculation:

$$\$227,010 \div 1.15 = \$197,400 \div 12 = \$16,450$$
amount available for monthly loan payments

With this information, you can calculate the amount of the loan using the minimodel (see Chapter 41):

```
FV  =
PMT = 16450
PV  = (?)              PV = 1810277
I   = 10 ÷ 12
N   = 25 × 12
```

Thus, $16,450 at 10 percent interest over 25 years pays off a loan of $1,810,277. The loan to value ratio (loan amount to appraised value) is an important requirement for a loan too. The lender will usually lend the largest amount that satisfies both of these ratios.

CALCULATIONS

The calculations done in Chapter 8 to determine the interest for loans can be reviewed to understand how to calculate the annual debt service. The annual debt service includes the interest calculated and the principal that is paid, if any.

INTEREST-ONLY LOAN

For an interest-only loan, the annual debt service is simply the interest paid. No principal is paid, so no principal is included in the debt service. The debt service is the same each year.

For a $1,000,000 loan at 10 percent interest, the annual debt service is $100,000.

PRINCIPAL PAYMENT LOAN

Both the payment of principal and the payment of interest compose the annual debt service for this type of loan. The debt service will decrease each year as the balance of principal declines and therefore the annual interest amount declines.

For a $1,000,000 loan at 10 percent interest with an annual principal payment of $50,000, the debt service the first year is $150,000. The second year, the debt service is $145,000. Interest is only paid on $950,000 the second year. The debt service declines over the term of the loan.

AMORTIZED LOAN

An amortized loan has level payments that are paid until the end of the term. Although the ratio of principal and interest changes with each payment, the debt service is the same amount each year.

A $1,000,000 loan at 10 percent interest payable monthly with the principal amortized over 25 years has a payment of $9,087 each month. The annual debt service is $9,087 × 12 = $109,044.

ONE-PAYMENT LOAN

This type of loan is paid in one payment of principal and interest at the end of the term. There is no interest or principal paid each year until the last year of the loan.

A $1,000,000 loan at 10 percent interest with all interest and principal due and payable at the end of five years has no annual debt service until the last year. Both the interest and principal should be included in the sale proceeds analysis if the loan is paid off as the result of a sale. If the loan is paid off prior to the year of the sale, the payment of principal and interest should be placed in nonoperating outlays and the interest amount in interest in the taxable income analysis.

ADJUSTABLE RATE MORTGAGE

Because the interest rate changes periodically and the loan is reamortized, the annual debt service is different each year. This type of loan is the same as an amortized loan. But since the interest rate changes, the amortization payments change upon the reamortization of the loan. Thus, the annual debt service can increase or decrease each year.

For the example used in Chapter 8, the monthly payment for the first year was $9,087. The monthly payment for the second year was $9,435. The debt service amounts for the first two years are

Year

1 $9,087 × 12 = $109,044

2 $9,435 × 12 = $113,220

The amount of debt service depends on the adjustment in the interest rate. The adjustment depends on the fluctuation of the market interest rate.

NEGATIVE AMORTIZATION LOAN

A negative amortization loan is an amortized loan in which the annual debt service is less than the annual interest. The payments are level, and the annual debt service remains the same—in theory. In practice, the negative amortization loan concept is usually combined with another type of loan to produce some formula for creative financing. It is likely, therefore, that the debt service for such loans will change as the provisions of the loan require a change in the payment schedule. These loans must be carefully reviewed to determine what the debt service will be for each year.

For the simple example given in Chapter 8 of a $1,000,000 loan at 10 percent with a monthly payment of $7,000 each month, the annual debt service is $7,000 × 12 = $84,000.

PARTICIPATION LOANS

The lender's participation on a participation loan is part of the debt service too. Calculations regarding participation loans are covered in Chapter 8. Because participation cannot be determined until after you know how the property performs, it is often paid after the fact. Since it is highly likely to be different each year, each year's debt service must be calculated individually.

IRREGULAR PAYMENT LOANS

These are creative loans designed to serve the needs of the parties to a transaction. You must carefully review the provisions of the loan to determine what the debt service is each year.

The loan used as an example in Chapter 8 has the following payments:

Year	Loan Payment/Month
1	$ 8,000
2	8,000
3	8,000
4	10,000
5	10,000
6	10,000
7	12,000
8	12,000
9	12,000
10	14,000 + $900,000 loan balance

The debt service for Years 1–3 is $8,000 × 12 = $96,000. The debt service for Years 4–6 is $10,000 × 12 = $120,000.

SUMMARY

For debt service, it is not important to make a distinction between principal and interest. They both compose the annual debt service. They are both paid out of the net operating income (NOI). They both decrease the cash flow available to the owner of the property.

CHAPTER 14

NONOPERATING OUTLAYS

Net Operating Income
- −Debt Service
- −**Nonoperating Outlays**
- −Capital Additions
- −Reserves
- +Reserves to Additions
  Cash Flow Before Tax
- −Tax Liability
  Cash Flow After Tax

Nonoperating expenses are covered in Chapter 10. Just as they are deductible for income tax purposes, most reduce cash flow too. They are subjective expenses that are associated with the specific ownership of the property and are not necessary to operating the property successfully. The example (used in nonoperating expenses) of the owner paying the MBA (college) tuition for the property manager (the niece) is relevant here too because such an expenditure comes out of the cash flow. For most expenditures, nonoperating expenses and nonoperating outlays are the same.

Like nonoperating expenses, however, nonoperating outlays is a catchall category. Some nonoperating outlays reduce cash flow but are not tax deductible, just as some nonoperating expenses do not reduce cash flow even though they are deductible for income tax purposes (see exceptions below). Thus, this category can be different than nonoperating expenses.

In most cases, nonoperating outlays are virtually identical to the nonoperating expenses in the income tax analysis. If nonoperating expenses were not deductible for income tax purposes, why would they be considered in the analysis of the property? Why would they not just be considered personal expenses of the owner? Why would they be entered into the real estate accounting? With a few exceptions, the nonoperating expenses in the income tax analysis and the nonoperating outlays in the cash flow analysis are often the same. Here are some exceptions:

1. Loan points are paid in advance, but they are amortized over the term of the loan for income tax deductions. The amortized amount is entered into nonoperating expenses each year, but no corresponding amount is entered into nonoperating outlays.

2. Paragraph 1 assumes that the loan was made for the acquisition of the property. If the loan is a refinancing or new money borrowed during the holding period of the investment, the entire amount of the loan points is placed in nonoperating outlays in the year of the new loan. In subsequent years, no amount appears in nonoperating outlays, but the amortized amount is entered into nonoperating expenses each year.

3. A balloon payment (principal balance) may be made on a loan during the holding period of the investment. Since principal is not a tax-deductible item, the balloon payment does not belong in the taxable income analysis and is not a nonoperating expense. But it decreases cash flow and is properly placed in nonoperating outlays.

Because nonoperating outlay is a catchall category like nonoperating expenses, each entry must be individually scheduled. Although most items will match corresponding nonoperating expense items, such is not always the case.

NEW FINANCING

When there is new financing during the holding period of the investment, the proceeds of the new financing are placed in a special line entry. Suppose an existing loan has a balloon payment (remaining balance) of $2,300,000. You are able to replace the loan but only in the amount of $2,200,000. There is a shortfall of $100,000 without considering the loan points charged. That shortfall must be covered by the cash flow. Thus, the $2,300,000 is entered into nonoperating outlays.

New financing should be placed in its own category: new financing. Suppose that in order to pay off the above $2,300,000 balloon payment, you obtain a loan of $2,400,000 giving you a gain of $100,000 without considering loan points. Since there is no category for income or cash received other than net operating income (NOI), there is no place to put the new financing proceeds. Thus, a special line entry is created:

Net operating income
−Debt service
−Nonoperating expenses
−Capital additions
−Reserves
+Reserves to additions
+**New financing**
Cash flow before tax

This same line entry should be used for an additional loan obtained on the property (e.g., a second loan) during the holding period but not at the beginning of the holding period.

GROUND LEASE RENT

When the buildings are on land that is not included in the ownership of the property, a ground lease will exist. The rent paid on the ground lease should be put in a special line entry (ground lease rent):

Net operating income
−Debt service
−**Ground lease rent**
−Nonoperating expenses
−Capital additions
−Reserves
+Reserves to additions
Cash flow before tax

A ground lease is similar to a loan. By giving the rent on a ground lease its own line entry, you will alert readers of the forecast that the land is not included in the property. Otherwise, you will have to include ground lease rent in nonoperating outlays.

LEASING EXPENSES

Certain leasing expenses are often incurred when new tenants are found for nonresidential buildings. Such expenses include leasing commissions (paid to brokers), lease buy-outs (paid to the landlords of the buildings from which the tenants are coming), and moving expenses (paid to the new tenants). These expenses are placed in nonoperating outlays. The amortized portion of these expenses is entered in nonoperating expenses in the taxable income analysis.

PARTICIPATION PAYMENTS

If a participation loan is based on an equity interest rather than including a provision for additional interest, the participations payments are categorized as a nonoperating outlay or under a separate line entry, participation payments.

SUMMARY

Keep in mind that the nonoperating outlays have to do with the ownership of the property, not the operation of the property.

CHAPTER 15
CAPITAL ADDITIONS

Net Operating Income
−Debt Service
−Nonoperating Outlays
−**Capital Additions**
−Reserves
+Reserves to Additions
Cash Flow Before Tax
−Tax Liability
Cash Flow After Tax

CHARACTERIZATION OF CAPITAL ITEMS

Whether an expenditure is an operating expense or a capital expense is a matter for rational judgment and custom. If the expenditure item lasts more than a year, it might be a capital addition. For instance, washing the walls of an apartment between a vacating tenant and a new tenant is usually not expected to last more than a year and is a maintenance expense item. Painting the walls of an apartment between tenants conceivably could last longer than a year and might be considered a capital item. In many markets, however, painting is routinely done between tenants and is considered a maintenance expense item—an operating expense.

Replacement carpeting installed in an apartment is expected to last longer than one year and is normally treated as a capital replacement. For tax purposes, however, it is conceivable that with aggressive accounting, replacement carpeting could be considered a maintenance expense. If the accounting for the property is done primarily for the purpose of maximizing tax benefits, some adjustments may have to be made to use that accounting as the basis for realistic real estate analysis. For instance, if you find an operating expense item for carpeting in a property manager's income and expense statement, consider recategorizing it as a capital replacement.

AMORTIZATION OF CAPITAL EXPENDITURES

Capital expenditures are, in effect, prepaid expenses. For tax purposes, the cost of the capital expense is recovered over its statutory cost recovery period (discussed in Chapter 9). Amortization of the cost is not relevant for cash flow purposes.

PAYMENT FOR CAPITAL EXPENDITURES

What is relevant is *when* the owner pays for the capital addition or improvement. Capital improvements and replacements are usually made by contractors or provided by vendors. Or capital improvements might be implemented by employees or property management staff. Therefore, payment is nearly simultaneous with the installation of the capital improvement. The payment affects the cash flow regardless of how the capital expenditure might be amortized for tax purposes.

ASSUMPTIONS ABOUT THE PROPERTY

Capital additions and improvements by definition last longer than a year. That means they do not occur every year. Some may occur only every 20 years (e.g., roof replacement). Thus, if they are included in the income and expense statement, they will potentially distort the income and expense for that year. That's why they are left out of the operating statement and relegated to the cash flow analysis. Projected capital improvements may vary widely for similar properties.

It can be argued that capital improvements must be made regularly, particularly to an older property, so why not include them in an operating statement? That is done, in effect, by appraisers and lenders when they subtract a reserve for replacements in their calculation of NOI. (See Chapter 16.) But many capital improvements are major one-time expenditures that may not occur again for many years.

That brings up the question of the condition of the property. Is a property with an NOI of $200,000 and no anticipated capital improvements anticipated in the next few years worth the same as a property with an NOI of $200,000 that requires a new roof in three years? In other words, do anticipated capital improvements tend to have a negative effect on value?

In some situations, the surprising answer may be "no." Many buyers expect to buy a property in prime condition with no deferred maintenance and with no capital improvements anticipated in the near future. Rather than adjust the market value downward, the buyer may insist that the seller put the property in prime condition as a requirement of closing the purchase transaction. It is simply assumed by the buyer that any property bought will be in prime condition or no purchase will be consummated.

There are buyers, of course, who will purchase a property at a below-market purchase price and put the property in prime shape at their own expense. For these buyers, anticipated capital improvements do affect value negatively.

Sooner or later, every property will require major capital additions. In every case, there is some assumption by a buyer about a length of time during which the property is expected to be in good shape. If the property is projected to be in good shape during that period, the buyer will pay market value for the property. If not, the buyer will insist that the deficient condition be remedied or the price be lowered. For example, is it acceptable to buy a property at full market value if the roof must be replaced in a year? Three years? Six years? Nine years? At some point, the projected repair will be so far in the future that it will have no economic effect on the purchase transaction. Your assumption about where that point is may affect your analysis.

CAPITAL IMPROVEMENTS

When major repairs include durable materials, such repairs are considered capital improvements. Replacing all the siding on a building, replacing a roof, installing new wiring, and similar improvements must be done from time to time for all buildings. They are capital improvements and are paid for when completed. If they are not paid out of the cash flow of the property, or the cash flow plus reserves, they must be paid out of the owner's pocket. Thus, a large capital improvement could cause a negative cash flow. It is not unusual, of course, for an owner to obtain additional financing or a refinancing to bankroll capital improvements.

CAPITAL REPLACEMENTS

Capital replacements are often personal property that is not attached to the real estate such as appliances or ongoing replacement items such as apartment carpeting. These generally have a shorter useful life than capital improvements and are most often made in partial amounts each year rather all at one time. The replacement of refrigerators is a good example. A few will be replaced each year as they wear out. In an apartment, they will not last as long as the roof.

CAPITAL ADDITIONS

Some improvements are actually expanded during the holding period of an investor. For example, a 40-unit apartment building with excess land might be expanded to 48 units. The additional eight units are a capital addition including the entire cost of building them.

Many capital improvements and replacements are considered like normal maintenance, and they maintain rather than enhance the value of the property. There is no corresponding increase in income after such capital expenditures are made. For capital additions, however, additional income is expected. Thus, in the case of the eight extra apartments units, additional rent is expected.

When normal maintenance gets so financially burdensome that the property deteriorates as a result, usually when the property gets old, the property may need a rehabilitation (rehab). A rehab might be considered a capital addition that results in an increase in income when completed.

TAX CONSIDERATIONS

As a practical matter, any expenditure that has a lasting effect spanning well over a year or multiple years should be considered a capital expenditure rather than an operating expense. This idea may have nothing to do with the accounting practices of owners. The Tax Code creates its own rules for designating operating expenses and capital expenses, and such rules may have little to do with reality in some situations. The accounting practices of owners are often designed to "beat" the IRS. Thus, neither the Tax Code nor the accounting practices of owners are consistent in their determination of what is a capital expense and what is an operating expense.

The game for many owners is to generate current income tax deductions rather than amortize the cost of a capital expenditure over a number of years. That has little to do with trying to create an objective analysis of the property. For example, an owner might replace the siding on one building each year in an apartment complex with 10 buildings. For each building, it is a major repair and should be treated as a capital improvement. But the cost—being only 1/10th what replacing the siding for entire complex would cost—is easily buried in the operating schedule provided to the IRS. But such a cost should not be characterized as an operating expense just because it is convenient for the owner to characterize it so in dealing with the IRS.

TENANT IMPROVEMENTS FOR AN OFFICE BUILDING

Although a minimum allowance is provided to tenants in a new office building to build a suite, most tenants go over the allowance. Usually the tenant is required to pay for the excess expenditures over the allowance, but in a weak rental market, the landlord often pays instead. The finish for an office suite can be very expensive but have little value to a tenant who succeeds the one for whom the improvements were made. Therefore, although the cost of the minimum suite is considered part of the cost of the building, the excess cost of the suite when borne by the owner should not be considered part of the cost of the new building. It is an extra. It is a tenant improvement (TI) and is treated as a TI provided to new tenants to an existing (but not new) building.

New tenants coming into an existing (but not new) building usually demand a suite that is in good condition, and the landlord usually incurs some expense getting the suite ready for the new tenant. Often, getting the suite ready means making capital expenditures. This is a complex situation in which it is negotiable who pays for what. It is assumed that some level of rehab will be done on all suites for new tenants. Some suites may require only minor work, and some may require extensive work. Such TIs become a recurring capital expenditure, perhaps in every year of operation. Because they recur so regularly, there is a temptation to consider their cost an operating expense. But the cost of TIs is not an operating expense, and the IRS will not allow it to be treated as such. It is properly categorized as a capital addition and amortized on a cast recovery schedule.

TENANT IMPROVEMENTS FOR A SHOPPING CENTER

Shopping centers should be treated as office buildings regarding TIs. The practice in shopping centers is for tenants to pay for their TIs. Only very minimal space improvements are normally provided by the owner, and TIs are less likely to be an annual recurring expenditure of the owner.

ANOTHER VIEW

There is a serious dilemma that has been accentuated in the weak real estate markets resulting from the savings and loan debacle. Should regularly recurring capital expenditures be treated as operating expenses regardless of how owners treat them?

Lenders require a reserve for replacements (capital replacements) to be subtracted in calculating NOI. The theory is that capital replacements recur every year, and, therefore, they are an expense that reduces the cash flow regularly, not just occasionally. They are to be treated as an operating expense regardless of how the IRS treats them because they affect the ability of the property to pay the debt service. The resulting NOI will be smaller than the NOI that is calculated in the normal manner. When the resulting NOI is used with a cap rate to value the property, the resulting value will be less. The reserves in this case, however, may not include reserves for large capital improvement items.

Buyers in a depressed market look at investment properties much more critically than in times of unrelenting appreciation. Often they conclude that the TIs in a building are also an ongoing expense that should be subtracted in calculating the NOI. This makes the NOI even smaller. When used with a cap rate to value the property, the resulting value will be less.

In fact, the lenders and bargain hunters have a valid point of view. Certain capital replacements or TIs are regular expenditures for many properties. Why shouldn't they be considered operating expenses? Since reserves tend to even out these uneven but regular expenditures, perhaps the best practice is to subtract reserves for replacements and TIs in calculating the NOIs of appropriate properties.

The fallacy here is that sophisticated investors use net present value (NPV) and internal rate of return (IRR) analysis to evaluate income properties. Such techniques take into account the expenditures forecast for replacements or TIs. Thus, it is not necessary to modify the NOI. But NPV and IRR analysis are complex techniques requiring many calculations for multiyear projections. (See Chapter 42.)

It is easier for many people to subtract the reserves for replacements or TIs in calculating NOI than to do a sophisticated analysis. Therefore, those who tend to rely on the capitalization of NOI to determine value are likely to subtract the reserves for replacements or TIs in calculating NOI. Real estate professionals who use discounted cash flow analysis techniques such as NPV and IRR are less inclined to alter the customary way of calculating NOI.

The main problem in altering the customary way of calculating NOI is that by including expenditures subject to cost recovery in the income & expense statement, two income & expense statements are needed for each year: one for the IRS and one for everyone else. The one for the IRS would not include a reserve for capital expenditures because the capital expenditures are amortized in the taxable income analysis under cost recovery. The one for everyone else would include a reserve for capital expenditures. But the one for everyone else would subtract the reserve for capital expenditures after the calculation of NOI, not out of the income & expense statement. By considering the replacements and TIs later in the analysis rather than earlier, such debatable items would be less likely to affect the essence of the calculations, but they would still receive their due consideration. (See Part 9, the book summary, for further comment.)

SUMMARY

Capital additions (expenditures, improvements, replacements) are entered in this line entry. The amortized portion is entered in the cost recovery line entry in the taxable income analysis.

CHAPTER 16
RESERVES

Net Operating Income
-Debt Service
-Nonoperating Outlays
-Capital Additions
-**Reserves**
+Reserves to Additions
Cash Flow Before Tax
-Tax Liability
Cash Flow After Tax

INDIVIDUAL CHOICE

Individual owners decide whether to maintain reserves for a variety of circumstances that may require funds:

1. Major capital additions known to be needed during the life of the investment.
2. Annually recurring capital replacements.
3. Regularly recurring capital expenditures for tenants.
4. Unexpected capital additions.

A reserve account includes any or all of the above reserve items. You subtract reserves from net operating income (NOI) in the cash flow analysis.

CAPITAL ADDITIONS

While compiling data for analysis, you learn many things about a property and its future operation. Take Maplewood Apartments, for example.

In three years, the roof will need to be rebuilt, and the cost will be about $81,000, an extraordinary amount. The owner will pay this capital expenditure at the time the work on the roof is done three years from now. The cost can be spread over three years, however, by setting up a reserve account and funding it. When the work is done, the funds in the reserve account offset the cost of the capital improvement.

CAPITAL REPLACEMENTS

Many replacements are predictable and are characterized as capital replacements. After the initial years of operation, for instance, almost every year the property manager will replace some of the ranges, refrigerators, and other appliances at Maplewood Apartments. Since these are capital additions, it is not appropriate to include them as an operating expense in the calculation of NOI. Nonetheless, these replacements directly affect cash flow every year.

Usually relatively small amounts of money cover these capital expenditures. The purpose of the reserve fund for these expenditures is not to save for future major capital expenditures that may strain the owner's financial resources. Rather, the reserve fund reduces the cash flow each year to reflect reality and to even out these annual expenditures that may vary widely from year to year.

LEASING EXPENSES

Certain capital improvements for nonresidential tenants known as tenant improvements (TIs) may occur on a regular basis as tenants turn over in a building. Although occurring regularly, the cost of TIs may vary widely from year to year. A reserve for TIs is a reasonable means of evening the annual expenditure. There are other leasing expenditures, too, such as leasing commissions, lease buy-outs, and moving expenses (see Chapter 15) for which the use of a reserve account makes sense.

CONTINGENCIES

The unexpected happens, and sometimes it's expensive. By putting funds in a reserve account each year, funds are available for unexpected capital expenditures. This type of a reserve account is different, because it's for extraordinary, unplanned expenditures.

In most cases extraordinary, unexpected expenditures are capital additions or replacements rather than operating expenses. Reserves customarily are not used to offset operating expenses in the calculation of NOI.

LENDERS AND APPRAISERS

Lenders take a different point of view regarding reserves for replacements. They look to the NOI of the property to provide the funds to make the loan payments. They regard any expenditure necessary for the operation of the property as being a direct adjustment to NOI. Because the annual capital replacements are similar to expenses, lenders see them as such. As a result, lenders require that reserves for replacements be included in the calculation of NOI rather than in the cash flow analysis. This is contrary to the customary practice of nonlenders.

No lender will lend funds on real estate without an appraisal. It is not surprising, therefore, that income property appraisers adopt the same point of view as lenders on reserves for replacement.

EXTRAORDINARY OPERATING EXPENSES

Reserves could be used to cover large, extraordinary, operating expenses, whether predictable or unpredictable, but it is not customary to use a reserve account for operating expenses. If you subtract reserves in the calculation of NOI, your income & expense statement and all the calculations that depend on NOI will be distorted. Such large, extraordinary operating expenses may turn out to be capital expenditures under close inspection. If not, the best practice may be to amortize them, showing a portion of the extraordinary operating expenses each year for a number of years in the NOI calculation, well footnoted, of course.

SOURCE OF FUNDS

Several ways an owner might cover the cost of extraordinary expenditures when the time comes are the following:

1. Obtain a second loan on the property.
2. Invest more money in the property.
3. Sell an investment share in the property.
4. Sell the property.
5. Set up and maintain a reserve account in anticipation of extraordinary expenditures. The account is funded out of the cash flow of the property.

All are equally valid. It's strictly a matter of owner preference. If the owner desires a reserve fund, you need to answer another question: How much will go into the reserve fund each year?

ANNUAL AMOUNT OF FUNDED RESERVES

Capital Additions

Assume that the construction on the $81,000 roof restoration at Maplewood Apartments starts at the end of the third year. That allows three years to accumulate the funds. That's $27,000 to be reserved each year. The reserve fund can then be reduced or eliminated after the third year, assuming no further capital additions are scheduled.

It might be worthwhile to account for interest earned on the reserve account in your cash flow projection. If you do, also escalate the cost of the capital addition with an inflation factor. But if you ignore both the interest to be earned and the inflation, they tend to cancel each other, and your estimate will be reasonably accurate under most circumstances.

Capital Replacements

For capital replacements, you make an estimate expressed as a percentage of potential rental income. Estimate the useful life of the capital replacement items and the cost of the items. Divide the useful life into the number of items to get the annual average. For example, Maplewood Apartment (100 units) has 100 refrigerators. If the useful life of a refrigerator is 12½ years, eight refrigerators each year will be replaced on the average. If they cost $585 each, that's $4,680 each year that goes into the reserve fund for replacements. Once you've estimated the annual cost of all the capital replacement items, calculate what percentage this is of the total of potential rental income and round to the nearest whole percentage. Use that percentage to fund your reserve for replacements.

Another way to estimate a reserve for replacements is to use experiential information. For instance, a property manager may have a good idea (based on experience) of what a reasonable reserve for replacements should be. It may be expressed as dollars per square feet (SF) or per unit or as a percentage of potential rental income.

Contingencies

Although capital additions and capital replacements have verifiable facts on which to base an estimate, a reserve for contingencies is purely a matter of judgment. The less the owner desires to cope with expensive surprises, the more desirable a larger reserve for contingencies is. And the older the property, the more appropriate a higher reserve for contingencies becomes.

Total Reserves

The reserves category includes all reserve accounts. It is difficult to find guidelines for estimating reserves, and a large measure of professional judgment is required. Property managers, architects, engineers, general contractors, and other professionals can assist you. A generous estimate for reserves may be conservative and even prudent. But it directly reduces cash flow, an important element of an investor's rate of return. Therefore, accuracy and detail, not a conservative guess, constitute the basis for a sound estimate.

It is worth noting that although many analysts find reserves expressed as a percentage of potential rental income to be convenient, reserves expressed as a percentage of effective rental income or gross operating income may be more realistic.

CHAPTER 17

RESERVES TO ADDITIONS

Net Operating Income
- Debt Service
- Nonoperating Outlays
- Capital Additions
- Reserves
+ **Reserves to Additions**
  Cash Flow Before Tax
- Tax Liability
  Cash Flow After Tax

The funds put into the reserve account stay there until they are applied to the appropriate expenditures. You must decide what the appropriate cash flow expenditures are. Usually, you will limit the application of reserve funds to those items covered in Chapter 16 (i.e., capital additions). When the appropriate expenditure is made, you pay part or all of the amount from the reserve fund to offset the decrease in the cash flow that would otherwise result. "Reserves to additions" is short for "reserves applied to pay capital additions."

The reserves category shows how much is added to the reserve account each year from cash flow. The reserves to additions category shows how much is subtracted from the reserve account each year and added to cash flow. And the reserve fund category in the sale proceeds analysis shows the year-end balance in the reserve account.

The reserves to additions category should be backed up with a schedule of funds applied to specific expenditures. Normally, reserve funds are applied to capital additions until the capital additions are completely paid or the reserve account is completely depleted.

Reserves are created by a subjective investment decision. They are not absolutely necessary for you if you have other liquid assets or ready borrowing power. Therefore, you can create whatever reserves will make you comfortable and can apply them in any way that will make you feel comfortable. For instance, you can set up guidelines requiring that reserves never drop below a set amount even though a capital addition is not completely covered (resulting in a negative cash flow).

CHAPTER 18

CASH FLOW BEFORE TAX

Net Operating Income
−Debt Service
−Nonoperating Outlays
−Capital Additions
−Reserves
+Reserves to Additions
Cash Flow Before Tax
−Tax Liability
Cash Flow After Tax

Cash flow before tax is the bottom line of the cash flow analysis unless your analysis includes tax calculations. The cash flow before tax is the amount that actually goes into your pocket from the investment, not the property. It is like the interest you earn on a certificate of deposit (CD). It is like the coupon interest payment you receive from a bond.

It is possible for your cash flow before tax to be a negative amount. A number of things may cause a negative cash flow:

1. A decreased NOI due to a decrease in rents or other income.
2. Too much financing (debt service) for the property to carry.
3. A large nonoperating expense.
4. A large capital improvement
5. Annual increases in expenses, nonoperating expenses, or capital replacements.

Sometimes investors intentionally purchase a property with a financing structure that causes a negative cash flow for one or more years. If you can increase your rate of return by maximizing borrowed funds, successive negative cash flows may be acceptable. As you cover such negative cash flows, it is like making your investment in the property later rather than sooner.

The cash flow before tax for each year is used for the before-tax net present value (NPV) and the before-tax internal rate of return (IRR) calculations. To make such calculations, you pick the annual cash flows before tax out of the cash flow analysis and input them into the flow model (see Chapter 42):

$$CF\ 0\ =$$
$$CF\ 1\ =$$
$$CF\ 2\ =$$
$$CF\ 3\ =$$
$$CF\ 4\ =$$
$$CF\ 5\ =$$
$$I\ \ \ =\ ?$$

You must also add the sale proceeds before tax to the cash flow for the last year of the projection. See Appendix I for the Maplewood Apartment cash flows before tax:

$$CF\ 0\ =\ (1783095)\quad\ \text{initial investment}$$
$$CF\ 1\ =\quad 26153$$
$$CF\ 2\ =\quad 47780$$
$$CF\ 3\ =\quad 54373$$
$$CF\ 4\ =\quad 93665$$
$$CF\ 5\ =\quad 117993 + 2854766$$
$$I\ \ \ =\ ?$$

The sale proceeds before tax is known as the "reversion." Before you can earn an internal rate of return (the most rational rate-of-return measurement for a multiyear projection), you must get back your investment. The IRR is a return of and a return on your investment. If the cash flows return less than your initial investment (investment base), you will earn a negative yield. Few short-term real estate investments get back the initial investment without the sale proceeds for the last year being included in the cash flow. So you can tell just by looking at your initial investment and the cash flows (and adding and subtracting) whether your IRR will be positive.

The equity return rate uses the first year's cash flow before tax (CFBT) as the divisor. Some real estate professionals use the first year's CFBT as the divisor for the cash on cash yield (making it identical to the equity return rate). In an attempt to be objective in calculating rates of return, some real estate professionals define CFBT as the net operating income (NOI) less only the debt service.

Although tax calculations add a dimension of analysis required by many investors, for many other investors, making a before-tax cash flow analysis is adequate. Tax calculations may be handled separately, because a precise tax analysis from the investor's accountant is desired or because portfolio considerations are paramount. If you are providing analysis for clients, don't always assume they will want after-tax analysis.

CHAPTER 19

TAX LIABILITY

Net Operating Income
−Debt Service
−Nonoperating Outlays
−Capital Additions
−Reserves
+Reserves to Additions
   Cash Flow Before Tax
−**Tax Liability**
   Cash Flow After Tax

In Chapter 11, you determined taxable income. Now you determine the investor's marginal tax rate, explained below, and apply it to taxable income (from the taxable income analysis) to calculate tax liability:

Taxable income	$120,889	
Marginal tax rate	28%	U.S. income tax
Tax liability	$120,889 × 28% = $33,849	Tax paid

A property showing a negative taxable income is said to have tax shelter:

Taxable income	($77,764)	Tax shelter
Marginal tax rate	28%	U.S. income tax
Tax liability	($77,764) × 28% = ($21,774)	Tax savings

To find the investor's highest marginal rate, look at the IRS tax rate schedules and talk with the investor's accountant. Just applying the U.S.

income tax marginal rate isn't accurate in states where there is a state income tax. You must also use the income tax marginal rate for the state in which the investor resides. Suppose the investor is in a state where his or her marginal tax rate is 11 percent. A more accurate representation of the tax to be paid is the combination of the U.S. and state (11% × 72% = 8%—see Chapter 32) income tax rates:

Taxable income	$120,889	
Marginal tax rate	36%	U.S. and state income tax
Tax liability	$120,889 × 36% = $43,520	Tax paid
Taxable income	($77,764)	Tax shelter
Marginal tax rate	36%	U.S. and state income tax
Tax liability	($77,764) × 36% = ($27,995)	Tax savings

These assumptions are commonly made in estimating tax liability:

1. The investor has other sources of income, and this property is not the sole source of income. It's additional income.

2. Therefore, income is taxed at the investor's highest marginal tax rate. In other words, the income is taxed in the investor's highest bracket.

3. The calculation of tax liability is only a rough estimate of the effect of income tax on the investor's real estate investment, not an attempt to file the investor's future tax return today.

Whether a person or a business entity, the investor is likely to have other income. Even tax-paying entities that own only real estate may own other real estate. Thus, the newly acquired property usually provides an addition to existing income or a loss that under certain circumstances can be applied against other income. Because the new property's income is added to existing income, each additional dollar added is taxed in the highest tax bracket in which the investor is paying tax; that is, the marginal tax rate is applied to each additional dollar. When there is only one tax rate, of course, there is no marginal rate.

The exception is the investor with no other source of income buying his or her first property. In this case, the full effect that the multiple tax brackets have on the property will have to be calculated to make an accurate estimate. But this is not a common situation. Most entities that own only one property and have no other source of income are limited partnerships. They are not tax-paying entities. They pass through the benefits of ownership to the individual partners. It is the partners who are taxed.

Determining tax liability for a tax return is a very precise calculation. Thus, even under the best of circumstances, it is difficult to determine accurately for the future years. Tax liability calculations as used in an investment analysis are only rough estimates. To try to estimate tax liability precisely is an effort that reaches diminishing returns quickly. It is best to use a simple method, intelligently applied, that will provide a rough estimate of the affect of the income taxation on the property. Leave the filing of tax returns and more precise analysis to accountants and other tax advisers.

An investor who has a specific need for precision in tax planning must work with his or her accountant or tax adviser in any reasonable attempt to realize such precision. It is well beyond the scope of this book and beyond the knowledge of most real estate professionals to achieve such precision. Accountants and tax advisers can make tax calculations and establish relevant assumptions with more skill but will have a difficult time predicting the future just as anyone will.

Tax liability can be either a positive or negative number. If it's a positive number, you have to pay tax, and it diminishes the CFBT. The resulting cash flow after tax (CFAT) is a smaller number. Here is an example where the taxable income and tax liability are positive:

CFBT	$129,771
−Tax liability	(33,849)
CFAT	95,922

If the tax liability is negative, you have a tax savings and there is tax shelter. When you subtract a negative number, the number changes to positive. Thus, when you subtract a negative tax liability from CFBT, the CFAT is increased, thus reflecting the effect of the tax shelter. In the following example, there is tax shelter, and the tax liability is negative ($21,774). Keep in mind that a negative subtracted becomes a positive; thus, the $21,774 becomes positive. The result is an increased CFAT:

CFBT	$ 86,449
−Tax liability	21,774
CFAT	108,223

Does tax shelter really increase cash flow? Tax shelter represents tax dollars that do not have to be paid. Those dollars stay in the investor's pocket instead of being paid in tax. The final result is more dollars in the investor's pocket, thus an increase in cash flow.

OTHER TAX CONSIDERATIONS

This straightforward tax formula to estimate the effect of income taxation on the real estate investment does not take into account other Tax Code provisions such as the alternative minimum tax or the tax credits that Congress from time to time allows. If you perceive that a special tax rule will have a significant effect on the after-tax performance of the property, you should include the calculations for such a rule in a systematic procedure that further refines the effect of taxes on the investment. For instance, when tax credits are allowed, they should be added to the cash flow before tax as a separate entry or should offset tax liability.

SUMMARY

Taxation of real estate income is well beyond the scope of this book. A general overview to illustrate how taxation can be incorporated into the analysis is the goal of this book. Without attempting to make precise calculations regarding tax liability such as is appropriate for filing a tax return, you can estimate the effect of income taxation on the after-tax performance of the real estate investment. The procedure is to apply a marginal tax rate to the taxable income from the taxable income analysis. Note that the book assumes a cash basis taxpayer. If you are an accrual basis taxpayer, the calculations are different in many cases.

CHAPTER 20

CASH FLOW AFTER TAX

Net Operating Income
- Debt Service
- Nonoperating Outlays
- Capital Additions
- Reserves
+ Reserves to Additions
  Cash Flow Before Tax
- Tax Liability
  Cash Flow After Tax

Once you have taken the cash flow before tax and subtracted the tax liability from it, you have calculated the cash flow after tax. This is the ultimate bottom line for you. Now you have taken everything into consideration regarding the operation of the property and the structure of the investment, except the sale. Although the calculation of tax liability may be just a rough estimate compared to the precise work that goes into doing detailed tax planning, including the tax liability is likely to make your internal rate of return (IRR) calculation more realistic. And there is nothing to prevent you from going beyond the scope of this book and incorporating more precise tax calculations into the calculations for the tax liability line entry.

Tax liability can be positive or negative, depending on whether taxable income is positive or negative. Tax liability is subtracted from the cash flow before tax to calculate the cash flow after tax. If tax liability is a positive number, it decreases the cash flow before tax, and the cash flow after tax is smaller. If tax liability is a negative number, it increases the cash flow after tax because a negative when subtracted changes signs to a positive. In other words, a tax saving (a negative tax liability) will increase the cash flow before tax to result in a larger cash flow after tax.

Although the above paragraph is true in theory, the Tax Code may limit the use of tax losses to generate tax savings. Nonetheless, if you own a number of other real estate investments that are currently generating taxable income, you can use the negative taxable income (tax shelter) from the property to offset the taxable income of the other properties. In such a case, you will show the negative taxable income, if any. The corresponding negative tax liability when subtracted from cash flow before tax will result in an increased cash flow after tax.

To calculate an after-tax IRR, you pick the cash flows after tax (CFATs) from the cash flow analysis and input them in the flow model (see Chapters 18 and 42).

$$CF \ 0 =$$
$$CF \ 1 =$$
$$CF \ 2 =$$
$$CF \ 3 =$$
$$CF \ 4 =$$
$$CF \ 5 =$$
$$I \quad = ?$$

You must add the sale proceeds after tax to the cash flow for the last year of the forecast. See Appendix I for the Maplewood Apartments cash flows after tax:

$$CF \ 0 = (1783095) \quad \text{initial investment}$$
$$CF \ 1 = \quad 26153$$
$$CF \ 2 = \quad 47780$$
$$CF \ 3 = \quad 54373$$
$$CF \ 4 = \quad 93665$$
$$CF \ 5 = \quad 117993 + 2337290$$
$$I \quad = ?$$

The cash flows for Maplewood Apartments are the same before tax and after tax except for the last year when the sale proceeds after tax is added. Maplewood Apartments generates tax shelter, but the Tax Code does not allow you to use it; thus, the tax liability is zero each year. In the last year when the property is sold, the profit on sale (and the suspended losses) is taken into account, resulting in a tax liability on sale of $517,476. Thus, there is a $517,476 difference upon sale between the before-tax and after-tax cash flow. The sale proceeds after tax are known as the "reversion."

The cash on cash rate of return uses the first year's cash flow after tax as the divisor. The cash flow after tax for the first year is also used as the divisor for the equity return rate. Because such rates of return take into account only the first year of the investment, they do not provide you with a comprehensive analysis of the investment. By using the cash flows after tax for each year of the holding period and the IRR or NPV analysis, however, a complete financial picture of the property's performance is realized.

The after-tax forecast can be easily erased from the forecast format without affecting any of the prior numbers. Therefore, you can create a computer program (spreadsheet template) that does the after-tax analysis, and the same program will automatically provide you with a before-tax analysis. Simply do not display the line entries after the cash flow before tax (in the cash flow analysis) and after the sale proceeds before tax (in the sale proceeds analysis):

Net operating income	
−Debt service	
−Nonoperating outlays	
−Capital additions	
−Reserves	
+Reserves to additions	
Cash flow before tax	
−Tax liability	DELETE
Cash flow after tax	DELETE
Sale Price	
+Reserve fund	
−Loan balances	
−Cost of sale	
Sale proceeds before tax	
−Tax liability on sale	DELETE
Sale proceeds after tax	DELETE

Changing your forecast from after tax to before tax is just that simple.

PART 4

SALE PROCEEDS ANALYSIS

The final concept in the analysis of a real estate investment is the analysis of the projected sale. This is essentially a cash flow analysis. It is subjective because it includes loan balances. It plays a role in calculating the overall performance of the investment. And like the cash flow analysis, it provides two bottom lines.

Chapters

21   Sale Price
22 +Reserve Fund
23 −Loan Balances
24 −Cost of Sale
25   **Sale Proceeds Before Tax**
26 −Tax Liability on Sale
27   **Sale Proceeds After Tax**

One bottom line is the sale proceeds before tax. The other is the sale proceeds after tax. These bottom-line figures are used along with the corresponding cash flow analysis figures to calculate either a before-tax net present value (NPV) or internal rate of return (IRR), or an after-tax NPV or IRR.

CHAPTER 21

SALE PRICE

Sale Price
+Reserve Fund
−Loan Balances
−Cost of Sale
Sale Proceeds Before Tax
−Tax Liability on Sale
Sale Proceeds After Tax

The anticipated sale price for a property is the market value for the property at the time of sale. This is a gross price from which certain disbursements must be made. The sale is assumed to be at the end of the year. For example, you purchase an apartment building for $4,800,000. The projected net operating income (NOI) for the year is $432,000, and the market capitalization rate (cap rate) is 9 percent. Inflation is 4 percent per year, and rents are going up with inflation. What is the sale price at the end of the first year?

One way to calculate the sale price is to calculate a year of inflation; that is, if inflation is 4 percent, increase the value by 4 percent. The sale price of the property at the end of the first year using this method is $4,992,000.

Another way is to use a cap rate. Since the end of the first year is the same as the beginning of the second year, the cap rate is applied to the second year's NOI. In this example, suppose you expect the NOI to go up more slowly than inflation due to a projected increase in the property management fee. The NOI for the second year is projected to be only $443,000. The normal technique is to assume that the cap rate will be the same for the duration of the holding period as it is for the purchase. Unless you have reason to believe the contrary in this case, you will use 9 percent for the cap rate. With a cap rate of 9 percent, the value of the property is $4,922,222 at the beginning of the second year (the end of the first year).

Keep in mind that the sale is assumed to be made at the end of the year with the sale price equal to the market value of the property at the end of the year. Because the end of the year is the same as the beginning of the next year, the cap rate method of determining a sale price applies a cap rate to the *next* year's NOI. Because buyers and sellers are anticipating the first year of the new ownership when they determine the value of the property for negotiation purposes (based on a pro forma NOI and a cap rate), the NOI for the *next* year is a logical determinate of value.

When rents and values are falling, your forecast should reflect that reality. Thus, the sale price in future years may be lower than the purchase price.

A third way to project the sale price is to assume that the sale price will stay the same for the entire holding period. This seldom reflects reality. But there are situations in which the value of the property may not follow the market. For instance, suppose you are purchasing an office building with one tenant and 10 years left to run on a lease (originally a sale and leaseback). The current rent of $14/SF/year will not change during the 10 years. The current market rent for similar buildings is $22/SF/year. What effect will the flat rent have on the value of the property during the next 10 years? In the early years, the effect will work to limit the value of the property. Undoubtedly, the closer to the end of the lease, the more the value of the property will approach the market value of similar buildings.

Assuming that the market rent will go up 4 percent per year with inflation, today's $22/SF/year will become $32.57/SF/year in 10 years. At the end of 10 years (the end of the lease), the rent for the office building will more than double from $14/SF/year to a potential $32.57/SF/year. In anticipation of this change, you may want to make a rough estimate for the sale price for each year of the 10-year period. That estimate will not be determined by an inflation rate, nor by the NOI and a cap rate, except perhaps for the end of the 10th year.

A sale and leaseback agreement often contains an option for the seller-tenant to repurchase the property. Due to the Tax Code, the option is usually one to repurchase at fair market value. But a sale and leaseback arrangement might give the seller-tenant an option to repurchase the property at the end of the lease term for a nominal amount. In such a case, the option arrangement will dictate the sale price. If the property is sold by the buyer to a third-party before the seller-tenant exercises the option to repurchase at a nominal price, the repurchase option will have a limiting effect on the sale price the third party is willing to pay.

The longer the holding period, the less important it is for a buyer to receive sale proceeds from a sale at the end of the holding period. For example, if a buyer invests in a 30-year sale and leaseback arrangement in which the seller-tenant has an option to repurchase the property for a nominal amount, the buyer can achieve a reasonable rate of return without significant sale proceeds. The buyer gets a reasonable return from 30 years of cash flow. Thus, there may be many long-term investment situations for which you will not receive significant sale proceeds. For such arrangements, the provisions of the agreement are more important for determining a sale price than anticipating market value.

CHAPTER 22

RESERVE FUND

Sale Price
+**Reserve Fund**
−Loan Balances
−Cost of Sale
Sale Proceeds Before Tax
−Tax Liability on Sale
Sale Proceeds After Tax

The reserve fund consists of the accumulated unused funds in the reserve account. Any funds that are applied to pay for capital improvements deplete the reserve account. The reserve fund, as it appears in the forecast, enables you to check the amount available to be applied to capital additions that may be required.

If a reserve account is funded and is used, there is likely to be some money in the reserve account upon sale. The funds in a reserve account and the capital improvements are seldom perfectly offsetting. When a capital improvement is made in the year that the sale transaction is closed, however, and the amount in the reserve fund is not sufficient to cover the cost of the improvement, the reserve account will empty.

If there is money in the reserve account, it is not conveyed to the buyer of the property. Therefore, the account is closed and the funds removed. In essence, the money increases the cash flow of the sale transaction. It is added to the sale price in the sale proceeds analysis.

Keep in mind that the forecast shows that the funds reserved are reserved on an annual basis. As a practical matter, funds may reserved on a monthly basis. A capital improvement early in the year may deplete the reserve fund to zero and require additional cash resources from the owner. Yet the reserve fund may begin building up again in the months after the capital improvement is finished.

CHAPTER 23

LOAN BALANCES

Sale Price
+Reserve Fund
−Loan Balances
−Cost of Sale
Sale Proceeds Before Tax
−Tax Liability on Sale
Sale Proceeds After Tax

Loan balances consist of the unpaid principal of the loans for the property. Annual interest is entered in the interest category of the income & expense statement. If interest other than the annual interest expense is unpaid on the loan, it is part of the loan balance too. The loan balances and the unpaid interest, if any, are entered in the loan balances category. Note that the unpaid interest that is part of a loan balance may receive a specific tax treatment not reflected in its placement in the loan balances category. Nonetheless, the placement of unpaid interest in the loan balances category accurately approximates the effect of its payment on the after-tax cash flow resulting from the sale.

To compute the loan balances, the following calculations are presented to correspond with the loan types in Chapter 8.

INTEREST–ONLY LOAN

The balance due on an interest-only loan is simply the loan amount. If no principal is paid, the loan balance is constant. But if the interest is paid annually, instead of monthly, and the property is sold in the middle of a future year, the accumulated interested is added to the principal to calculate the loan balance.

PRINCIPAL PAYMENT LOAN

For this type of loan, add together all the principal payments that have been made and subtract them from the loan amount. For instance, for a $1,000,000 loan that requires annual principal payments of $50,000, the loan balance after three years will be

$$3 \times \$50,000 \qquad = \$150,000$$
$$\$1,000,000 - \$150,000 = \$850,000$$

Thus, $850,000 is the loan balance after the third year's payment has been made.

AMORTIZED LOAN

When the term of the loan is shorter than the amortization term or when the loan is paid off before it is completely amortized, you will need a financial calculator to calculate the balance of the principal due for the payoff. This is called a *balloon payment* or simply the mortgage balance due. Because each amortization payment contains a different ratio of principal and interest, an easy calculation of the loan balance is not possible—without a financial calculator. Use the amortization function (i.e., the AMORT function of many calculators) to calculate loan balances. For instance, the balance on a $1,000,000 loan at 10 percent interest amortized over 25 years after 36 monthly payments have been made is $968,510.

Another method of calculating the loan balance is to take the present value (PV) of the remaining payments at the interest rate of the loan. (This method is illustrated in Chapter 41.)

ONE–PAYMENT LOAN

For a one-payment loan, all the interest and all the principal are due in one payment at the end of the term. If the interest is simple interest, the interest remains constant for each period of the loan and accumulates. A $1,000,000 at 10 percent simple interest at the end of three years has a balance of $1,300,000:

$$10\% \times \$1,000,000 = \$100,000$$
$$\$100,000 \times 3 = \$300,000$$
$$\$300,000 + \$1,000,000 = \$1,300,000$$

The balance for a $1,000,000 loan at 10 percent compounded annually can be calculated on a financial calculator using the minimodel (see Chapter 41):

```
FV  = (?)              FV = 1331000
PMT =
PV  = 1000000
I   = 10
N   = 3
```

The balance of $1,331,000 for compounded interest is $31,000 more than the balance calculated with simple interest.

ADJUSTABLE RATE MORTGAGES

Treat adjustable rate mortgages the same as amortized loans. Because the interest rate changes every year (or sometimes more often), however, the loan has to be reamortized each year for the remaining portion of the amortization term to calculate the new payment. Thus, a loan balance can be calculated as an amortized loan based on the current year's loan characteristics. For instance, suppose a 25-year, $1,000,000, adjustable rate loan with monthly payments has a balance of $982,118 at the end of three years. The rate for the current year (fourth year) is set at 10¼ percent. The loan payment is now calculated for a $982,118 loan at 10¼ percent amortized over 22 years using the minimodel (see Chapter 41):

```
FV  =
PMT = (?)              PMT = 9382
PV  = 982118
I   = 10.25 ÷ 12
N   = 22 × 12
```

Therefore, the new loan payment is $9,382. Now you can determine the balance at the end of any month during the year or at the end of the year by calculating the loan balance for an amortized loan as you normally would using a financial calculator. For instance, the loan balance of this loan at the end of the fourth year is $969,620.

NEGATIVE AMORTIZATION LOAN

If the unpaid interest on a negative amortization loan is compounded, you can calculate the balance due with a financial calculator. Suppose you have a $1,000,000 loan at 10 percent with an annual payment of $90,000. Use the amortization function on your financial calculator to compute the balance after five years: $1,061,051.

If the unpaid interest is not compounded, however, it accumulates, and a financial calculator cannot calculate the balance using the normal financial functions. Here is how you can calculate the balance:

Annual interest	$100,000
−Annual payment	90,000
Accumulation/year	10,000

$$5 \times \$10,000 = \$50,000$$
$$\$1,000,000 + \$50,000 = \$1,050,000 \text{ balance due}$$

The examples above for an accumulated interest mortgage and a negative amortization mortgage are simple ones because the interest rate stays the same. For an adjustable rate mortgage with a fixed payment, the interest calculations have to be made for each year in order to determine the loan balance. The variations are too diverse to cover all possibilities, but the basic calculations included here can be applied to many different loan arrangements.

PARTICIPATION LOAN

A common participation agreement in a loan allows the lender to obtain a percentage of the sale proceeds. Usually a calculation is made to determine what the sale proceeds would be in a theoretical sale if the property were sold immediately after the purchase. The participation agreement covers the excess sale proceeds over the sale proceeds of the theoretical sale. For instance, suppose the sale proceeds in the theoretical sale are $2,700,000. What is the participation amount in a sale at the end of the fifth year if the sale proceeds are projected to be $4,100,000 and the participation amount is 10 percent?

$$\$4,100,000 - \$2,700,000 = \$1,400,000 \times 10\% = \$140,000$$

If the assumption becomes true, the participation amount will be $140,000. This amount is subtracted in the calculation of tax on ordinary income and is included in loan balances.

Some participation loans take their participation not as additional interest but rather as an equity interest. In such a case, the participation payment upon sale is subtracted in the calculation of capital gain rather than in the calculation of tax on ordinary income. It is also included in loan balances or entered as a separate line entry. The annual participation payments for such a loan are categorized as a nonoperating expense rather than as interest.

IRREGULAR LOAN PAYMENTS

These loans must be analyzed on a custom basis with the techniques covered above. It's likely that each year will have to be analyzed separately to calculate a balance at the end of the holding period.

SUMMARY

Some loans can be so complicated that the most reasonable way to calculate a loan balance is to use a computer program specifically designed to process a particular type of loan. But without such a program, some combination of the above techniques in conjunction with discounted cash flow analysis can be applied to calculate a loan balance. (See Chapters 8 and 13 for additional information on making loan calculations. And see Chapters 41 and 42 for discounted cash flow analysis techniques.)

CHAPTER 24

COST OF SALE

Sale Price
+Reserve Fund
−Loan Balances
−**Cost of Sale**
Sale Proceeds Before Tax
−Tax Liability on Sale
Sale Proceeds After Tax

The cost of sale includes broker's commissions, marketing costs, transactions expenses, closing costs, professional fees, and the like. Because a broker's fee is usually a contingent fee that is a percentage of the sale price, the cost of the sale is often calculated as a percentage of the sale price larger than the anticipated broker's fee. For example, if a broker's commission of 2 percent is anticipated, 3 percent might be a reasonable estimate for the cost of sale.

If it is anticipated that the property can be sold without a broker involved, there may be a savings. But in such a case, a substantial amount for marketing expenses and for the salaries of personnel performing marketing services should be included in the cost of sale.

Because the sale is anticipated at the end of the holding period, it is difficult to predict market conditions. When the market is not favorable to sellers, abnormally high marketing expenses may result from the effort to sell the property. When the market is favorable to sellers, the cost of sale may be lower than anticipated. Because it is not certain what the cost of sale will be, it is practical to make a rough percentage estimate rather than compile a potential list of expenses. Thus, the broker's anticipated commission plus an additional percentage factor may be as accurate as you can expect to be.

CHAPTER 25

SALE PROCEEDS BEFORE TAX

Sale Price
+Reserve Fund
−Loan Balances
−Cost of Sale
Sale Proceeds Before Tax
−Tax Liability on Sale
Sale Proceeds After Tax

The sale proceeds analysis is essentially a cash flow analysis for the sale transaction. As such, it has two possible results: a before-tax cash flow and an after-tax cash flow. This chapter covers the before-tax cash flow. It is simply the cash flow resulting from the sum of the cash flows involved in the sale of the property. The loan balances and the cost of sale are subtracted from the sale price. The reserve fund is added. The result is the cash that goes into the investor's pocket before tax is paid.

The sale proceeds analysis assumes that the owner receives cash. This is true when the buyer pays all cash or obtains a loan and pays cash to the loan. However, when the owner is required to finance a small part or a major part of the sale price to induce the buyer to make the purchase, this sale proceeds analysis does not accurately analyze such a sale transaction. You must make an additional analysis regarding the owner carryback loan. Such an additional analysis has the effect of extending the holding period of the investment to the end of the term of the carryback loan arrangement. It also has complex tax consequences (see Chapter 27).

The sale proceeds are normally an important part of the investor's rate of return from the real estate investment. The sale proceeds are often referred to as the reversion, analogous to the return of capital in a securities investment. You use the before-tax cash flows for each year and the sale proceeds for the last year along with the initial investment to do a before-tax net present value (NPV) analysis or to calculate a before-tax internal rate of return (IRR).

When the lender participates in the loan, participation in the sale proceeds is usually handled as a separate line entry:

Sale Price

+Reserve Fund

−Loan Balances

−**Participation Payments**

−Cost of Sale

Sale Proceeds Before Tax

This alerts readers of the forecast that there is a participation loan without having to use a separate schedule or a footnote.

Calculating the tax on the sale of the property is a complex analysis covered in the next chapter. For people, the after-tax analysis of a real estate investment is more realistic than the before-tax analysis, and the sale proceeds after taxes are covered in Chapter 27. But for other investors, an after-tax analysis is not required. The investor could be a limited partnership for which all the tax benefits are passed through to the limited partners. The effects of the limited partnership arrangement must be analyzed first before proceeding to do an after-tax analysis. The investor could be an entity that does not pay tax (e.g., a pension fund). Or the investor could be a business in which the tax department handles all tax matters, and the real estate department does only before-tax calculations. For these cases and others, a before-tax analysis may be all that is required.

CHAPTER 26

TAX LIABILITY ON SALE

Sale Price
+Reserve Fund
−Loan Balances
−Cost of Sale
Sale Proceeds Before Tax
−Tax Liability on Sale
Sale Proceeds After Tax

There are a number of steps in the calculation of tax liability on sale. First, you have to determine the adjusted tax basis of the property. You start with the basis upon acquisition (purchase price). You add capital additions (cumulative). You subtract cost recovery (cumulative). The result is your adjusted basis:

Basis

Basis at acquisition
+Capital additions
−Cost recovery
Adjusted basis

The basis at acquisition is generally the purchase price along with acquisition costs. (See Chapter 32.)

Next you determine excess cost recovery. This is necessary only if you have taken cost recovery under a provision of the Tax Code that requires that the excess be recaptured.

The cost recovery is the sum of all cost recovery taken over the holding period. The straight-line cost recovery is the sum of all cost recovery over the holding period, calculated as if it had been straight-line cost recovery.

Excess Cost Recovery

Cost recovery

−Straight line cost recovery

Excess cost recovery

The calculation of recapture can be complicated by Tax Code provisions that required *all* of a certain type of cost recovery to be recaptured, not just the excess over straight line. You must carefully review the Tax Code to determine whether the recapture is the excess over straight line or the entire amount of accelerated cost recovery taken.

To determine the capital gain, you start with the sale price. You subtract the costs of sale. Then subtract the adjusted basis. These calculations yield the total gain:

Capital Gain

Sale price

−Costs of sale

−Adjusted basis

Total gain

−Recapture of cost recovery

−Suspended losses

Capital gain

The resulting total gain is further reduced by the recapture of cost recovery, if any. This is because excess cost recovery is treated separately. It is transferred, in effect, to the calculation of tax on ordinary income. Suspended losses are also subtracted from total gain to directly reduce the total gain. Suspended losses are the deferred tax shelter losses that have been accumulating in a suspense account (a cumulative account). These are legitimate losses that could not be taken fully in the year they occurred because of limitations in the Tax Code. These losses were not lost; however, they were deferred in a suspended losses account. Now they are subtracted from the total gain to reduce the gain and thus reduce the amount of tax paid on that gain.

You are now ready to calculate the tax. Ordinary income and capital gains are calculated separately. For the tax on ordinary income, you start with recapture of cost recovery from which is subtracted the unamortized expenditures and interest participation payments. That gives you the taxable ordinary income that you multiply by the investor's tax rate on ordinary income. The result is the tax on ordinary income:

Tax on Ordinary Income

Recapture of cost recovery
−Unamortized expenditures
−Participation payments
Ordinary taxable income
×Tax rate on ordinary income
Tax on ordinary income

The recapture of cost recovery comes from your calculations above. The unamortized portion of amortizable nonoperating expenses are subtracted here to diminish the excess cost recovery. A good example is unamortized loan points. The unamortized loan points may cause ordinary taxable income to be a negative number, especially when there is no recapture of cost recovery.

This negative number when multiplied by the tax rate creates a tax savings rather than a tax liability. It can be used to offset other tax liability.

The tax on capital gain is calculated by multiplying the capital gain by the tax rate for capital gain:

Tax on Capital Gain

Capital gain
×Tax rate for capital gain
Tax on capital gain

Through these various calculations you finally get the final calculation. The tax liability on sale is simply the tax on ordinary income and the tax on capital gain added together:

Tax Liability on Sale

Tax on ordinary income
+Tax on capital gain
Tax liability on sale

This number, tax liability on sale, is used in the calculation of sale proceeds after tax:

Sale proceeds before tax
−**Tax liability on sale**
Sale proceeds after tax

There may be some variations to the above calculations. For instance, if there was a partial sale of the property preceding the sale being analyzed, the basis must be allocated to the portion of the property sold in the partial sale. Such a portion of basis must be subtracted in determining adjusted basis:

Adjusted Basis

Adjusted basis
+Capital additions
−Cost recovery
−**Basis of partial sale**
Adjusted basis

If the loan included non-interest participation payments, such payments are subtracted in the calculation of the total gain:

Capital Gain

Sale price
−Costs of sale
−**Participation payments**
−Adjusted basis
Total gain

If investment tax credits were taken, they may be required to be recaptured at the time of sale. The recapture of investment tax credits is subtracted in the calculation of sale proceeds after tax:

Sale proceeds before tax
−Tax liability on sale
−**Recapture of investment tax credits**
Sale proceeds after tax

If the loan included interest participation payments, such payments are subtracted in the calculation of ordinary income:

Tax on Ordinary Income

Recapture of cost recovery

−Unamortized expenditures

−**Participation payments**

Ordinary taxable income

×Tax rate on ordinary income

Tax on ordinary income

If the sale includes a loan carried back by the seller, the tax treatment of the loan is that of an installment sale. Such tax calculations are well beyond the scope of this book. But the carry-back loan obviously extends the cash flow until the carry-back loan is paid off.

This book assumes that a taxpayer is on a cash basis. If you are on an accrual basis for your tax accounting, the tax calculations may be different in some situations.

CHAPTER 27

SALE PROCEEDS AFTER TAX

Sale Price
+Reserve Fund
−Loan Balances
−Cost of Sale
Sale Proceeds Before Tax
−Tax Liability on Sale
Sale Proceeds After Tax

Just as cash flow after tax is the ultimate bottom line for the cash flow analysis, sale proceeds after tax is the ultimate bottom line for the cash flow analysis of the sale transaction. The tax liability is calculated in a complex analysis (see Chapter 26) and is subtracted from the sale proceeds before tax. The result is the cash that actually flows into the investor's pocket, tax and all other things considered.

The sale proceeds after tax and the cash flow after tax along with the initial investment are used in after-tax net present value (NPV) analysis and to calculate the after-tax internal rate of return (IRR). For example, for a five-year forecast, the cash flow after tax for the first four years is entered into the NPV/IRR cash flow scheme. The last entry is the sum of the last (fifth) year's cash flow after tax and the sale proceeds after tax for the fifth year. The first entry is the initial investment at the beginning of the first year of the investment. A financial calculator or a computer program will allow you to calculate a after-tax NPV or IRR with these entries. Here is the T-chart for the cash flows for Maplewood Apartments (Appendix I):

Maplewood Apartments

0	(1,783,095)
1	26,153
2	47,780
3	54,373
4	93,665
5	117,993 + 2,337,290

$i = (?)$

Note: See Chapter 41 for information on T-charts.

With a computer program, it is easy to assume a sale at the end of each year. You can then have the program calculate the NPV and IRR for each year. For instance, in a five-year projection, you can have the program calculate the NPV or IRR assuming a sale at the end of the third year. In that case, you program the computer to consider the initial investment, the first two years of cash flow after tax, and the cash flow after tax for the third year added to the sale proceeds after tax for the third year. The T-chart for the first three years of the operation of Maplewood Apartments follows:

Maplewood Apartments

0	(1,783,095
1	26,153
2	47,780
3	54,373 + 1,964,036

$i = (?)$

For more detailed information on NPV and IRR calculations and T-charts, see Chapters 41 and 42.

SUMMARY

With this chapter, the forecast portion of this book is completed. The ultimate bottom line for the annual cash flow is the cash flow after tax. The ultimate bottom line for the sale transaction is the sale proceeds after tax. Together these give you the ultimate bottom lines for the entire forecast. And the NPV and IRR will show you the significance of these bottom-line numbers by measuring them in a way that you can compare them not only to other real estate investments but also to non-real estate investments.

In the following chapters, much background information and analysis are presented to allow you to make the best use of the sophisticated forecasting you have learned in the preceding chapters.

PART 5

INCOME & EXPENSE REFINEMENTS

The initial chapters gave an elementary view of the operation of apartment buildings, offices, and shopping centers to acquaint you with their character and to show you how they begin operations immediately after development. This part of the book treats these real estate investments in their complexity and maturity. It considers operations after maximum occupancy has been reached. Additionally, this part of the book considers additional types of properties and real estate investment opportunities.

Chapters

CHAPTER 28

APARTMENT FORECAST

You are going to close a purchase transaction as the buyer on Maplewood Apartments in one month. There is a contingency clause in the purchase agreement allowing your client a period to complete the due diligence investigation on the property. If your analysis is satisfactory and the remainder of the information obtained on the property shows no compelling reason to reject the property, you will remove the contingency and close the transaction.

Maplewood Apartments is a five-year old suburban garden apartment complex with 100 units. There are no units higher than two and one-half stories above grade, so there are no elevators.

POTENTIAL RENTAL INCOME

Here is the current rent schedule for Maplewood Apartments:

Units	Rooms/SF		Rent	Rent/SF	Total
11	1BR/575		$604	$1.05	$ 6,644
9	1BR/630	loft	686	1.09	6,174
23	2BR/805		773	.96	17,779
29	2BR/880		836	.95	24,244
8	2BR/945	loft	926	.98	7,408
15	3BR/985		906	.92	13,590
5	3BR/1,065		947	.89	4,735
100	Total				$80,574

All tenants are on month-to-month tenancies. Two months ago all rents were raised to the current levels with advanced notice to the tenants. Every six months the rents are raised 2½ percent according to the property manager. She indicates that with inflation and the stable local market, she has been able to raise the rents 2½ percent semiannually for the past few years, as her records confirm.

For your income and expense statement, you assume that rents will continue at their current level for three months after the closing. Your market research indicates that the rents can continue to be raised between 2 percent and 2½ percent every six months on all sizes of units. You will use 2 percent increases (compounded) for the first year as 2 percent more closely approximates the general inflation rate. Thus, three months from the closing, you will raise rents 2 percent for the next six months. Nine months from the closing, you will raise rents 2 percent again. Here is the rent scheduled for the first year:

Month	Rent	Months	Total
1–3	$80,574	×3	$241,722
	+2%		
4–9	82,185	×6	493,110
	+2%		
10–12	83,828	×3	251,484
1–12	Annual rent		$986,316

This analysis gives an estimate of the rents for the first year of operation after the transfer of ownership. For subsequent years of the projection, the first year's rent can be raised at the inflation rate: 4 percent (compounded).

In an apartment project where the rents are not raised simultaneously, the analysis is more difficult. For instance, suppose tenants are on six-month rental agreements (leases) in Maplewood Apartments. At the end of the term of the lease, it is automatically renewed (at the tenants' option) with the rent increasing to the current rent charged to new tenants (i.e., the rent increases 2 percent). In this case, the only way for you to accurately determine the total annual rent is by charting all the leases—100 of them! This would also apply to tenants on month-to-month tenancies who have been promised that their rent will increase only once every six months. The easiest way to do the volume of work it takes to chart 100 tenants is to put them into six monthly groups and chart each group.

Regardless of what the rental agreements are and when the rent changes, you will only establish the potential rental income for the year by making a chart to fit the situation. The charting should fit the current situation as well as any future changes you are planning for the first year.

In the rent schedule for Maplewood Apartments, the size of each unit appears to be the essential correlation to rent. In many apartment complexes, other factors may be the determinants. Fireplaces, extra appliances, proximity to facilities, and views may command higher rents. Special characteristics that command a higher rent should be noted on the rent schedule (e.g., mountain view, fireplace, loft).

It is useful to determine the rentable square feet of the project too for comparative purposes and for statistical analysis.

Units × Size		Square Feet
11 × 575	=	6,325
9 × 630	=	5,670
23 × 805	=	18,515
29 × 880	=	25,520
8 × 945	=	7,560
15 × 985	=	14,775
5 × 1,065	=	5,325
Total		83,690 rentable square feet

There may be additional rental income that should be scheduled. For example, at Maplewood Apartments, each tenant gets one covered parking space included in the apartment rent. There are 150 covered parking spaces and 50 more spaces in the open. If a tenant wants a second covered parking space, there is an additional rent of $34 per month charged if a space is available. If available, a second space in the open is free. Here is the schedule with the rent increased 2 percent every six months:

$$50 \text{ spaces} \times \$34 = \$1,700$$

Months		
1–3	$1,700 × 3 =	$ 5,100
4–9	$1,734 × 6 =	$10,404
10–12	$1,768 × 3 =	$ 5,304
Total		$20,808

This is rent paid for the use of real property. It is proper to schedule it just like the rent for the apartment units. It does not belong in other income.

Maplewood Apartments also has a small number of storage spaces on the premises. These are rented to tenants who need additional storage space.

$$10 \text{ storage units} \times \$57 = \$570$$

Months		
1–3	$570 × 3 =	$1,710
4–9	$581 × 6 =	$3,486
10–12	$592 × 3 =	$1,776
Total		$6,972

This is a borderline categorization. If this figure is a substantial amount, it may be more appropriate to place it in other income. Most apartment projects are not in the business of providing storage space in addition to the storage included in each apartment. A large amount of rent for storage units may distort the potential rental income for the purpose of comparison to other apartments. It would reflect business income from a nonapartment business (i.e., business income from a storage business). If the storage units were separate from the apartments but adjacent, separate analysis may be more appropriate than including the storage income in other income. For Maplewood Apartments, you determine that the small number of storage units available does not require special treatment, and you add the rent to the rent schedule.

The potential rental income from the property is the sum of the rent for the units, covered parking spaces, and storage units assuming 100 percent occupancy:

Apartments	$986,316
+Covered parking	20,808
+Storage units	6,972
Potential rental income	**$1,014,096**

The example used in this chapter is more complex than the example given in Chapter 1. Maplewood Apartments illustrates that to estimate the first year's potential rental income for an apartment project, you must consider rents, rent fluctuations, and timing. The Maplewood Apartments analysis does not consider differences in rent paid by different tenants because the rents are raised for all tenants at the same time. If that were not the case, a further complication of the timing analysis would require a more complex rent schedule. Seldom is an actual situation as clear-cut as the one presented for Maplewood Apartments, but the ideas covered here will give you a better idea of the considerations it takes to estimate the rental income for the first year of ownership.

INCENTIVES

In competitive markets, particularly ones for which vacancy is high, incentives (concessions of abatements) may be given to tenants to move in—or to stay in—an apartment project. These incentives may come in various forms. However they are accounted for by the property manager, they must reduce potential rental income if they are not part of a start-up promotion.

For example, suppose tenants at Maplewood Apartments who sign a one-year lease are given a free trip to Hawaii if they stay and pay rent for the full year. If the property manager buys a packaged Hawaiian trip for $625, the rent for the year for each unit for which the trip is awarded is decreased by $625.

When an apartment project is being leased for the first time after initial construction or after a thorough rehabilitation, there is usually a budget for nonoperating (start-up) promotional expenses. If this Hawaiian trip is a legitimate promotional expense used to fill the apartment project quickly at market rents, then this expense is properly written off as a special nonoperating promotion expense. If, however, the trip incentive is used to lure tenants into units at rents above market, the cost of the trip must somehow decrease the income of the property rather than be written off as a promotional expense.

When the trip incentive is written off as a normal operating expense, the net operating income (NOI) is the same as if potential rental income had been reduced. And there is no distortion. But if in the next year of the projection, the prior year's rent is the same (or increased for anticipated inflation) and the incentive is not projected as an expense, the forecast may be misleading. The rent for the next year may not be realized without the incentive continuing through the next year. The best practice to avoid distortion in future projections is to decrease potential rental income by the amount of the incentive.

Of course, if the incentive is "free rent" instead of a Hawaiian trip, the principle is the same. It must decrease the income of the property or be a one-time promotional expense associated with a lease-up program. Since Maplewood Apartments offers no incentives to lease, this issue is not considered in the Maplewood Apartments analysis.

VACANCY & CREDIT LOSS

Your market research indicates that the rents for Maplewood Apartments are well within the range of current market rents. The historical vacancy of 6 percent for Maplewood Apartments is within the range of market vacancy rates. There is little differentiation in the market between different sizes of units. All are experiencing approximately the same vacancy rate. The balance between an acceptable vacancy and the enjoyment of high rents is the goal of a property manager. If rents are too low, vacancy will be low. If rents are too high, vacancy will be high. Because the property has had a stable 6 percent vacancy and the property manager has been able to raise rents 2½ percent every six months, it is probable that a reasonable balance exists. So long as the current economic stability of the local market is expected to continue, the vacancy rate of 6 percent is reasonable to use in a forecast.

The property manager calculates the total number of unit-days that the property has in one year. The actual total unit-days of occupancy for which rent is paid is determined from the property management records. The difference is the vacancy & credit loss. Surveys, whether formal or informal, accumulate information on vacancy determined by property managers using this logical method. When free rent is used as an incentive, a unit may be occupied without any rent being paid. The unit-days during which units are occupied under such an incentive plan should not be included in the vacancy & credit loss.

OTHER INCOME

Maplewood Apartments offers laundry facilities on the premises to tenants. The facilities include coin-operated washers and dryers that are provided, managed, and maintained by a contractor specializing in that business. The revenue is split 50/50 with the property owner. Last year the property owner's share of the revenue amounted to $11,061. If you increase that amount by 4 percent inflation to $11,503, it is a reasonable estimate of such income for the next year. This income is entered in other income. It is nonmanagement-intensive income appropriate for the operation of the property (i.e., the owner of the property does not have the management responsibility).

IREM INCOME

The Institute of Real Estate Management (IREM) publishes statistics on the operating performance of various types of apartment projects. Here are the income categories in the IREM *Income/Expense Analysis Conventional Apartments* (1991 edition):

IREM	*Real Numbers*
Gross possible rental income	Potential rental income
−Vacancies and rent loss	−Vacancy and credit loss
Total rents collected	Effective rental income
+Miscellaneous income	+Other income
Total collections	Gross operating income

The gross possible rental income includes all the rent paid in the operation of the property and is further divided into subcategories.

Gross Possible Rental Income

Apartment rentals
Garage and parking income
Stores and offices

Because expenses for apartments are often discussed in terms of percentages of the rental income, IREM calculates a special figure to use as the basis of such percentage discussions.

IREM	*Real Numbers*
Gross possible rental income	Potential rental income
+Miscellaneous income	+Other income
Gross possible income	**Gross possible income**

Gross possible income is the maximum rent to be collected by the property assuming 100 percent occupancy and the collection of nonrental income. It is used as the divisor to calculate percentages. For example, maintenance expense divided by gross possible income calculates a percentage for maintenance expense that you can compare to other properties.

The IREM statistics for income are not as current as the market information you can obtain by doing your own market research. Find locally published statistics that are more current. Do your own survey by calling property managers. The IREM income analysis is included here only because it accompanies the IREM expense statistics, which are very useful.

IREM EXPENSES

The Annual Property Operating Data (APOD) form includes a convenient generic list of expenses to use in preparing a pro forma income & expense statement. It is useful, however, to use the specialized list of apartment expenses established by IREM that allows easy comparison to other apartment projects. If you use the same expense categories as IREM, you will be able to easily compare your property to the national, regional, or local statistics. Here are the categories in the IREM *Income/ Expense Analysis Conventional Apartments* (1991 edition):

Administrative

Management fee
Other administrative

Operating

Supplies
Heating fuel (common are only)
Heating fuel (common area and apartments)
Electricity (common area only)
Electricity (common area and apartments)
Water/sewer (common area only)
Water/sewer (common area and apartments)

Gas (common area only)
Gas (common area and apartments)
Building services
Other operating

Maintenance

Security
Grounds maintenance
Maintenance-repairs
Painting/Decorating

Tax—Insurance

Real estate taxes
Other tax/fee/permit
Insurance

Recreational/amenities
Other payroll

The statistics are based on surveys of property managers, and IREM furnishes specific definitions that show how to categorize various expenses. By using the special divisor *gross possible income,* you can calculate what percentage any one expense is of the maximum rent achievable by the property.

Usually you will have to take the operating statement provided by a property manager and rearrange the expenses to make them fit into the above categories. The IREM definitions are important to consider carefully in recategorizing the expenses to fit the IREM format. (There is more information on doing this in Chapter 34.)

INTEREST

Only that part of the loan payment that is interest is deducible as an expense in the calculation of tax liability. For the amortized 30-year loan on Maplewood Apartments, the ratio of interest and repayment of principal changes with each monthly payment. With a financial calculator or computer program, you can compute the interest and principal portions of each payment or group of payments (e.g., 12 payments = one year for the loan). For the first year of the new loan on Maplewood Apartments, the amount of interest paid is $489,299.

COST RECOVERY

You have agreed in the purchase contract, based on some relevant data, that the purchase price shall be apportioned to the improvements and personal property, as follows:

Improvements	5,010,500
Personal property	39,500

The improvements will be depreciated straight line over 27½ years (28 years to approximate the Tax Code cost recovery table). The personal property consisting of refrigerators for the apartment units will be depreciated over seven years with straight-line depreciation. Additionally, you expect to replace refrigerators at the rate of about eight each year at a cost of $585 each.

A roofing contractor has indicated that the roofs of many of the buildings will have to be replaced within three to four years. The contractor estimated a cost of $81,000 for such replacements, and you schedule it to be done in the third year of ownership with a cost recovery schedule of 28 years based on straight-line depreciation.

NONOPERATING EXPENSES

This is a catchall for subjective, tax-deductible expenses that are not properly included in the income & expense statement. For example, the loan that will be used to purchase Maplewood Apartments has a loan fee of 1½ percent. It is deducible for tax purposes but only if amortized over the term of the loan. The fee amounts to $71,775. The term of the loan is 30 years. Thus, 1/30th of the fee ($2,393) is deductible each year as a nonoperating expense. This expense item is similar to cost recovery.

Do not categorize it as a cost recovery item, however. Because it is not added to basis, it does not reduce the basis of the property as cost recovery does.

DEBT SERVICE

Unlike interest, which is just a portion of each loan payment, the annual debt service is the entire payment of interest and principal. The entire payment must be made each month to the lender, and the amount paid comes out of the cash flow of the property. For Maplewood Apartments, the monthly loan payment is $42,878. Thus, the annual debt service is $12 \times \$42,878 = \$514,536$.

NONOPERATING OUTLAYS

Normally the amount in nonoperating outlays is identical to nonoperating expenses. Most nonoperating expenses are out of pocket, and they must be subtracted from the cash flow. In the case of Maplewood Apartments, however, the loan points are a prepaid expense, not an out-of-pocket expense. So the amortization amount is properly deducted for tax purposes in the income tax analysis, but it is not paid out of cash flow. Thus, it is not included in nonoperating outlays.

CAPITAL ADDITIONS

The roof replacements will cost $81,000 and will be done in the third year. This is not a minor repair. It is a replacement of the roofs on many of the buildings. It is a capital improvement that can be expected to last for more than one year and likely for many more. Thus, it is a capital addition. Even though it is depreciated for tax purposes, it is paid at one time out of cash flow. Capital additions can severely deplete cash flow or even cause a negative cash flow. One way to alleviate such an expenditure is to build a reserve fund in anticipation of the capital addition.

RESERVES

You need a reserve account to ameliorate the effect of the roof replacements on the projected cash flow. But you do not want to be overly cautious and cause a significantly lower investment return by substantially reducing the cash flows into an unnecessarily large reserve account. You estimate that a reserve of 2½ percent of potential rental income is about right. Without the reserve fund, the property would have a very meager cash flow in the third year. The reserve fund has the effect of evening the cash flows of the projection.

TAXATION

You are in the 28 percent marginal tax bracket for federal income tax and in the 8⅓ percent marginal tax bracket for state income tax for both ordinary income and capital gain. Thus, you use 34 percent as the tax rate for both. (See Chapter 32.) You are not an "active" investor.

SALE

The cap rate of 8.8 percent has been stable, and you anticipate that using such a cap rate to determine the sale price for each year of the projection is going to be a reasonable guess. The sale price is calculated by dividing the cap rate into the next year's NOI since the hypothetical sale takes place at the end of the year (beginning of the next year). For instance, the sale price for the end of the first year of $6,689,578 is the second year's NOI of $588,683 divided by the cap rate of 8.8 percent.

Notice that there is $48,817 in the reserve fund at the time of the sale in the fifth year. If no future large capital expenditures are expected after the third year, the reserve amount for each year may be too high. Perhaps it should be reduced after the roofs are replaced.

The normal cost of selling a property like Maplewood Apartments, including brokerage commissions and promotional expenses, you estimate to be about 5 percent.

PURCHASE PRICE

The purchase price for Maplewood Apartments is $6,432,000. You are purchasing the property on a capitalization rate of 8.8 percent, which is the current cap rate for apartments locally. You anticipate that the total acquisition costs will be about 1 percent, which amounts to $64,320.

The investment base consists of the equity required for the investment in Maplewood Apartments in addition to the cost of acquisition and the loan points. The investment base is used as the initial investment in calculating the internal rate of return (IRR).

LOAN

A lender will make a loan on the property at an interest rate of 10¼ percent amortized with monthly payments over 30 years. The lender requires a 75 percent loan to value ratio and a 1.1 debt coverage ratio. The property has been appraised at the purchase price.

Loan to Value Method	
Appraised value	$6,432,000
Loan to value ratio	× 75%
Loan amount	$4,824,000
Debt Coverage Ratio Method	
NOI	$566,041
Debt coverage ratio	÷ 1.1
Maximum debt service	$514,582
	÷ 12
Maximum monthly loan payment	$42,881

Loan Amount Calculation

FV =
PMT = (42881)
PV = ?   PV (loan amount) = 4785284
I   = 10¼ ÷ 12
N   = 30 ÷ 12

Note: This is the minimodel covered in Chapter 41.

Because the loan amount calculated by the debt coverage ratio is lower, that will be the maximum loan available from that lender. You agree with the lender that the loan amount will be $4,785,000 with a 1.5 percent (1½ points) loan fee.

ASSUMPTIONS

Based on historical data, you believe that a 4 percent inflation rate for both rent and expenses may be expected.

PROJECTION

The five-year forecast for Maplewood Apartments is in Appendix I. The projection consists of seven pages. The first includes a pro forma income & expense statement along with loan information, purchase information, and the assumptions made for the creation of the projection. The second page contains the forecast for five years. These two pages give you a clear picture of how the property will perform if the input and assumptions turn out to be accurate. These two pages also provide you with adequate information to compare Maplewood Apartments to other investment properties.

Subsequent pages include the sales proceeds after tax analysis, which is a refinement of the tax calculations regarding the projected sale of the property for each year. That is backed up with the cost recovery schedule.

One page, comparative statistics, is the comparison of Maplewood Apartments with IREM statistics. The IREM statistics provided are fictitious ones for an undisclosed city in which the fictitious Maplewood Apartments are located. IREM statistics provide national, regional, and local (a selection of cities) statistics. Additional columns could be created, if desired, to include additional IREM statistics. (See Chapter 34 for more information on the comparison.)

Two mathematical sensitivity analyses are also included. One shows how NOI is sensitive to vacancy & credit loss and to gross rental income. Investors who do not agree with your assumptions regarding the performance of the property have 187 NOIs from which to choose based on different assumptions about vacancy & credit loss and gross rental income. Notice that the pro forma NOI is in the center of the sensitivity analysis and that the NOIs increase from the upper left-hand corner to the lower right-hand corner.

The other sensitivity analysis shows how the value will be affected by changes in NOI or the cap rate. It is useful in determining an offering price for the property as well as for getting a picture of what might happen in the future. It gives 153 choices. Notice that the pro forma value is in the center of the sensitivity analysis and that the values increase from the upper left-hand corner to the lower right-hand corner (see Chapter 43).

All together, these pages provide you with a definitive amount of information on the potential performance of the property. However, the main part of the information is included in the first two pages composing the pro forma/assumptions and the forecast. These two pages cover the essentials for understanding the property.

CHAPTER 29

OFFICE BUILDING FORECAST

You will close a purchase transaction on Ridgeline Office Tower, a five-story office building with 60,000 square feet, in one month on July 1 if the due diligence on the building supports the purchase decision. You are analyzing the investment potential of the property. Your anticipated holding period is five years. You estimate the acquisition costs to be about 1 percent, and such costs are added to both the tax basis and the initial investment (investment base).

POTENTIAL RENTAL INCOME

Although the rent calculations for a new office building may be simple, for an existing office building there is only one way to do them: chart the leases. That is, read each lease and put each one in a multiyear rent schedule. Leases are staggered. They start and end at different times. They have different rents and different provisions. Each lease must be analyzed and its financial effects abstracted for the rent schedule.

You must make some assumptions as to what happens at the end of the lease term. Will the tenant renew the lease? If not, how long will the space be vacant? What tenant improvements will have to be provided to get a new tenant? What will the new rent be? Part of the basis for such assumptions can be established by interviews with the existing tenants. Other information comes from the market.

If you consider the information that you have on the leases and the tenants complete and reliable and it shows little or no vacancy for most years, you must decide whether to trust the information or use a market vacancy rate in your projection. The leases for this property are gross leases (no reimbursements to the landlord for any expenses). Here's the abstract of the leases for Ridgeline Office Tower:

Space 1: Transland Insurance, Inc. (a credit tenant), 12,762 SF, fifth year of a 12-year lease, option to renew on the same terms for an additional three years, current rent $12.07/SF/year, escalation 3 percent (compounded) every other year, utilities paid by the landlord, lease started January 1, used as an administrative office.

Space 2: IBC, Inc. (International Business Computers, a credit tenant), 12,030 SF, second year of a five-year lease, option to renew on the same terms for an additional five years, current rent $12.05/SF/year, escalation 8 percent (not compounded) of base rent for the fourth year and 4 percent (not compounded) of base rent each year thereafter starting in the fifth year, utilities paid by the landlord, lease started July 1, used as an administrative and sales office. The base rent is $12.05/SF/year.

Space 3: Bledsoe & Gatmier, 5,664 SF, fourth year of a three-year lease, option to renew for three years on same terms and conditions (option has been exercised), current rent $12.29/SF/year, escalation determined each year by Consumer Price Index (CPI), 50 percent of the pro rata share of the utilities paid by tenant, lease started April 1, used as a law office.

Space 4: Travel Time, Ltd., 958 SF, fifth year of an eight-year lease, no option, current rent $15.52/SF/year, escalation 4 percent (compounded) each year, utilities paid by the landlord, lease started January 1, used as a walk-in travel agency. A surcharge of $.75/SF/year for heavy customer traffic is paid by tenant.

Space 5: James R. Luddington, CPA, 1,435 SF, fourth year of a four-year lease, option to renew for four years on same terms and conditions, current rent $14.44/SF/year, escalation 4 percent (not compounded—the base rent is $12.89) each year, utilities paid by the landlord, lease started October 1, used as an accounting office.

Space 6: Harvest Sales, Inc. (food importer), 12,729 SF, second year of a four-year lease, no option, current rent $12.74/SF/year, escalation determined each year by CPI, utilities paid by the landlord, lease started July 1, used as a central administrative office.

Space 7: Future Stock Corporation (software publisher), 12,236 SF, third year of a four-year lease, no option, current rent $12.83/SF/year, escalation 2 percent (compounded) each year, utilities paid by the landlord, lease started January 1, used as a publishing office.

Space 8: Vacant space, 2,186, SF, the utilities paid by the landlord.

The goal of abstracting the leases is to determine the rent for each unit, each year. All the rents are added to get the potential rental income for the building each year. When a vacancy will occur, assumptions are made on an individual basis as to whether the space will be leased to a new tenant or re-leased to the existing tenant. Look at each situation individually.

Before you can create a rent schedule for the space in the building, you must make some assumptions as to how space will be leased based on the expiration of current leases. The current owner has determined that there is a rent differential between tenants that take under 4,000 square feet and those that take over 4,000 square feet. The larger tenants also seem to require longer lease terms. Your research confirms this view of the market and provides you with information regarding current market rents. Therefore, you will assume that in the first year of your client's ownership, the rent will be $14.23/SF/year escalated at 4 percent (compounded) annually for space under 4,000 SF. The term will be three years:

Year	$/SF/year
1	$14.23
2	14.80
3	15.39
4	16.01
5	16.65
6	17.30

For space over 4,000 SF, the term will be six years, and the rent during the first year of ownership will be $12.97/SF/year escalated at 4 percent (compounded) annually:

Year	$/SF/year
1	$12.97
2	13.48
3	14.01
4	14.57
5	15.15
6	15.75

When space becomes vacant, you will use the above assumptions to determine the lease rate for the purposes of the projection. Additionally, you will assume a vacancy period of three months for space under 4,000 SF and six months for space over 4,000 SF.

You proceed to schedule each lease according to the information you have obtained in your due diligence investigation. You are doing a five-year holding period starting July 1, and you will schedule six years of leases with the years of your projection running from July 1 to June 30. The reason that you need six full years is that for a five-year projection, you will need the NOI for the sixth year to determine the value at the beginning of the sixth year (end of the fifth year).

Over the last few years, the CPI has increased about 4 percent (compounded).

Transland Insurance (Space 1) has a lease that will not run out during the six-year projection that you will do. Escalation is every other year. The rent was escalated to its current level at the beginning of the fifth year. The lease started in January, and when you close the purchase transaction, the tenant will be starting the second half of its fifth year:

Year	Portion	$/SF/year	Total SF	Annual Rent	Comment
1	0.5	$12.07	12,762		
	0.5	12.07	12,762	$154,037	
2	0.5	12.07	12,762		
	0.5	12.43	12,762	156,352	
3	0.5	12.43	12,762		
	0.5	12.43	12,762	158,668	
4	0.5	12.43	12,762		
	0.5	12.80	12,762	161,010	
5	0.5	12.80	12,762		
	0.5	12.80	12,762	163,352	
6	0.5	12.80	12,762		
	0.5	13.18	12,762	165,777	

IBC (Space 2) also has a lease that will not run out during the six years of your projection if the option is exercised. You have talked to the office manager, who indicates that the long-range plan for its local operation requires no additional office space. IBC is satisfied with the location and expects to exercise the option. The second year of the lease will be over when you close the purchase transaction, and the third year will begin. The rent is same until the fourth year of the lease when it escalates 4 percent above the base rent each year thereafter.

Year	Portion	$/SF/year	Total SF	Annual Rent	Comment
1	1	$12.05	12,030	$144,961	
2	1	13.01	12,030	156,510	escalation starts
3	1	13.49	12,030	162,284	
4	1	13.97	12,030	168,059	
5	1	14.46	12,030	173,953	
6	1	14.94	12,030	179,728	

Bledsoe & Gatmier (Space 3) is in the fourth year for this lease started on April 1. It has almost three years until the renewal term on this lease runs out. You have talked to the managing partner, who indicates that it is very unlikely that the firm will continue its occupancy in the building at the end of the current lease term. The firm anticipates moving to a larger office building that has more potential and flexibility for accommodating its long-term growth. You will use 4 percent (compound) to escalate this rent because that approximates the yearly CPI increases.

Year	Portion	$/SF/year	Total SF	Annual Rent	Comment
1	0.75	$12.29	5,664		
	0.25	12.78	5,664	$70,303	
2	0.75	12.78	5,664		
	0.25	13.29	5,664	73,107	
3	0.75	13.29	5,664		
	0.25	14.01	5,664	76,293	vacant (three months)
4	0.25	14.57	5,664		vacant (three months)
	0.75	14.57	5,664	82,524	new tenant
5	0.25	14.57	5,664		
	0.75	15.15	5,664	84,988	
6	0.25	15.15	5,664		
	0.75	15.75	5,664	88,358	

Travel Time (Space 4) likes the building and the location very much. It definitely plans to stay in the building and negotiate a new lease at the end of its current lease term. Because its space is relatively small, it agreed to pay 5 percent over the market lease rate set by the prior owner for space under 4,000 SF. It is willing to negotiate a similar arrangement for a new lease.

Year	Portion	$/SF/year	Total SF	Annual Rent	Comment
1	0.5	$15.52	958		
	0.5	16.14	958	$15,165	
2	0.5	16.14	958		
	0.5	16.78	958	15,768	
3	0.5	16.78	958		
	0.5	17.45	958	16,395	
4	0.5	17.45	958		
	0.5	16.81	958	16,409	new lease
5	0.5	16.81	958		
	0.5	17.48	958	16,423	
6	0.5	17.48	958		
	0.5	18.17	958	17,075	

James R. Luddington, CPA (Space 5), is the suburban office of a downtown accounting firm. The firm's long-range plans call for a consolidation of all suburban offices into a downtown office building in which the firm will have an ownership interest. Construction on its new building will not start until late next year, so it will exercise its four-year option to renew in your client's office building. But it does not anticipate staying in your building at the end of the option term. The firm's rent is escalated at 4 percent (not compounded). Its base rate is $12.89/SF/year. The continuation of this lease upon the exercise of its option will start October 1.

Year	Portion	$/SF/year	Total SF	Annual Rent	Comment
1	0.25	$14.44	1,435		
	0.75	14.95	1,435	$21,269	
2	0.25	14.95	1,435		
	0.75	15.47	1,435	22,012	
3	0.25	15.47	1,435		
	0.75	15.98	1,435	22,747	
4	0.25	15.98	1,435		
	0.75	16.50	1,435	23,490	
5	0.25	16.50	1,435		
	0.25	16.65	1,435		vacant (three months)
	0.5	16.65	1,435	23,838	
6	0.5	16.65	1,435		
	0.5	17.30	1,435	24,358	

Harvest Sales (Space 6) is happy with the building and has no plans to move. It expects to negotiate a new lease at the end of the current lease term. You will escalate this rent by 4 percent (compounded) each year. It will start the third year of its current lease on July 1.

Year	Portion	$/SF/year	Total SF	Annual Rent	Comment
1	1	$13.24	12,729	$168,531	
2	1	13.76	12,729	175,151	
3	1	14.01	12,729	178,333	new lease
4	1	14.57	12,729	185,461	
5	1	15.15	12,729	192,844	
6	1	15.75	12,729	200,481	

Future Stock (Space 7) is a software publishing company that is growing very rapidly. It has indicated that it will leave the building at the end of the present lease term. It needs to move to an office building where it can double its space. Its rent escalation is 2 percent (compounded) each year. Its current rent is $12.83/SF/year. Its fourth and last year starts January 1.

Year	Portion	$/SF/year	Total SF	Annual Rent	Comment
1	0.5	$12.83	12,236		
	0.5	13.09	12,236	$158,577	
2	0.5	13.09	12,236		
	0.5	13.48	12,236	162,554	vacant (six months)
3	1	14.01	12,236	171,426	new tenant
4	1	14.57	12,236	178,278	
5	1	15.15	12,236	185,375	
6	1	15.75	12,236	192,717	

You anticipate that the vacant space (Space 8) can be filled within the first three months of your client's ownership. You will project the lease starting October 1 at the lease rate and term you have set for space under 4,000 SF. Upon the expiration of a three-year lease term, you will project another three-month vacancy and then another lease.

Year	Portion	$/SF/year	Total SF	Annual Rent	Comment
1	0.25	$14.23	2,186		vacant (three months)
	0.75	14.23	2,186	$31,106	
2	0.25	14.23	2,186		
	0.75	14.80	2,186	32,040	
3	0.25	14.80	2,186		
	0.75	15.39	2,186	33,319	
4	0.25	15.39	2,186		
	0.25	16.01	2,186		vacant (three months)
	0.5	16.01	2,186	34,657	
5	0.5	16.01	2,186		
	0.5	16.65	2,186	35,696	
6	0.5	16.65	2,186		
	0.5	17.30	2,186	37,106	

Once all the leases are properly scheduled, they are summarized in a lease schedule. (See the lease schedule for Ridgeline Office Tower in Appendix II.) The lease schedule shows the potential rental income (the sum of the scheduled rents) and the scheduled vacancy. The vacancy percentages (of potential rental income) for the six-year projection are 1, 10, 2, 3, 1 and 0 percent. That's an uneven projection for vacancy, and the sixth year may be overly optimistic.

VACANCY

Market statistics indicate a vacancy rate for this type of office building to be stable at 4 percent currently. The average vacancy for the property is less than 3 percent. The leases run out on all the space in the building during the next six years except for the one credit tenant. The assumptions you made about such space being leased may not be as accurate as the market vacancy rate. It may be more prudent and realistic to use the market vacancy rate for your projection. However, if the property's projected vacancy had been higher than the market vacancy rate, it may have been more prudent to use the property's vacancy. Such questions come up when analyzing office buildings. You must consider the quality of your information and the local market situation, and then use your best judgment to determine the vacancy & credit loss amount you will use in your projection.

In this case, your review of the lease schedule shows that the credit tenants will be close to the end of their lease terms at the end of your projection (assuming IBC exercises its option). Everything else being similar, a prospective buyer at that time may not view the property's income as being as secure as it is now with two credit tenants in the building for the length of your holding period. Additionally, the sixth year shows a vacancy of 0 percent. In any case, a prospective buyer five years from now is not likely to calculate an income & expense statement with a 0 percent vacancy rate. Therefore, you decide to use the market vacancy rate of 4 percent for your forecast.

OTHER INCOME

Bledsoe & Gatmier agreed to pay 50 percent of its pro rata share of the utilities for the building. You estimate that the utilities are $1.47/SF/year. Its pro rata share is $5,664 \times 1.47 \times 50\% = 4,163$ in the first year, which you escalate at the 4 percent inflation rate. Normally, expense reimbursements are considered other income. It is not possible to determine what the utility costs are going to be by reading the lease. They must be estimated. In this case, however, it is a troublesome categorization. Bledsoe & Gatmier is the only tenant paying an expense reimbursement. Placing this reimbursement in other income may distort potential rental income. If the leasing practices in the market and for the building do not include reimbursement arrangements, this expense is probably better placed in potential rental income (after estimating it). But since it is only a small amount, you decide to ignore the anomaly and place it in other income where it would normally be expected to go.

Travel Time has retail walk-in traffic in its suite, which is a travel agency. Because this causes more wear and tear on the building than is caused by other tenants, Travel Time has agreed to pay a traffic surcharge of $.75/SF/year so long as its suite is open to the general public. The idea behind such a surcharge is that it covers the extra maintenance costs resulting from the extra pedestrian traffic. Although the surcharge is clearly stated in the lease and might be considered scheduled rent, it may not be paid by the next tenant in that space. Additionally, if Travel Time were to cease its walk-in business, it would no longer be obligated to pay the surcharge. In fact, there is a possibility that Travel Time will cease its walk-in business during its lease term. The travel agency does most of its business with corporate and commercial customers rather than consumers. Such customers do not require a walk-in facility. Travel Time is considering eliminating its consumer business. If it does so, the walk-in traffic will cease, and the obligation to pay surcharge will also cease. Therefore, it is reasonable to place the surcharge in other income because it may distort potential rental income if it is in the scheduled rent. But it will not distort NOI. Presumably, the surcharge goes to pay for extra expenses, and the surcharge and the extra expenses will be a wash.

The projection for other income is

Year	Reimbursements	Surcharge	Total
1	$4,163	$718	$4,881
2	4,329	718	5,047
3	4,502	718	5,220
4	4,682	718	5,400
5	4,869	718	5,587
6	5,063	718	5,781

Were there to be a retail store on the ground floor of the Ridgeline Office Tower, you might be able to charge the tenant percentage rent (a percentage of the gross retail sales) like tenants in a shopping center are normally required to pay. If so, the amount of percentage rent in excess of base rent should be entered in other income. This avoids distorting the potential rental income category for office buildings that is not expected to include percentage rent.

There is no additional other income for the Ridgeline Office Tower.

IREM INCOME

The Institute of Real Estate Management publishes annual statistics on office buildings in *IREM Income/Expenses Analysis Office Buildings Downtown & Suburban*. Here are the income categories (1991 edition):

IREM

Gross possible rental income
+Pass-throughs
+Percent rent
+Miscellaneous
Gross possible income
−Vacancy
Total collections

Real Numbers

Potential rental income
−Vacancy & credit loss
Effective rental income
+Other income
Gross operating income

IREM gross possible rental income includes the following categories:

Gross Possible Rental Income

Office rentals

Retail stores

Garage and parking

This IREM scheme for office operating statements appears to be different from both the *Real Numbers* scheme and from the IREM scheme for apartments. It is not. IREM vacancy is not a percentage that is applied to potential rental income in one case and to potential rental income + other income in the other case. Rather, it is just a numerical difference between what is possible to collect and what is collected. Therefore, it is the equivalent of vacancy and credit loss. There is no *Real Numbers* category equivalent to gross possible income in the IREM scheme, but rather the IREM gross possible income is the equivalent of two *Real Numbers* categories added together: potential rental income plus other income. Likewise, there is no IREM equivalent to the effective rental income category of *Real Numbers*.

Note that the IREM vacancy amount reported for both apartments and offices is determined by the difference between gross possible rental income and the actual portion of the gross possible rental income that is collected. That amount is reported as a percentage by the IREM statistics.

Confusing though it may be, it is not a problem until you do a comparison to IREM office statistics. In a comparison, however, it is not the income statistics in which you will be interested. You can get more accurate and up-to-date market income information and vacancy rates locally than you can from IREM statistics. Rather, the IREM statistics are invaluable for the expense analysis, and comparing expenses is the primary reason to use them.

IREM EXPENSES

The Annual Property Operating Data (APOD) form includes a list of expense categories that accommodate a wide range of properties. The IREM list of office expenses is longer and more specific:

Utilities
>   Electricity
>   Water
>   Sewer
>   HVAC fuel
>   Combination electricity
>   Self-contained energy plants

Janitorial
>   Janitorial payroll or contract
>   Cleaning supplies
>   Miscellaneous

Maintenance and repair
>   Payroll-maintenance
>   Supplies
>   HVAC repairs
>   Electrical repairs

  Plumbing repairs

  Elevator repairs and maintenance contracts

  Exterior repairs

  Roof repairs

  Parking lot repairs

  Decorating

  Miscellaneous repairs

Administrative

  Payroll—administrative

  Advertising

  Management fee

  Other administrative costs

Other payroll costs

  Payroll taxes

  Employee benefits

Insurance

Services

  Landscape services

  Trash removal

  Security

  Window washing

  Snow removal

  Miscellaneous services

Taxes

  Real estate taxes

  Other taxes, fees, and permits

This list of expenses can be condensed into the following categories to summarize the IREM format:

Utilities

Janitorial/maintenance and repair

Administrative/other payroll costs

Insurance/services

Net operating costs   (a subtotal)

Real estate taxes

Total operating costs   (operating expenses)

This abbreviated format is used for a substantial portion of the statistics published by IREM. Note that the IREM abbreviated format does not include the category of other taxes, fees, and permits, although this category is also included in the calculation of total operating costs.

BOMA EXPENSES

The Building Owners and Managers Association (BOMA) also publishes statistics for office buildings in the *BOMA Experience Exchange Report*. Like IREM, BOMA makes no attempt to calculate and provide statistics on net operating income. It furnishes statistics on income in a slightly different format than IREM, but its format for expenses is almost identical to IREM's except for leasing expenses. These are BOMA's expense categories:

Cleaning

    Payroll

    Contract

    Supplies/materials/miscellaneous

    Trash removal

Repairs/maintenance

    Payroll

    Elevator

    HVAC

    Electrical

    Structure/roof

    Plumbing

    Fire/life safety

    Other maintenance/supplies

Utilities
  Electrical
  Gas
  Fuel oil
  Purchased steam
  Purchased cold water
  Coal
  Water/sewer
Roads/grounds/security
  Roads/grounds payroll
  Roads/grounds contractor
  Roads/grounds other
  Security payroll
  Security contractor
  Security other
Administrative
  Payroll
  Management fees
  Professional fees
  General office expenses
  Other administrative expenses
Fixed expenses
  Real estate tax
  Building insurance
  Personal property tax
  Other tax
Leasing expenses
  Advertising/promotion
  Commissions
  Professional fees
  Tenant alterations
  Buy-outs
  Other leasing

MORTGAGE

The loan you have obtained for the purchase of the property is in the amount of $3,656,000 at 9½ percent interest amortized over 30 years. The lender is charging a 1 percent loan fee (one point). The loan fee amount of $36,560 is amortized over 30 years as a nonoperating expense.

COST RECOVERY

The purchase agreement contains an allocation of $4,047,250 to the improvements on the property. The improvements are depreciated over 31½ years (32 years to approximate the Tax Code cost recovery tables). The tenant improvements (TIs) are depreciated identically.

CAPITAL ADDITIONS

There are no major repairs or replacements anticipated for the Ridgeline Office Tower building. The suite improvements scheduled for upgrades during vacancy are the only capital additions. Tenants are expected to take care of their suites. Normal cleaning is provided through the janitorial service. Much of the cleaning and minor repairs required between new tenants and prior tenants could be paid as operating expenses. But often more work and materials are needed to get the space in good shape.

In a projection, you can have any number of levels of tenant improvement costs to fit all situations. For this projection, you choose two levels that you have labeled "minor refurbishing" and "rehab." These are capital improvements (capital additions). For income tax purposes, you may be able to write off part of these costs as operating expense items. That can get very detailed and complicated. For the purposes of doing the projection efficiently, you will categorize these expenditures as capital additions and depreciate the complete cost of the work and materials required to complete these tenant improvements over 31½ years (32 for convenience).

Treatment of Tenant Improvements

Office suites are created with standard construction. It is the finish (carpeting, wall covering, etc.) and extra partitioning that makes one suite more expensive to build than another. Medical offices that require extensive plumbing are more expensive too. Most new office space is offered with an allowance for suite improvements. That allowance will normally build an adequate but "plain vanilla" suite. Many tenants want a little more, if not a lot more. The cost of suite improvements over the allowance is borne by the tenant. Often the tenant finances this excess cost through its bank. Sometimes the building owner finances the excess cost. If so, the excess cost is a capital addition incurred in the year the lease starts. The payment for this excess cost might be included in the lease as rent. This has the effect of increasing the rent with no increase in operating expenses. Thus, the NOI is higher, and the value of the building is higher. In effect, it's similar to a rent concession, and it may be difficult to detect.

The same situation exists when a new tenant moves into an existing suite vacated by another tenant. The suite seldom needs to be gutted, but it must be refurbished or rehabed to accommodate the new tenant. Normally the minimum is done, just enough to correspond to the allowance. The excess cost above the minimum is borne by the tenant. When it is borne by the owner, accounted for as a capital addition, and paid for in future rent, it can distort the financial performance of the property. It should be treated much the same as a substantial rent concession. If it is accounted for separately in the lease (or under a separate agreement) and not included in rent, it is not deceptive. Otherwise, the original excess cost of the suite improvements must be determined and the rent reduced accordingly.

When the supply of office space becomes abundant and owners compete fiercely for tenants, the payment of these excess costs for suite improvements by the owners is often the first major rent concession given. Soon every building owner is giving it. In this case, the payment of such excess costs is definitely a rent concession. Like any other rent concession, it has the effect of reducing the rent, even though the rent was never increased to pay for it.

Another way of looking at this excess cost is to see it as income-producing construction that is capitalized. Unfortunately for a buyer, however, the excess suite improvements will last only a few years but the building will last much longer. It doesn't make sense to capitalize them both with the same capitalization rate. So paying for these excess costs with rent under the lease rather than under a separate agreement is a distortion of the performance of the property. It is a distortion regardless of what the remainder of the market is doing.

If the excess suite improvements are handled under a separate agreement, what do you do with the income? It may be best to account for the income outside the real estate analysis completely. After all, it is essentially a loan to the tenant. It should, at least, be capitalized at a higher rate for valuation purposes.

Cost of Tenant Improvements

The cost of tenant improvements is not an operating expense. The cost of providing tenant improvements within an allowance is part of the construction cost when an office building is new. The cost of refurbishing or rehabing a vacated suite within an allowance for a new tenant is a capital addition. It would be tedious and speculative to evaluate each suite to anticipate what might need to be done when the tenant moved out to prepare the suite for the next tenant. Usually, a cost per square foot is estimated for a minor refurbishing and another cost estimated for a more substantial rehab. You assign the appropriate cost to each suite for the year in which there is to be an anticipated change in tenants.

For instance, for Ridgeline Towers you estimate that the average minor refurbishing will cost $5 per square foot. A major rehab will cost $11 per square foot. You consider each tenant's situation individually. For tenants exercising options, you may have to provide some minor cleaning and painting, but you expect to cover these costs in normal operating expenses.

The Transland Insurance and IBC spaces will require no expenditures for suite improvements. The space for Bledsoe & Gatmier will require only a minor refurbishing when it becomes vacant in the third year of your ownership. Travel Time has indicated that it expects a minor refurbishing when it negotiates a new lease in the fourth year of your ownership. The space for James R. Luddington, CPA, will require a minor refurbishing when it becomes vacant in the fifth year of your ownership. The space for Harvest Sales will not require any expenditure for suite improvements. The Future Stock space is partitioned so unusually that it will likely require a rehab to prepare it for a new tenant in the third year of your ownership. The current vacant space has already been cleaned and painted, but you may have to do more to accommodate a new tenant. Thus, you schedule a minor refurbishing for the first year of your ownership. This suite is anticipated to be vacant again in the fourth year of your ownership, so you schedule another minor refurbishing. The tenant improvement schedule (with escalation for inflation) follows:

Year	Minor Refurbishing	Rehab
1	$5.00	$11.00
2	5.20	11.44
3	5.41	11.90
4	5.63	12.38
5	5.86	12.88
6	6.09	13.40

Below the costs are applied to the appropriate spaces:

Year	Space	Minor	Rehab	Size	Capital Additions
1	8	$5.00		2,186	$ 10,930
2	7		$11.44	12,236	139,979
3	3	5.41		5,664	30,658
4	4	5.63		958	5,393
	8	5.63		2,186	12,307
5	5	5.86		1,435	8,409

LEASING COMMISSIONS

Leasing commissions in your market are normally 3 percent of the base rent for the term of the lease and are paid at the commencement of the lease. Also, 1½ percent of the base rent for the term of each lease renewal by a tenant exercising an option is paid upon exercise of the option. When a lease ends without an existing option to renew and the tenant will stay in the building, you assume that no commission will be paid. Here is the schedule of leasing commissions paid:

Space	Year 1	Year 2	Year 3	Year 4	Year 5
1	–0–	–0–	–0–	–0–	–0–
1A	–0–	–0–	–0–	–0–	–0–
2	–0–	–0–	–0–	$12,604	–0–
2A	–0–	–0–	–0–	2,520	$ 2,520
3	–0–	–0–	–0–	14,854	–0–
3A	–0–	–0–	–0–	2,475	2,475
4	–0–	–0–	–0–	–0–	–0–
4A	–0–	–0–	–0–	–0–	–0–
5	$1,287	–0–	–0–	–0–	2,150
5A	321	$ 321	$ 321	321	716
6	–0–	–0–	–0–	–0–	–0–
6A	–0–	–0–	–0–	–0–	–0–
7	–0–	30,856	–0–	–0–	–0–
7A	–0–	5,142	5,142	5,142	5,142
8	2,799	–0–	–0–	3,149	–0–
8A	933	933	933	1,049	1,049
Total	$4,086	$30,856	–0–	$30,607	$2,150
Cumulative	$4,086	$34,942	$34,942	$65,549	$67,699
Total (A)	$1,254	$6,396	$6,396	$11,507	$11,902
Cumulative	$1,254	$7,650	$14,046	$25,553	$37,455
Unamortized	$2,832	$27,292	$20,896	$39,996	$30,244

Note: "A" designation indicates amortization of lease commissions.

These expenditures are categorized as nonoperating outlays in the cash flow analysis. However, they are not deducted in one year as non-operating expenses in the taxable income analysis. Rather, they are amortized over the term of the lease like amortized loan points are amortized over the term of the loan.

RESERVES

The largest anticipated expenditure is the low cost of the rehab for the Future Stock suite in the second year. There is going to be a negative cash flow in the second year regardless of what the reserve amount is. Perhaps the best way to even the cash flows is to limit the negative cash flow years to just one: the second year. Therefore, 5 percent is the reserve amount chosen.

TAX LIABILITY

You are in the 28 percent bracket and will be a passive investor in this property. The state income tax is 8⅓ percent.

COST OF SALE

You estimate the cost of sale for this property to be 4 percent, including real estate commissions and other costs.

PROJECTION

The five-year forecast for the Ridgeline Office Tower is in Appendix II. The projection consists of five pages. The first includes a pro forma income & expense statement along with loan information, purchase information, and the assumptions made for the creation of the projection. The second page contains the cash flow analysis over five years. These two pages give you a clear picture of how the property will perform if the input and assumptions turn out to be accurate. These two pages also provide you with adequate information to compare the Ridgeline Office Tower to other investment properties.

Subsequent pages include the sales proceeds after tax analysis, which is a refinement of the tax calculations regarding the projected sale of the property for each year. That is backed up with the cost recovery schedule. The lease schedule is the last page.

All together, these pages provide you with a definitive amount of information on the potential performance of the property. However, the main part of the information is included in the first two pages composing the pro forma/assumptions and the cash flow analysis. These two pages cover the essentials for understanding the property.

CHAPTER 30

SHOPPING CENTER FORECAST

You are doing research and analysis to decide whether you will close a purchase transaction in one month on Crossroads Plaza Shopping Center. If your due diligence investigation shows the property to be acceptable, you will close October 1. The shopping center is a three-year-old 60,000 square feet neighborhood shopping center with a supermarket anchor tenant. Sales for shopping center tenants have stabilized and are increasing with inflation, which you calculate is about 4 percent (compounded) per year. Currently, the shopping center is 100 percent leased. You are doing a before-tax analysis only.

POTENTIAL RENTAL INCOME

Because the landlord is providing a special retail environment conducive to a high volume of business for tenants, the landlord takes a percentage of the gross sales of the tenants as rent (percentage rent). Although a percentage of gross sales should protect the landlord against inflation (retail prices go up with inflation), landlords sometimes put escalation clauses into the lease just to be sure.

But it is more than just the collective retail stores that create a draw. Usually one or more large tenants (e.g., an anchor tenant such as a supermarket or a department store) attract many customers that the smaller retail stores would not be able to attract collectively without the anchors. Thus, anchor tenants pay low rent while other tenants pay high rent. The anchor tenants are subsidized, in effect.

You assume that the sales for each tenant will increase 4 percent each year with inflation. Because there are percentage rent clauses in each of the leases, it is important to be able to do a projection of future sales. Some of the tenants are still paying base rents. The leases are as follows:

Space 1: Market Fair (supermarket) 38,940 SF, fourth year of a 20-year lease, percentage rent of 1½ percent, sales in the third year of the lease were $15,838,096, lease started July first.

Space 2: Christie's Cleaners (dry cleaner) 1,602 SF, percentage rent of 6½ percent (base rent is $13.63/SF/year with no escalation), third year of a five-year lease, option to renew on same terms for an additional five years, sales in the second year of the lease were $274,163, lease started January 1.

Space 3: Primavera (beauty shop) 1,107 SF, percentage rent of 7 percent (base rent is $13.85/SF/year with no escalation), third year of a five-year lease, option to renew on the same terms for an additional five years, sales in the second year of the lease were $180,224, lease started October 1.

Space 4: Fallbrook's (ice cream store) 943 SF, percentage rent of 6½ percent (base rent $12.17/SF/year escalated at 2 percent compounded), second year of a six-year lease, option to renew on the same terms for an additional three years, sales in the first year of the lease were $171,893, lease started October 1.

Space 5: Screen Scene (video rental) 1,429 SF, percentage rent of 6 percent, fourth year of a six-year lease, option to renew on the same terms for four years, sales in the third year of the lease were $262,441, lease started July 1.

Space 6: Electronic Emporium (consumer electronics store) 2,510 SF, percentage rent of 4½ percent (base rent is $9.23/SF/year with no escalation), fourth year of a five-year lease, option to renew on same terms for five years, sales in the third year of the lease were $376,560, lease started October 1.

Space 7: Trimart (drugstore) 9,891 SF, third year of a 20-year lease, percentage rent of 2½ percent, sales in the second year of the lease were $2,491,771, lease started April 1.

Space 8: Yorkshire Table Restaurant, 3,578 SF, percentage rent of 5 percent (base rent is $11.83/SF/year escalated at 4 percent compounded), second year of a 10-year lease, sales in the first year of the lease were $831,556, lease started April 1.

Crossroads Plaza is a thriving neighborhood shopping center where most of the tenants enjoy acceptable sales. You have spoken with all the tenants, and all who have lease options, except one, expect to exercise their options.

Market Time (Space 1) is a national chain of supermarkets and a credit tenant. This is the anchor tenant of Crossroads Plaza. Market Time is currently paying percentage rent. Your discussion with the manager indicates that current sales are running about 4 percent ahead of last year.

		Percentage Rent	Sales		
Year	Portion	$/SF/year	Total SF	Annual Rent	Comment
1	0.75	1¼%	$16,471,619		
	0.25	1¼%	17,130,483	$207,953	
2	0.75	1¼%	17,130,483		
	0.25	1¼%	17,815,702	216,272	
3	0.75	1¼%	17,815,702		
	0.25	1¼%	18,528,330	224,923	
4	0.75	1¼%	18,528,330		
	0.25	1¼%	19,269,463	233,920	
5	0.75	1¼%	19,269,463		
	0.25	1¼%	20,040,241	243,276	
6	0.75	1¼%	20,040,241		
	0.25	1¼%	20,841,850	253,007	

Christie's Cleaners (Space 2) is a local chain of dry cleaners. Currently, the tenant is not paying percentage rent, but sales are rising with inflation. Your talk with the manager confirms that a 4 percent increase over last year's sales is likely.

		Percentage Rent	Sales		
Year	Portion	$/SF/year	Total SF	Annual Rent	Comment
1	0.25	$13.63	1,602		
	0.75	13.63	1,602	$21,835	
2	0.25	13.63	1,602		
	0.75	13.63	1,602	21,835	
3	0.25	13.63	1,602		
	0.75	13.63	1,602	21,835	
4	0.25	13.63	1,602		
	0.75	13.63	1,602	21,835	
5	0.25	13.63	1,602		
	0.75	6½%	$346,901	22,363	percentage rent starts
6	0.25	6½%	346,901		
	0.75	6½%	360,777	23,224	

Primavera (Space 3) is an independent beauty shop. Currently, the tenant is not paying percentage rent. The owner tells you sales will increase at least 4 percent this year and likely more than that.

		Percentage Rent	Sales		
Year	Portion	$/SF/year	Total SF	Annual Rent	Comment
1	1	$13.85	1,107	$15,331	
2	1	13.85	1,107	15,331	
3	1	13.85	1,107	15,331	
4	1	13.85	1,107	15,331	
5	1	7%	$219,268	15,348	percentage rent starts
6	1	7%	228,038	15,962	

Fallbrook's (Space 4) is a national chain. Currently, the tenant is not paying percentage rent. The manager indicates that sales should increase at least 4 percent above last year.

		Percentage Rent	Sales		
Year	Portion	$/SF/year	Total SF	Annual Rent	Comment
1	1	$12.66	943	$11,938	
2	1	6½%	$193,357	12,568	percentage rent starts
3	1	6½%	201,091	13,070	
4	1	6½%	209,134	13,593	
5	1	6½%	217,499	14,137	
6	1	6½%	226,198	14,702	

Screen Scene (Space 5) is a local chain. The tenant is currently paying percentage rent. The manager confirms that a 4 percent increase in sales is likely.

Year	Portion	Percentage Rent $/SF/year	Sales Total SF	Annual Rent	Comment
1	0.75	6%	$272,938		
	0.25	6%	283,855	$16,539	
2	0.75	6%	283,855		
	0.25	6%	295,209	17,201	
3	0.75	6%	295,209		
	0.25	6%	307,017	17,889	lease renewal
4	0.75	6%	307,017		
	0.25	6%	319,297	18,604	
5	0.75	6%	319,297		
	0.25	6%	332,068	19,348	
6	0.75	6%	332,068		
	0.25	6%	345,350	20,123	

Electronic Emporium (Space 6) is a national chain. Percentage rent is not being paid. The manager tells you that a 4 percent increase in sales is probable but that sales have been disappointing due to excess competition in the market area. At the end of the lease term the tenant will move out and will not exercise the option to renew the lease.

Year	Portion	Percentage Rent $/SF/year	Sales Total SF	Annual Rent	Comment
1	1	$ 9.23	2,510	$23,167	
2	0.0833	12.60	2,510		one-month vacancy
	0.9166	12.60	2,510	31,626	new tenant
3	0.0833	12.60	2,510		
	0.9166	5½%	$576,898	31,716	percentage rent starts
4	0.0833	5½%	576,898		
	0.9166	5½%	599,974	32,889	
5	0.0833	5½%	599,974		
	0.9166	5½%	623,971	34,204	
6	0.0833	5½%	623,971		
	0.9166	5½%	648,932	35,573	

Trimart (Space 7) is a national chain of drug stores and a credit tenant. Trimart is currently paying percentage rent. Your talk with the manager indicates that it's too early to predict total sales for the year, but sales usually increase each year with inflation.

| | | Percentage Rent | Sales | | |
| | | $/SF/year | Total SF | | |
Year	Portion	$/SF/year	Total SF	Annual Rent	Comment
1	0.5	2½%	$2,591,441		
	0.5	2½%	2,695,098	$66,081	
2	0.5	2½%	2,695,098		
	0.5	2½%	2,802,901	68,724	
3	0.5	2½%	2,802,901		
	0.5	2½%	2,915,017	71,473	
4	0.5	2½%	2,915,017		
	0.5	2½%	3,031,617	74,332	
5	0.5	2½%	3,031,617		
	0.5	2½%	3,152,881	77,306	
6	0.5	2½%	3,152,881		
	0.5	2½%	3,278,996	80,398	

Yorkshire Table Restaurant (Space 8) is a local chain of family restaurants. The tenant is not currently paying percentage rent. The manager indicates that the increase in sales this year will be a little higher than 4 percent over last year.

| | | Percentage Rent | Sales | | |
| | | $/SF/year | Total SF | | |
Year	Portion	$/SF/year	Total SF	Annual Rent	Comment
1	0.5	$12.31	3,578		
	0.5	12.80	3,578	$44,921	
2	0.5	12.80	3,578		
	0.5	13.31	3,578	46,710	
3	0.5	13.31	3,578		
	0.5	13.84	3,578	48,570	
4	0.5	13.84	3,578		
	0.5	5%	$1,011,716	50,051	
5	0.5	5%	1,011,716		
	0.5	5%	1,052,184	51,596	
6	0.5	5%	1,052,184		
	0.5	5%	1,094,271	53,660	

The space that Electronic Emporium will vacate in your client's second year of ownership can be easily leased to a new tenant. Every month the property manager gets inquiries from prospective tenants desiring to lease space for a liquor store. From your inquiries, it appears that there will be no political opposition to a liquor store being located in Crossroads Plaza. Based on your research, you estimate that a liquor store would generate sales of $212/SF/year next year were it an established one. It is likely it will be well established by the second year of the lease and enjoy normal sales. A 5½ percentage rent is appropriate, and you estimate a base rent of $12.60/SF/year will be the current market rent for liquor stores in the first year of the new tenant. You will start the new lease one month after the termination of the old. That will allow you time to clean the space and will allow the new tenant time to prepare the space for retail liquor sales. (See Chapter 1 for a sample detailed schedule of base rents and percentage rents for a shopping center.)

VACANCY

If the tenants in a shopping center are experiencing healthy sales and the shopping center continues to do well, tenants are not likely to leave. It is more likely that you will want to replace certain tenants at the end of their lease terms with other tenants that have potential for higher sales (and higher rent). On the other hand, it is not unusual for local tenants to close their retail businesses because of poor sales or insolvency. Some tenants may even disappear overnight. For these reasons, it is prudent to include a vacancy factor in your projection even though Crossroads Plaza is 100 percent leased. Your research indicates that neighborhood shopping centers in your region have a 3 percent vacancy, so you will use a 3 percent vacancy factor.

OTHER INCOME

The miscellaneous income for small shopping centers normally is nominal. For Crossroads Plaza, there is no income other than the rent and tenant reimbursements for certain expenses. In the leases, the tenants have agreed to reimburse the owner for a pro rata (based on square feet of space) share of the common area maintenance (CAM), the real estate taxes, and the insurance costs. Those expenses are expected to be as follows:

CAM	$ 46,893
Real estate taxes	51,783
Insurance	11,901
Total	$110,577

You will escalate these reimbursements at 4 percent per year for your projection.

ULI INCOME

The Urban Land Institute publishes a number of statistical books for different types of shopping centers. One, *Dollars and Cents of Shopping Centers,* includes neighborhood shopping centers, community shopping centers, regional malls, and super regional malls. The income is expressed in a statistical format rather than in a format for calculations.

Under total rent, the categories are minimum rent (base rent) and overages (rent in excess of the base rent). No vacancy statistics are provided. The rent statistics provided are based on actual collections, not on a rent schedule. So, total rent is, in effect, an after-vacancy figure and is the equivalent of effective rental income. In addition to rent are the following categories:

Total rent
+Common area charges
+Other charges
+Miscellaneous income
Total operating receipts

Common area charges are tenant reimbursements for CAM. Other charges include property taxes and insurance, which are also reimbursed by tenants in many shopping centers. Where there is a central HVAC system, utility costs are often passed on to tenants also. These pass-throughs are entered in other income and are not subject to vacancy calculations.

The bottom line of the income statistics is total operating receipts. These statistics for income are more valuable than their counterparts for residential and office income properties. Shopping center owners frequently turn to these national statistics as a guide to set rents. Renting to a variety of national chains and local tenants in a variety of different retail businesses and charging percentage rent is too complex for relying on local information and statistics (see Chapter 1). Nonetheless, shopping center rents are affected by local markets, and ULI income statistics are not blindly followed.

Keep in mind that minimum rent (base rent) and overages (percentage rent in excess of base rent) are often presented separately and capitalized with different capitalization rates (cap rates) to reflect different risks.

ULI EXPENSES

In *Dollars and Cents of Shopping Centers*, the expenses are placed in a few simple categories:

Total operating receipts
> Building maintenance
> Parking lot, mall, and other common areas
> Central utility systems
> Office area services
> Advertising and promotion
> Real estate taxes
> Insurance
> General and administrative
> Management agent fees
> Leasing agent fees
> −Total operating expenses
> Net operating balance

The total for operating expenses is labeled "total operating expenses." This total is not the same as the operating expenses category in the *Real Numbers* scheme. But if the leasing agent fees were extracted and placed in nonoperating outlays (and amortized in nonoperating expenses) instead, total operating expenses (ULI) would be equal to operating expenses (*Real Numbers*). ULI's net operating balance, likewise, would be the equal of net operating income if leasing agent fees were extracted from expenses and placed in nonoperating outlays (and amortized in nonoperating expenses) instead. But that is not how the statistics are published, and net operating balance is not the equivalent of net operating income.

ICSC EXPENSES

The International Council of Shopping Centers publishes *SCORE: ICSC's Handbook on Shopping Center Operations Revenues & Expenses*, which offers statistics on shopping center expenses. The expense categories for strip centers are as follows:

Recoverable common area M&R

  Landscaping

  Parking lot cleaning/sweeping/repairs

  Snow removal

  Trash removal

  Other

Nonrecoverable building owner M&R

  Roof repair

  Other

Common area utilities

  Electricity

  Other

General administrative and marketing

  On-site payroll and benefits

  Professional services

  Management fee

  Leasing fees and commissions

  Marketing

  Bad debt allowance

  Other

Insurance

    Liability insurance

    Property insurance

    Special coverages

    Other

Tax

For enclosed malls, there are different expense categories to express the different expenditures required by buildings substantially different than the buildings in strip centers:

Recoverable common area M&R

    Housekeeping

    Elevator/escalator

    HVAC equipment

    Landscaping

    Parking lot cleaning/sweeping/repairs

    Snow removal

    Trash removal

    Other

Nonrecoverable building owner M&R

    Roof repair

    Other

Common area utilities

    HVAC energy

    Other

General and administrative

    Professional services

    On-site payroll and benefits

    Management fee

    Leasing fees and commissions

    Bad debt allowance

    Other

Marketing

    Advertising

    Promotions/special events

    Christmas decor/events

    Administrative

    Other

Insurance

    Liability insurance

    Property insurance

    Special coverage

    Other

Tax

SCORE offers a detailed spread of statistics on expenses, which will facilitate a detailed comparison.

NONOPERATING OUTLAYS

The leasing fees for Crossroads Plaza could be scheduled but might be misleadingly low. Local tenants in the retail business can become insolvent unexpectedly and leave without notice. Sometimes that happens with national chains too. For a shopping center that is 100 percent occupied, it may appear that no leasing commissions will be paid in most years. In reality, leasing fees might be incurred. Therefore, it might be prudent to use a statistical figure for leasing fees. For instance, ULI includes such an expense in *Dollars and Cents of Shopping Centers*, and ICSC includes this expense in *SCORE*. You will use a factor of $.24/SF/year obtained from your market research. The first year the expenditure will be $14,400, and it will be escalated at the normal inflation rate of 4 percent per year.

CAPITAL ADDITIONS

In shopping centers, each retail business is responsible for providing and paying for its space improvements and decor. Since retail decor spans a wide range from plain to glitzy, and since a new tenant is unlikely to be able to use the decor of a prior tenant, improvements are customarily the tenant's responsibility. The landlord usually provides only the basics (e.g., roof, floor, heating and cooling, and demising partitions).

Because tenants provide their own space improvements, there are not capital additions for such improvements. Crossroads Plaza has no major repairs or replacements that are known to be needed in the next six years, and no capital additions are planned.

RESERVES

Without any requirements for capital additions, you will use a 1 percent annual reserve amount to cover general contingencies. Since there is a positive cash flow, this reserve may not be necessary. If there is an unexpected capital expenditure, however, it will tend to even the cash flows.

PURCHASE PRICE

The purchase price for Crossroads Plaza is $4,696,000. You are purchasing the property with the price based on a current market capitalization rate of 8.4 percent. You estimate that the cost of acquisition will be about 1¼ percent, which is $58,700. The investment base for this purchase is the equity (down payment) required plus the loan points and the acquisition costs.

MORTGAGE

You can obtain a loan at 9½ percent interest amortized over 30 years. The loan will be $3,522,000 and requires the payment of two points in loan fees.

ASSUMPTIONS

Your believe that a 4 percent inflation rate for both income and expenses may be expected based on historical data. You will purchase the property on a capitalization rate of 8.4 percent, and you will use an 8.4 percent cap rate to estimate future sale prices.

COST OF SALE

You estimate the cost of sale at 4 percent of the sale price. This estimate includes closing expenses and real estate commissions.

PROJECTION

The five-year projection for Crossroads Plaza is in Appendix III. The projection consists of three pages. The first is the pro forma income & expense statement and includes purchase information, loan information, and the assumptions made. The second page contains the five-year forecast. These two pages cover the essentials for understanding the property. The third page is the lease schedule. The five-year projection is a before-tax projection only, as the client requested.

Note that even though you may have a spread sheet computer program that calculates both before-tax and after-tax cash flows, it is easy to convert to a before-tax cash flow projection that excludes after-tax information. You simply do not print the income tax analysis: that portion of the cash flow analysis after cash flow before tax, and that portion of the sale proceeds analysis after sale proceeds before tax. You also do not have to supply the required inputs for the after-tax calculations, but if you did, it would not make any difference. In other words, you do not need a separate spread sheet program.

Note that the forecast for Crossroads Plaza was calculated on the same computer spreadsheet model that calculated the other forecasts. For Crossroads Plaza, certain lines were eliminated in printing the forecast to create a before-tax forecast rather than an after-tax forecast. (See Chapter 20.)

CHAPTER 31

OTHER REAL ESTATE INVESTMENTS

FOUR-PLEX

You have found a four-plex (four-unit apartment building) a few years old to purchase. You have made a verbal agreement with the owner that you will sign a purchase contract in two days contingent on processing the information you have regarding the property and the local real estate market and on making the decision to invest. The units are all the same size, each with two bedrooms, a refrigerator, washer, and dryer. The property manager very recently raised the rents to $642 per unit, and the rents have been raised once a year for the last few years. The tenants pay their own utilities except for water, sewer, and electricity for the common area lighting. Two parking spaces are provided to each tenant at no additional rent. The market is stable, and the vacancy rate has been in the 4 percent to 6 percent range for a long time. Over the past few years, the vacancy rate has consistently been 4 percent to 5 percent in this building. There is no indication that the market conditions will change, and there is a new municipal moratorium on building new multifamily residential units. It will not be lifted until a new sewer treatment plant is built. The sewer treatment plant is in the preliminary planning stage and is unlikely to be built for at least four or five years.

You decide to use the Annual Property Operating Data (APOD) form of the Commercial Investment Real Estate Institute to calculate your pro forma. There is no on-site management. Contract services include some minimal landscaping work, and supplies are primarily for maintenance, repairs, and landscaping. (See Appendix IV for the APOD pro forma.)

Because this property can be financed with widely available residential loan programs, you are able to get an 80 percent loan at 9½ percent interest amortized with monthly payments over 30 years. The loan payment is $1,286 per month. The loan fees amount to 1½ points. You will use 4 percent for an inflation rate for both income and expenses, although the moratorium on multifamily construction may have the effect of inflating rents at a higher rate. The carpeting has just been replaced in all the units, and no significant capital additions are planned during your anticipated five-year holding period. Nonetheless, you will reserve 1 percent of potential rental income per year for a contingency fund. Since you are purchasing the property for $191,250 on a 9.8 percent capitalization rate (cap rate), you will assume a 9.8 percent cap rate for the sale of the property. You anticipate the cost of sale to be 6 percent. The cost of acquisition will be nominal, and you estimate it at ¼ of 1 percent of the purchase price.

The allocation of values for cost recovery purposes is in the purchase agreement. The personal property including the appliances is $2,800. You decide to depreciate the personal property straight line over seven years. The improvements on the property are valued at $157,850, which you will depreciate straight line over 27½ years (28 years to approximate the IRS cost recovery table).

You plan to be actively involved in the management of the property, although you will have a property management firm take care of the day-to-day management for a fee of 8 percent of gross operating income. You are in the 28 percent tax bracket, and the income from the real estate will not put you into the 33 tax bracket. There is no income tax in your state.

The loan points are a nonoperating expense. They must be amortized over the term of the loan (30 years). Because they are prepaid, they are not a nonoperating outlay.

The forecast based on the above information in Appendix IV clearly shows that this forecast format is applicable to small properties as well as to large ones. The forecast provides you with a complete picture of the performance of the property over your five-year holding period.

Keep in mind that the primary use of the forecast is not predictive; that is, its best use is not to predict the performance of the property. The future is difficult to predict accurately. Rather, its best use is comparative. If a forecast is done for each property being considered for investment, such forecasts provide a sound basis on which to judge the financial performance of the alternative investment opportunities. By using computers, small properties can be analyzed quickly, efficiently, and cost-effectively.

SINGLE-FAMILY RESIDENCE

A single-family residence is not too small for the APOD form. When rented for income, a single-family residence is a one-unit residential income property, and the forecast format is appropriate to use. Vacancy rates and expense ratios may be difficult to predict, but using this investment analysis format to analyze single-family rental investments will give you the confidence you need to make reasonable investment decisions.

SALE AND LEASEBACK

A sale and leaseback transaction usually includes a credit tenant (a corporate tenant with excellent credit) that sells the property to you and becomes the sole tenant. The sale is made because the corporation can invest the funds invested in the building at a higher rate of return in its own business than it gets from the real estate. The lease term is usually a minimum of 10 years, often 20 or 30 years. For the buyer, the investment in the real estate is usually almost risk free, so the capitalization rates (cap rate) for such transactions are usually low. The seller-tenant continues to occupy the building and continues to treat it much as if it still owned the building. In fact, the seller-tenant usually agrees to pay all the expenses of occupying and using the building including maintenance, property taxes, and casualty insurance.

The sale and leaseback idea can also work with noncredit tenants (corporate tenants that are not strong financially even though they may have good credit records) too. With noncredit tenants, however, the investment is no more secure than the ownership of a building with a normal selection of tenants. The investment may even be less secure because if the seller-tenant vacates, the investor has the entire building to re-lease.

A sale and leaseback can be either a normal sale in which the seller becomes the sole tenant, or it can be a means of financing for the seller. The terms of the transaction agreement and the lease will indicate which it is.

If the sale and leaseback transaction is a means of financing, the lease will contain an option to repurchase the property at the end of the lease term. Such a lease and option must be written carefully to provide each party with the tax benefits it seeks; and the option is usually one to repurchase the property at fair market value at the end of the lease. In such cases, it is the intention of the seller-tenant to repurchase the property. Keep in mind that one of the attractions of the sale and lease-back used as a means of financing is that it is 100 percent financing. The sale price is high due to the low cap rate and the security of the long-term lease. Seller-provided financing is rare in sale and leaseback transactions.

If the sale and leaseback is a means for the seller-tenant to raise capital, and there is no intention to repurchase, the sale is identical to a normal sale. The only difference is that the building has only one tenant. Although the lease may have a long term, the buyer must assume that the seller-tenant will vacate the building at the end of the lease term. In this situation, the lease provisions may be different than in the financing situation. But in both situations, the seller-tenant takes responsibility for the operation of the building.

For the purpose of calculating a forecast, you can use the format in this book. The income will be the agreed rent. It may be a flat rent, or it may be escalated over the term of the lease. There is no vacancy & credit loss. There is no other income. And there are no expenses. As a practical matter, there may be some minor expenses even in normal situations when the seller-tenant agrees to pay all the expenses. For instance, there may be bookkeeping and accounting expenses. Whatever the expenses, they will be nominal. The income & expense statement may be as simple as the following:

Gross operating income	$1,449,930
−Expenses	$3,650
Net operating income	$1,446,280

The taxable income analysis and the cash flow analysis will be normal. If the buyer obtained a loan to purchase the property, the interest deduction will be taken and the debt service paid. The buyer will take cost recovery and will amortize the loan points. Capital additions may be the responsibility of the seller-tenant and may not need to be included in the forecast. Reserves are not likely to be needed, at least in the early years of the lease. In the later years of the lease, reserves can help the buyer prepare for rehabing the building for new tenants if the seller-tenant intends to vacate.

The building can be sold by the buyer at any time. If the sale is before the end of the lease term, the provisions of the lease may substantially affect the probable sale price. If the sale is made by the buyer to the seller-tenant under a repurchase agreement, the provisions of the agreement may affect the probable sale price. The repurchase agreement could be for a repurchase at a nominal sum. It is more likely, however, that the repurchase agreement will stipulate fair market value. Otherwise, substantial tax benefits may be lost. It is important to carefully review the transaction agreement and the lease to understand what affect, if any, they may have on a future sale price. Any agreements affecting the transferability of the property are likely to be of record.

LAND

Unimproved land held for future development is not considered income property. It is speculative property. Sometimes there is nominal income, often from an agricultural user or a transient user. But such income cannot be taken seriously, and it is often unreliable. It is probably better to leave it out of your analysis in many cases. The primary consideration with investing in raw land is the carrying cost. The main expenses are the property taxes and the debt service. The investment return, if any, is made upon the sale of the property for a higher price—a substantially higher price—than the purchase price.

In the income & expense statement, income can be expressed as an estimated amount per year if perceived to be reliable. It usually doesn't make sense to subject it to a vacancy & credit loss or to augment it with other income. If there is a lease on the property with a reliable tenant, however, you can treat the income like any rental income, even if nominal.

The operating expenses are likely to be modest. The primary expense is the property tax. But liability insurance may be needed. The land may have or need fencing and other minor improvements that must be maintained. Only a thorough investigation will reveal existing or potential expenses.

In the taxable income analysis, the interest expense may have restrictions on tax deducibility. There is no cost recovery for land. And nonoperating expenses are not likely except for amortized loan points, if any. In the cash flow analysis, the debt service must be paid. Nonoperating outlays are not likely, and capital additions will be modest, if any are required, except in special cases. Reserves are not applicable because there is not likely to be any cash flow to reserve.

The sale is what makes a land investment attractive. The appreciation in price must pay the carrying costs and provide a return of and on investment. The sale is calculated in the normal manner except the price is seldom appreciated at the normal inflation rate. The value of the property must appreciate dramatically to make a speculative land investment provide a reasonable rate of return commensurate with the risk.

In some situations, expensive capital improvements must be made to the property to realize the maximum on sale. For instance, if sewer and water lines are brought to the property line or if sewer and water infrastructure are installed on the property, the sale price may increase substantially more than the cost of the improvements—even for unsubdivided land. These capital expenses should be anticipated prior to purchasing the land and should be included in the analysis.

It makes sense to use the forecast format of this book to analyze a land investment. But it is likely that many of the line entries will not require any input.

OTHER REAL ESTATE INVESTMENTS

Apartments, office buildings, and shopping centers are the meat and potatoes of real estate investing. There are many other types of buildings that may be sound investment opportunities too. Warehouses, hotels, motels, special-use buildings (e.g., banks, auto repair facilities), corporate headquarters, government buildings, retail buildings, restaurants, fast food restaurants, convenience stores, ministorage units, and day-care centers are a few that are widely available.

PART 6

FORECAST ANALYSIS

The analyses provided thus far in the book have focused on the first year of operation or on individual years of operation. This part of the book treats taxation, the general operation of real estate, and the creation of multiyear analyses, which more realistically fit the holding periods of investors. The forecasts conceived in these chapters form a basis for measuring investment performance with sophisticated techniques.

Chapters

32 Taxation
33 Property Management
34 Comparative Statistics
35 Assumptions
36 Inflation Factors
37 Initial Investment
38 Projections

CHAPTER 32

TAXATION

In the other chapters of the book, the effect of income taxation on real estate analysis is illustrated with enduring tax concepts to show how taxation fits into the analytic scheme. Those concepts are subject to change, but an attempt was made to use tax concepts that are unlikely to change and to exclude tax concepts that appear to be more ephemeral. In this chapter, the 1992 tax laws are reviewed with the hope that when the tax laws change, this chapter will be the only chapter of the book that is outdated.

Although this chapter is more specific regarding the current tax laws, it is not meant to be a definitive treatment of income taxation as it applies to real estate investments. Rather, it is an incomplete overview designed to illustrate, in the most general way, how considerations of income taxation can be incorporated into real estate investment analysis. Every transaction and every property have individual idiosyncrasies, which often require complex tax analysis. For every tax guideline, there are many exceptions. Thus, even the few concepts presented here must be viewed as just barely enough for you to get your conversation started with your client's accountant, tax attorney, or other tax adviser.

You can treat the incorporation of income taxation into the real estate analysis as merely a rough estimate of the effect tax will have on the investment performance. This is what most real estate professionals do if they even take the trouble to include tax calculations. Or you can make the tax analysis so meticulous that it is almost the same as filing a tax return. If you are going to analyze so meticulously, you should do so in a joint effort with your client's tax adviser. Even for just a rough tax estimate similar to that illustrated in this book, you should at least seek input from your client's tax adviser.

ACQUISITION COSTS

Some acquisition costs may be deductible in the year of purchase. Such costs are deductible as nonoperating expenses. Acquisition costs such as title insurance, real estate commissions (buyer's broker), option payments, attorney's fees, appraisal costs, inspection fees, and surveys are added to the tax basis of the property and are not categorized as nonoperating expenses. It may not be worth the time and effort to distinguish between the deductible acquisition costs and the acquisition costs that must be added to basis. This is particularly true when the investor cannot use the tax shelter that may be generated in the first year of the investment by the deductible acquisition costs. Therefore, the best practice for efficient analysis may be simply to add all the acquisition costs to the basis.

LOAN POINTS

Loan points are not added to basis. Neither are they deductible as an expense when incurred. They must be amortized over the term of the loan. If loan points are paid on a loan used to acquire the property, they are added to the initial investment (investment base) and amortized as a nonoperating expense. If loan points are paid on a loan obtained during the holding period of the property, they are a nonoperating outlay and are amortized as a nonoperating expense.

INITIAL INVESTMENT (INVESTMENT BASE)

The down payment (equity) or the cash purchase amount for the property is one component of the initial investment. The other two components are the loan points, if any, and the acquisition costs. The initial investment is necessary to calculate an internal rate of return (IRR) for the real estate investment. *The initial investment (investment base) has no tax significance. Do not confuse it with tax basis.*

BASIS

The tax basis of the property is the purchase price. Capital additions increase basis. Cost recovery decreases basis. Some of the acquisition costs must be added to the purchase price to increase the basis rather than being currently deductible. A normal practice for analysis is to add all the acquisition costs to the basis.

INTEREST

Interest is deductible when paid. If interest is not an adequate amount, the imputed interest rules may apply. The imputed interest provisions of the Tax Code are quite complicated. Prepaid interest is not deductible except on an amortized basis.

COST RECOVERY

Real estate cost recovery is clearly defined in the Tax Code. For residential income property, a 27½-year period is allowed. For commercial property, a 31½-year period is allowed. The actual allowable amount of annual cost recovery is determined by tables included in the Tax Code. The tables reflect an adjustment for the first year on the assumption that the property is not purchased exactly at the beginning of the year on January 1. You can approximate the tables with simple mathematics, so you don't have to use them. A longer cost recovery period of 40 years may also be elected for both residential or commercial property.

For personal property, there are many classifications and corresponding cost recovery tables. Accelerated cost recovery (150 percent or 200 percent declining balance) is allowed for personal property. Check the tables in the Tax Code. For instance, refrigerators belong in the personal property classification that allows a seven-year cost recovery period and 200 percent declining balance. The mathematics of approximating these tables is more complex than the mathematics for the real estate tables, but using mathematics may be simpler than incorporating the tables into your computer program or spreadsheet.

Capital additions are put on a cost recovery schedule in the year that they are added to the property. They are also added to the basis. The cost recovery period for capital improvements is the same as it is for the original real estate in most cases (i.e., 27½ and 31½ years). For tenant improvements that may wear out before the end of such long periods, this is a harsh rule. But there is no provision that allows tenant improvements provided by the landlord to be amortized over the term of the lease. As a practical matter, tenant improvements can be divided between currently deductible expenses and expenditures that must be capitalized. But this must be done carefully. In this book, it is assumed that the entire amount spent for tenant improvements is capitalized and depreciated over the normal cost recovery period for real estate.

Real Property

For the commercial property in Chapter 9, the allocation of value to improvements (less personal property) is $740,000. Here are the depreciation calculations for that commercial property:

$$\$740,000 \div 31.5 = \$23,492/year$$

The IRS cost recovery is calculated from the cost recovery table, which uses a midmonth convention. Thus, if you purchase the property on January 1, the factor for the first year is 0.03042:

$$\$740,000 \times 0.03042 = \$22,510 \text{ first year}$$

The second year the factor is 0.03175:

$$\$740,000 \times 0.03175 = \$23,495 \text{ each year after first year}$$

A quick and easy method to approximate the IRS table without using the table itself is simply to change the cost recovery period to 32 years and use simple division:

$$\$740,000 \div 32 = \$23,125$$

Otherwise, you will have to use the entire IRS cost recovery table in your computer spreadsheet for each type of cost recovery. When doing a partial year, divide by 12 and multiply by the remaining months for the purchase or the elapsed months for the sale. This method is not absolutely accurate, but it's easier to calculate. The discrepancy will have an insignificant effect on your forecast.

Personal Property

For the commercial property reviewed in Chapter 9, the cost recovery for personal property permits accelerated depreciation. Accelerated depreciation allows you to take more depreciation in the beginning years and less in the later years of the term. The allocation to personal property is $40,000. Suppose the personal property can be depreciated on a seven-year cost recovery schedule. Currently, the Tax Code allows 200 percent declining balance for a seven-year period. That means that in the first year, 200 percent of the straight-line cost recovery for the first year may be taken for a cost recovery deduction in the first year. Straight line is a

$$\$40,000 \div 7 = \$5,714$$

And 200% declining balance is

$$\$5,714 \times 200\% = \$11,428$$

Theoretically, to calculate the remaining years, you use a percentage factor applied to the adjusted basis of the asset. The straight line multiplication factor is

$$1 \div 7 = 0.14286$$

The 200 percent declining balance multiplication factor is

$$0.14286 \times 200\% = 0.28571$$

The second year the cost recovery is recalculated:

$$\$40,000 - 11,428 \text{ [cost recovery taken]} =$$
$$28,572 \text{ [adjusted basis]} \times 0.28571 = \$8,163$$

The third year the cost recovery is recalculated:

$$\$11,428 + 8,163 = \$19,591 \text{ [cost recovery taken]}$$
$$\$40,000 - 19,591 = 20,409 \text{ [adjusted basis]} \times 0.28571 = \$5,831$$

Unfortunately, these calculations are just theoretical. The Tax Code allows only straight-line cost recovery the first year (half-year convention) or one-quarter of straight line (midquarter convention for property placed in service in the fourth quarter). The half-year convention and midquarter convention cost recovery tables are in the Tax Code. Thus, the above theoretical calculations must be modified as follows for the half-year convention:

Year

1 $40,000 ÷ 7 = $5,714
2 $40,000 − 5,714 = 34,286 × 0.28571 = $9,796
3 $34,286 − 9,796 = 24,490 × 0.28571 = $6,997

The mid-quarter convention are as follows:

Year

1 $40,000 ÷ 7 = 5,714 ÷ 4 = $1,428

2 $40,000 − 1,428 = 38,572 × 0.28571 = $11,020

To further complicate matters, as soon as the accelerated cost recovery for the year is less than the annual straight-line cost recovery, the cost recovery table switches to straight line. Therefore, a comparison must be made each year to the annual straight-line cost recovery amount to determine when the switch is to be made. Nonetheless, it may be easier to reproduce the contorted mathematics than to use the cost recovery tables in a computer spreadsheet program.

You can elect to use straight-line cost recovery for personal property. This is desirable when the use of accelerated cost recovery will result in suspended losses or there are other reasons that maximum current losses are not beneficial.

CAPITALIZATION OF EXPENSES

You can elect to capitalize certain expenses (e.g., interest) for property under development. This means that such expenses will not be deductible currently. For certain situations, this may be a benefit to a taxpayer.

RECAPTURE

For personal property all cost recovery is recaptured on sale. Real property cost recovery is not recaptured on sale unless accelerated cost recovery has been taken. If taken, the excess of accelerated cost recovery over straight line cost recovery is recaptured. Currently, accelerated cost recovery is not allowed. Therefore, there is no recapture.

For personal property, all cost recovery is recaptured on sale. But the recapture is limited to the amount of the gain on the personal property. Because there is seldom any gain on the sale of personal property, recapture for personal property can be safely ignored in most situations.

NONOPERATING EXPENSES

These are expenses not appropriate to subtract from income to determine NOI. Nonetheless, they are tax deductible expenditures. They are subtracted from NOI to determine taxable income.

Certain of these expenses may have to be amortized. If so, they are not added to basis and put on a cost recovery schedule. Rather, they are placed on an amortization schedule, and the amortized portion for the year is deducted as a nonoperating expense. Loan points and leasing commissions are good examples of an amortizable nonoperating expense. Like unamortized loan points, the unamortized portion of these amortizable nonoperating expenses are deducted at sale.

ACTIVE/PASSIVE INCOME

The character of the income is created by the activities of the investor. To be characterized as an "active" investor, a taxpayer must satisfy these criteria:

1. Play a material role in the management of the property.
2. Have a taxable income less than $100,000. A taxable income over $150,000 precludes a taxpayer from claiming to be an active investor. A taxable income between $100,000 and $150,000 allows less than $25,000 of tax loss on a progressive basis.

   Note: A limited partner in a limited partnership cannot be an active investor.

This is a complex part of the Tax Code, and these criteria provide only a simple outline of the rules. But the rules have significant impact on tax shelter, as you will see.

TAXABLE INCOME

Taxable income is the bottom line of the taxable income analysis. The analysis starts with NOI and subtracts interest, cost recovery, and nonoperating expenses. The result is the amount of income that is taxable. If the taxable income is negative, it is tax shelter and can be potentially used to offset income from other sources. But it is also subject to certain limitations in the Tax Code. An "active" investor can apply up to $25,000 (per investor) of tax shelter to income from other sources. A "passive" investor cannot apply any tax shelter unless the income from other sources is passive real estate income.

Because of the intricacies of the current Tax Code and the distinction between passive and active income, the normal number expressed for the taxable income line entry is altered as follows:

1. If taxable income is a positive number, there is no alternation.
2. If taxable income is a negative number and it is passive income, the line entry is zero. All tax loss is suspended until the sale. In this case, all tax loss is added to a suspended losses account and carried forward to the time of sale. (See Appendices I and II.)
3. If taxable income is a negative number and it is active income, the line entry can be between 0 and (25,000). But the negative number cannot be larger than (25,000) due to the Tax Code limitation ($25,000 limit per year per investor, not per property). Additional tax loss is added to a suspended losses account and carried forward to the time of sale. (See Appendix IV.)
4. If taxable income is a negative number and the investor has other passive real estate income, the tax loss may be applied to such other passive income. The limitation in this case is all of the other passive real estate income of the investor. If there is excess tax loss after applying it against the investor's other passive income, the excess is suspended until sale.
5. Suspended losses may also be applied against the passive real estate income in any succeeding year before sale.

The suspended losses are subtracted from the sale price at the time of sale to compute the capital gain. Thus, when the current tax loss (tax shelter) is not allowed in the year it occurred, it is deferred until the property is sold, at which time it is permitted to reduce the amount of gain resulting from the sale.

TAX RATE

Taking into account the various tax tables, a *rough* approximation of the current federal tax brackets for a married couple follows:

Taxable Income	Bracket
Under $30,000	15% lowest
30,000 to 75,000	28%
75,000 to 150,000	33%
Over 150,000	28% highest

The real estate income is taxed as additional income in the taxpayer's highest tax bracket. Because state tax is deductible, the state tax rate is reduced by the federal tax rate (e.g., $0.72 \times 11\% = 8\%$ where the state tax rate is 11% and the taxpayer's federal bracket is 28%).

OTHER CONSIDERATIONS

This straightforward tax formula to estimate the effect of income taxation on the real estate investment does not take into account other tax schemes such as the alternative minimum tax or the tax credits that Congress from time to time allows. If you perceive that one of these tax rules will have a significant affect on the after-tax performance of the property, you should include such extraordinary calculations in a systematic procedure that further refines the effect of taxes on the investment.

INVESTMENT TAX CREDITS

There are no investment tax credits currently allowed.

TAX LIABILITY ON SALE

To determine the tax liability on sale, the following general analysis procedure will produce a reasonable estimate in many cases:

    Basis at acquisition
   +Capital additions
   −Cost recovery
    Adjusted basis

Sale price
−Costs of sale
−Adjusted basis
−Recapture of cost recovery
−Suspended losses
Capital gain or loss
×Tax rate for capital gain
Tax on capital gain (savings)

Recapture of cost recovery
−Unamortized expenditures
Ordinary taxable income
×Tax rate on ordinary income
Tax on ordinary income (savings)

Sale price
+Reserve fund
−Cost of sale
−Loan balances
Sale proceeds before tax
−Tax on capital gain
−Tax on ordinary income
Sale proceeds after tax

Adjusted basis is calculated by adding capital additions and subtracting cost recovery from the original basis at purchase. The capital gain or loss is calculated by subtracting the cost of sale, the adjusted basis, the recapture of cost recovery, and the suspended losses from the sale price. Note that the recapture of cost recovery is subtracted so that it may be used with the ordinary income marginal tax rate to calculate the ordinary income tax. Once the capital gain or loss has been calculated, the capital gain marginal tax rate can be applied. Under the current tax law, ordinary income and capital gains are taxed at approximately the same rate. Nonetheless, ordinary income and capital gains are still kept separate in the Tax Code.

At the present time, accelerated cost recovery is not allowed for real estate improvements. Accelerated cost recovery is allowed, however, for personal property. The current rule requires that 100 percent of accelerated cost recovery be recaptured at sale. The recapture of cost recovery (100 percent of cost recovery for personal property) is subtracted from the sale price in the calculation of capital gain. But it is subtracted only because it is converted to ordinary income. As ordinary income, it is taxed at the ordinary income tax rate. Before applying the tax, the recapture of cost recovery is reduced by unamortized expenditures (e.g., unamortized loan points), if any:

> Recapture of cost recovery
> −Unamortized expenditures
> Ordinary income on sale

Then the ordinary income marginal tax rate is applied to the resulting ordinary income on sale.

You are now ready to calculate the total tax liability on sale. As you have seen, capital gains and ordinary income are calculated separately. Although they have been taxed at approximately the same rate for years, it is still best to keep them separate. Congress has kept them separate in the Tax Code, looking toward the day when they may be taxed at different rates again.

> Tax on capital gain
> +Tax on ordinary income
> **Tax liability on sale**

The tax liability on sale is the number that goes into the forecast.

INSTALLMENT SALE

An installment sale (owner carryback loan) of a property extends the cash flow from the closing on the sale until the end of the loan term. The tax treatment of installment sales is indecently complicated and is beyond the scope of this book. The Commercial Investment Real Estate Institute offers an installment sale worksheet and an installment sale cash flow analysis to bring some order to such tangled calculations.

OVERVIEW

Do not look on the specific tax considerations in this chapter and in Chapters 8, 9, 10, 11, 19, and 26 as being the essence of the information presented. Rather, you should perceive how the tax considerations can be incorporated into the forecast to make a reasonable estimate of the effect of taxation on investment performance. The details of the tax treatment are purposefully covered in a general manner. The provisions of the Tax Code briefly discussed in this chapter will likely change. But whenever subsequent provisions are legislated, they can be intelligently incorporated into this analysis format. As you can see, currently the calculation of taxable income is straightforward. So is the application of a marginal tax rate to determine tax liability. The complications result from the abundant rules regarding active and passive income, the amount of tax shelter that may be permitted, and the deferral of tax losses.

Unfortunately, many properties do not fit the general application of the Tax Code. If your property is an exception, you may have to do your tax calculations more precisely after taking into account many of the diverse and complex provisions of the Tax Code.

SUMMARY

This chapter has presented in a brief and general manner some of the aspects of the 1992 Tax Code most relevant to real estate analysis. Many of these tax concepts are likely to change. In the other chapters that present taxation concepts, the ideas presented are the more enduring ones that are not likely to change. Anything but the most superficial treatment of the income taxation of real estate is well beyond the scope of this book. The primary reason for even superficial coverage is to demonstrate how tax calculations can fit into your analysis to estimate the effect of the Tax Code on the performance of an investment.

CHAPTER 33

PROPERTY MANAGEMENT

PROPERTY MANAGEMENT

Proper analysis assumes that the property is well managed by professional property managers who are free to manage it efficiently. This is not always the case. There are at least two situations when this is not true, and there are undoubtedly many more.

INCOMPETENT PROPERTY MANAGEMENT

You find a property that is operating so far below local and national norms that it sparks your curiosity. On further investigation, you attribute the lackluster performance to poor property management. Because you can provide professional property management, you see an opportunity to improve the performance substantially if you acquire the property.

SUPERCOMPETENT PROPERTY MANAGEMENT

You find a property that is being operated very well by an aggressive and competent local property management firm. The property performs well above the norm in an unstable local market.

Your employer is a bureaucratic national financial institution with an office outside the locale of the property. If your employer acquires the property, you will hire a resident manager. But the professional property management will be done from your office with your staff property managers flying to the property occasionally to supervise the resident manager. Considering the inefficiencies of managing from afar and the quick entrepreneurial reaction to market changes required by the unstable local market, you perceive that the performance of the property will decline under your ownership.

YOUR PROPERTY MANAGEMENT

Both of the preceding descriptions are objective. The first observation is easy to make. Everyone likes to think that he or she or his or her company does things better than others. The second observation is much more difficult. Who wants to admit that someone else can do a better job? Yet it is important to be objective about how you will be able to manage the property when you become the owner.

Property management covers a lot of ground. It takes much attention to detail, a broad spectrum of skills, and an ability to keep long-range objectives in mind. Property managers do everything from keeping the books to acting as general contractors for rehabilitations.

Properties managed by well-trained professional property managers do well. But income properties are businesses just like any other business. When the market is stable, good management usually maintains profitability. When the market is unstable and in decline, it may take a measure of entrepreneurship to keep a property profitable. Not all property managers make good entrepreneurs or promoters.

You have to assess the property management capabilities of the current management and yourself accurately. If your skills are better than the existing manager's, there may be an opportunity for you to increase the investment yield of the property by improving the property management. If your skills are less agile than the existing management, the performance of the property may fall off under your ownership—unless you retain the current management. If this reality is ignored in your analysis, whether it be for acquisition or for asset management, the property may perform substantially under expectations.

SPECIALIZED PROPERTY MANAGEMENT

Today some income properties specialize in niche markets. For instance, there are specialized types of shopping centers such as "power centers." Their success depends on getting and maintaining a esoteric tenant mix and on promoting the center to create a specific image. It may take specialized property management to effectively manage some of these speciality properties. Normal professional property managers may not have the requisite skills without further education.

THE MANAGEABILITY OF THE PROPERTY

Some properties are easier to manage than others. A one-story office building with central heating/cooling may require more intensive management than another one-story office building in which each tenant has its own heating/cooling system. The property manager is responsible for maintenance in the former while the tenants may be responsible in the latter. Building design has a direct effect on the scope of the property management effort.

Tenants are a consideration too. Apartments in declining areas generally require more intensive management than that for other areas. Tenant turnover may be high. Collecting rent may take more attention. On-site crime and vandalism may be an ongoing problem. And keeping maintenance up-to-date may be difficult. Likewise, a specialty apartment such as a singles apartment for the more affluent may require extra attention. Social activities may have to be planned and managed. An assortment of specialized services and facilities may have to be provided. Each property has its own relationship to tenants that determines the intensity of the management.

MANAGEMENT SCOPE

Property management activities may have to be expanded and reduced to accommodate local conditions. For instance, when apartment occupancy is high, new tenants can often be handled administratively. Minimal marketing is required. When apartment occupancy is low, a gang of aggressive leasing agents as well as an aggressive marketing campaign may be necessary just for average success.

You must be cognizant of the scope of management required. Expanded management activities may mean additional expenses (e.g., promotion) or an increased property management fee. More importantly, it could be disastrous to your investment to misjudge the extent of management required.

RELEVANCY

Your research to provide sound data for your analysis may be successful, and your investment analysis calculations may be correct. But a realistic evaluation of the prospective property management is relevant to the future performance of the property too. Unfortunately, it is sometimes difficult to evaluate such an intangible. But, since investment analysis assumes competent property management, you must make a judgment as to·whether the skills of the property manager are matched to the management requirements of the property.

SUMMARY

You cannot take property management for granted. If the property is to perform as forecast, you must ensure that the property management fits the property and the situation.

CHAPTER 34

COMPARATIVE STATISTICS

The different categories and formats for operating expenses proliferate. There is no industry standard. You can choose between an arbitrary format published by an organization or institution, or devise your own arbitrary arrangement. For instance, the Commercial Investment Real Estate Institute's Annual Property Operating Data (APOD) form is widely used. But perhaps the best method is to follow the formats in published statistics. By doing this, you will be able to compare your property to the statistics directly and easily.

EXPENSES

The following organizations publish useful operating expense statistics:

Apartments
  Institute of Real Estate Management (IREM)
Offices
  IREM
  Building Owners and Managers Association (BOMA)
Shopping Centers
  Urban Land Institute (ULI)
  International Council of Shopping Centers (ICSC)

These statistics are published regularly and are available for a reasonable price. In each book, the categories and formats of expenses are carefully explained. This allows you to accurately categorize and arrange the operating expenses for your property the same way. A comparison of your property to the statistics can be revealing.

There are three ways you can use these comparisons. First, you can take the last year's income and expense statement for the property and compare it to the statistics. If certain expenses are out of proportion, it is cause for further investigation. It may indicate a problem with the property that you had not detected, or it may indicate an opportunity to manage the property better and increase the net operating income (NOI).

Second, after you have created your pro forma income & expense statement, you can compare it to the statistics. Again, if certain expenses are out of proportion, you may be able to identify problems and opportunities that you might have missed otherwise.

Third, you can use the statistics as the basis for your pro forma income & expense statement. This is most appropriate when the property is new and has no operating data. There is, however, a danger in doing this. A property always has its own specific operating characteristics that may not fit a statistical profile well. Thus, input from local property managers is always necessary when basing your pro forma income & expense statement on statistics.

INCOME

The organizations identified above provide statistics on income too, but these statistics are not as reliable as expense statistics. Income tends to have occasional periods of volatility. The statistics in these organizations' publications may be two years old or more by the time you use them. Rent may be substantially higher or lower, depending on extremes of supply and demand in the locale of the property. Additionally, specific properties in specific locales may command rents that do not fit a generic profile. So a local source of information regarding rents is better to use than these statistics. One exception is the rent statistics for shopping centers. The rent is different for each type of tenant. There may not be enough local data for each tenant type to determine appropriate market rents. Therefore, a combination of local information and national statistical data must be used.

On the other hand, expenses are more stable. Thus, the expense statistics are helpful in these statistical publications.

ANALYZING THE STATISTICS

The statistics are presented in various ways. One useful way is in dollars per square foot. Another is in a percentage of total income. Your first consideration is understanding the type of square footage that the statistics use. It is rentable square feet, not gross square feet. You will have to calculate the square feet for your property matching the method used by those property managers who compiled the published statistics. The method is often outlined in the publication. The second consideration is understanding the divisor used in calculating percentages. When using percentages of total income, the question is what is the total income. Pay attention to the publication's definition of total income, or whatever term is used. For instance, IREM uses *gross possible income* for apartments (Gross possible income = Potential rental income + Other income). You will have to calculate your total income the same way to use the IREM percentage statistics.

Always learn as much about the statistics as possible. For instance, some publications will tell you how many properties were included in compiling the particular statistic you desire to use. When the number is as low as four or five properties, the sampling is somewhat thin and may not be representative. Watch for anomalies. In a particular locale, a certain expense might be abnormally high due to some local phenomenon (e.g., the water expense tripled due to a local drought).

Statistics are published for the entire country, for regions, and for certain metropolitan areas. Usually the statistics for the entire country have a large sampling. But such statistics will not reflect local deviations. The statistics for local areas will reflect local deviations but may have a sampling too small to be reliable. Each property is unique, too. Your property may have an anomaly that doesn't fit the local statistics, yet such an unusual expense may be a reasonable and appropriate operating expense.

Comparing your property with groups of properties that are similar in location, character, size, and age will give you better results than comparing them to national statistics. For instance, if the properties providing the supporting data for the statistics are in the same city, about the same size and character, and about the same age, the statistics may be very accurate in regard to your property, particularly if the sampling is large. But this situation is not always the case.

APPLICABILITY

Because there is so much room for deviation and error, these statistics are not a means of fine tuning your income & expense pro forma. It's better to do that with information from reliable local statistics or from local property managers. These statistics are useful for detecting operating problems by comparing your property to the published statistics. If an anomaly jumps out at you from the comparison, it deserves further investigation. However, if the differences are only 20 percent or 30 percent, or even 50 percent in some cases, there may be no significant deviation.

MAPLEWOOD APARTMENTS

To create the pro forma forecast for Maplewood Apartments, you obtain operating information from the property manager. Your research and your conversations with the property manager lead you to believe that the property is well managed. Therefore, you will rely on the information you have obtained. Because the operating statement format from the property manager for Maplewood Apartments is not the same as IREM's, you must create a worksheet in the IREM format to rearrange your income and expenses to conform to the IREM scheme. The operating statement on page 209 for last year is provided to you by the property manager.

After reviewing the operating statement, you call the property manager and determine the following from your conversation:

1. The supplies entry is related only to maintenance and repairs.
2. The painting entry is broken down into interior and exterior.
3. The siding replacement entry is for the complete replacement of siding on one of the buildings. You decide that this is a capital expenditure.
4. The new appliances entry is for replacement of old appliances. You decide that this is a capital expenditure.
5. The utilities entry is for electricity and gas. The electricity is for the common areas. The gas is for centrally supplied hot water for consumption, not for heat.

MAPLEWOOD APARTMENTS
Operating Statement

Income:

Rental income	$911,810
Other income (laundry)	11,061
Total	$922,871

Operating expenses:

Trash	$ 8,028
Real estate taxes	44,663
Yard care	20,169
Supplies	20,695
Telephone	1,809
Postage and shipping	907
On-site manager	19,185
Management fee	49,053
Painting	29,596
Pool service	6,039
Siding replacement	18,732
Cable TV	9,963
New appliances	9,428
Advertising	9,552
Utilities	39,314
Legal fees	3,761
Maintenance and repairs	38,833
Mileage	1,591
Payroll taxes	1,384
Water and sewer	13,783
Office and clerical	22,998
Cleaning	15,484
Public relations	953
Insurance	16,521
Floor covering replacement	64,970
License fee	216
Miscellaneous	1,148
Total	$468,775

6. The mileage entry is for mileage reimbursements for the on-site manager and other employees.

7. The cleaning entry is broken down into interior, exterior, and carpets.

8. The insurance entry is broken down into property insurance and worker's compensation insurance.

9. The floor covering replacement entry is for the replacement of worn-out floor coverings for the first time in many years. You decide that it is a capital expenditure.

10. The vacancy and credit loss was 6 percent.

11. The apartment complex has 83,690 rentable square feet.

The notes from your telephone conversation show the following figures for the break-downs of the following specific entries:

Maplewood Apts—Conversation with Property Manager

Painting	
Interior	$26,504
Exterior	3,092
Utilities	
Electricity	12,922
Gas	26,392
Cleaning	
Interior	10,235
Exterior	1,093
Carpets	4,156
Insurance	
Property	15,100
Worker's Compensation	1,421

The first thing you do is remove the following line items because it is not appropriate to include capital additions and replacements in an income and expense statement:

Siding replacement	$18,732	Capital addition
New appliances	9,428	Capital replacement
Floor covering replacement	64,970	Capital addition

IREM provides the following format for its residential income property expense statistics. You reorganize the operating statement line items to fit into the IREM format. Next, you place the remaining line items into the IREM format from *Income/Expense Analysis Conventional Apartments:*

Management fee	$49,053	
Other administration		
Telephone	1,809	
Postage and shipping	907	
Advertising	9,552	
Legal fees	3,761	
Mileage	1,591	
Office and clerical	22,998	
Public relations	953	
Subtotal administration		**$90,624**
Supplies	–0–	
Heating fuel	–0–	
Electricity	$12,922	
Water/sewer	13,783	
Gas	26,392	
Building services		
Trash	8,028	
Other operating		
Miscellaneous	1,148	
Subtotal operating		**$62,273**
Security	–0–	
Grounds maintenance		
Yard care	$20,169	
Maintenance–repairs		
Supplies	20,695	
Painting (exterior)	3,092	
Maintenance and repair	38,833	
Cleaning (exterior)	1,093	
Painting/decorating		
Painting (interior)	26,504	
Cleaning (interior)	10,235	
Cleaning (carpets)	4,156	
Subtotal maintenance		**$124,777**
Real estate taxes	$44,663	
Other tax fees/permit	216	
Insurance	15,100	
Subtotal tax—insurance		**$59,979**
Service		**$16,002**
Pool service	$6,039	
Cable TV	9,963	
Other payroll		**$21,990**
On-site manager	19,185	
Payroll taxes	1,384	
Insurance (workmens comp)	1,421	
Total expenses		**$375,645**

You have already learned from the property manager that the potential rental income from last year was $970,011. Consequently, you calculate IREM's *gross possible income* for the property to be $970,011 + $11,061 = $981,072. This is the divisor for calculating expense percentages for comparison.

		Maplewood (%)	City (%)
Administrative	90,624 ÷ 981,072 =	9.2%	9.0%
Operating	62,273 ÷ 981,072 =	6.3%	6.1%
Maintenance	124,777 ÷ 981,072 =	12.7%	6.8%
Tax and insurance	59,979 ÷ 981,072 =	6.1%	6.2%
Recreation/amenities	16,002 ÷ 981,072 =	1.6%	0.3%
Other payroll	21,990 ÷ 981,072 =	2.2%	2.9%
Total	375,645 ÷ 981,072 =	38.3%	34.7%

Now you are able to compare the expense percentages for the property to the expense statistics for the city (38 apartment projects with a total of 6,216 units) in which the property is located. The first anomaly is the high cost of maintenance. The cost is almost double that of the statistic for the city. This leads you to investigate further. You find the reasons for the high maintenance and determine that the maintenance cost is not an obstacle to purchasing the property. The other anomaly is the high recreational amenities expense. This property, however, offers above average amenities, and the higher cost is justified. Other than these two deviations, the property appears to be operating as would be expected from reading the statistics. You can also refine your comparative analysis more by breaking down the categories and making comparisons to the additional statistics available in the IREM publications. The subcategories are compared to IREM statistics as follows:

	Maplewood (%)	City (%)
Management fee	5.0%	4.7%
Other administrative	4.2	3.9
Supplies	–0–	0.3
Heating fuel	–0–	2.1
Electricity	1.3	0.8

	Maplewood (%)	City (%)
Water/sewer	1.4	1.6
Gas	2.6	1.4
Building services	0.8	1.4
Other operating	0.1	1.6
Security	–0–	0.3
Grounds maintenance	2.0	2.1
Maintenance—repairs	6.4	2.4
Painting/decorating	4.1	1.7
Real estate taxes	4.5	4.4
Other tax fees/permit	—	0.1
Insurance	1.5	1.4

In this case, you use the operating statement from the property manager as the basis for creating your pro forma forecast (see Appendix I). Essentially, you inflate the expenses 4 percent for your pro forma except when you have specific knowledge that an expense should be treated differently for the future. For instance, you anticipate that the property taxes will jump considerably after the purchase transaction, but you think you can save on the management fee. Although you believe that you can decrease the cost of maintenance substantially in the future, you decide that it is prudent to continue to project the high cost of maintenance. Once you complete your pro forma income and expense statement, you make another comparison to the IREM statistics as part of your analysis (see Appendix I).

SUMMARY

Comparing your property to operating statistics is easy and is a productive method of identifying operating anomalies. The statistics can also provide you with confidence when your property's percentage expenses are similar to the norms. The IREM publications also provide per-square-foot statistics, and you can make your comparisons on that basis too.

CHAPTER 35

ASSUMPTIONS

You must make various assumptions when you create a real estate pro forma because you are predicting the future. The facts of the future are not known yet. Therefore, all assumptions must be well researched to foster maximum accuracy. For instance, a written loan commitment from a reputable lender is assurance that such a loan will be made on the property being analyzed. Seldom will you have the commitment at the time of analysis, however, and you will have to research the current mortgage market to determine what types of loans and terms are available.

All assumptions should be stated in your analyses. Some of the assumptions won't show up in the report format, but they are in the calculations, nonetheless. By providing a section or a page where all assumptions are identified, the reader is better able to understand the real estate (see Chapters 28–31 and Appendices I, II, III, and IV). Any assumption that is not expressed on a schedule of assumptions or in the investment analysis narrative should be identified in a footnote. Footnotes are especially important when their omission will cause misunderstanding, or worse, misrepresentation.

Although the word *assumption* should never mean "unresearched," it seldom means "well researched" either. Most real estate professionals are not allowed enough time to make well-researched assumptions unless a feasibility analysis is specifically required. If they did, every investment analysis would be a feasibility analysis instead. A feasibility analysis combines the features of a market study and a marketability study into an investment analysis (see Chapter 43).

Every selection process for real estate acquisition starts broadly. Some of the rates of return and ratios in Chapter 40 can be used to weed out unsuitable properties. Then full analyses will be done on certain promising properties. The one that's the most promising becomes the focus of negotiation. If a purchase agreement is reached, there is usually a contingency period to complete a "due diligence" investigation. During the due diligence period, the underlying assumptions for the investment analysis will usually be researched more thoroughly. But the focus of the due diligence investigation is not necessarily developing more and better information for the investment analysis. On the contrary, it often focuses only on confirming information already in use and on examining the physical and legal characteristics of the property. Many investors are not knowledgeable enough to develop market and marketability information, and they don't want to bear the cost of obtaining it. So, for many transactions, the investment analysis is based on market data that is not as thoroughly researched as a feasibility study. But times are changing. As real estate investing becomes institutionalized (e.g., by pension funds and other institutional investors), the requirements for more and better information will become the rule rather than the exception. There will be fewer investment analyses, and there will be more full-fledged feasibility studies.

Many investors believe they can avoid making assumptions and, therefore, will not run the risk of erroneous analysis. The underlying premise in that approach is that no assumptions means a "conservative" analysis that is more likely to be accurate. Unfortunately, by not making assumptions affirmatively and knowledgeably, assumptions are made inadvertently and unknowledgeably. In such a situation, it is difficult to bring objectivity and rationality to the analysis process.

For instance, some investors assume by using the same net operating income (NOI) and value (sale price) for the entire holding period of the investment that this approach will foster successful investments. However, this approach has at least two pitfalls. First, rents may be declining and may result in lower NOIs in the future. Only the use of market data will alert you to a potentially disastrous real estate investment in this situation. Second, when rents and values are increasing, the practice of using static assumptions may provide a "worst case" analysis rather than an investment analysis. You may miss prime investment opportunities. Market data should always be the driving force of an investment analysis. And it takes market research and affirmative assumptions to generate the most accurate investment analysis. Although there is nothing wrong with doing a worst case analysis, it should be developed after a rational investment analysis has been completed.

The saving and loan crisis of the '80s discredited investment analysis to some degree. Virtually every income property loan that ended up in default was originally documented with an investment analysis. Most of those deficient investment analyses, however, were backed up with poorly founded, optimistic assumptions rather than objective market research. Rational market research might have shown the investments to be unwise, and the loans might never have been made. The ultimate effect of the saving and loan crisis will be more stringent requirements in the future for objective feasibility information and investment analysis.

Regardless of the predictive quality of investment analysis, no one believes the future will happen for the property exactly as the analysis predicts. The investment analysis is just an intelligent guess. The real value of investment analysis is comparing real estate investment opportunities. Each property is analyzed under the same guidelines using assumptions appropriate to the property and its market. The properties that provide the highest rates of return are favored. Thus, the comparative use of investment analysis is essential for making rational choices.

CHAPTER 36

INFLATION FACTORS

Each year, economic forces grind on, almost always resulting in inflation. Real estate income and expenses usually inflate too. Occasionally,
an oversupply of real estate makes rents decline in a countertrend that
may last several years. When you calculate multiple-year projections,
your task is to anticipate such inflation or decline.

Most inflation figures come from the Consumer Price Index (CPI).
When researching inflation rates, keep in mind there may be more than
one CPI, and you must choose the one that is the most relevant. Comparable state or local statistics may be available too. Although national
economic forces will usually cause expenses to increase at a steady rate,
local economic forces may cause rents to decline or fluctuate. You can
find such information regarding rents only by thorough local research.

POTENTIAL RENTAL INCOME

If national inflation has been stable, you can pick a national inflation
rate (rounded to the lowest half percent) that best represents the normal
annual inflation. Once you have picked a rate, stick with it for the entire
projection unless you have information that leads you to believe something else will happen. For instance, if the inflation rate is increasing
each year and the federal government has started another round of un-
restrained spending, you may be justified in using a different rate for
later years of the projection. In this case, the rate would be higher.

Local economic forces can cause rents to increase or decline at a
different rate than the national inflation rate. Therefore, local historical
statistics on rents must always be researched. Whatever rate of increase
or decline you choose for your projection, it should be well substantiated
by local research. If an oversupply of real estate is causing rents to

decline regardless of inflation, you need to gather information on that trend to determine a rate of decline. It is difficult to determine exactly what rents are in an unstable market and where they are going. To determine whether a trend will continue in the future, look at the underlying causes for the trend. If the causes continue, the trend is likely to continue too.

If a rate of increase or decline is to be used, you apply it to the potential rental income for the first year to calculate the potential rental income for the second year, and so forth. This is especially appropriate for apartments. But other types of income properties have leases that may dictate exactly what potential rental income will be in the years ahead.

When leases determine the future potential income, certain assumptions must be made regarding rental rates for lease renewals and for new tenants. Usually, the current base rent is inflated (or decreased), and it is assumed that new tenants in future years will pay such an inflated or decreased based rent. If your only tenants are credit tenants on long-term leases that will not expire during your holding period, the leases will dictate exactly what the rent will be in your projection.

Shopping centers are in a special category due to leasing practices. Most leases include percentage rent (i.e., rent determined by a percentage of the gross sales of the tenant). As the dollar volume of retail sales increases with inflation, the rents increase too. No special inflation factor is required. Some tenants, however, are likely to be paying the minimum rents in their leases rather than percentage rents. In such cases, the leases dictate what the rents will be until the tenants' sales volumes are high enough to activate the percentage rent clauses. Shopping center turnover is more complicated too. Instead of one or several base rents, there are multiple base rents determined by tenant category. Each base rent for an anticipated future tenant must be individually inflated (see Chapter 30).

VACANCY & CREDIT LOSS

If you are using a specified amount for vacancy & credit loss, inflate it at the same rate as potential rental income unless you have reason to believe something different will happen. Perhaps better, convert it to a vacancy rate (divide the vacancy amount by potential rental income). Use the vacancy rate for the entire projection unless you have information to indicate that something else is more likely to happen. If you are already using a vacancy rate (a percentage), keep it constant through your entire projection. The actual amount for vacancy & credit loss will increase and decrease as potential rental income increases or decreases. If local research indicates that there is a trend showing the vacancy rate itself increasing or decreasing, you can adjust your vacancy rate accordingly over the projection.

The vacancy may be determined by the leasing situation of the property rather than by the market. If the property is 3 percent vacant when there is 8 percent vacancy for similar buildings in the market, it may not be rational to project a higher vacancy rate for the property. Nonetheless, you have to assume that when leases are not renewed or tenants otherwise vacate the property, the vacant space created will tend to take the property toward market vacancy.

EFFECTIVE RENTAL INCOME AND GROSS OPERATING INCOME

These are resultant numbers and will inflate (or decline) automatically. You do not have to use inflation factors.

OTHER INCOME

Inflate or decline this number as you would potential rental income unless you have information that supports another conclusion. In some cases, other income may be from contractual income (e.g., a lease or agreement) and is determined by the terms of the agreement.

OPERATING EXPENSES

Expenses in general often inflate at a different rate than rents. You should not assume that income and expenses inflate at the same rate without supporting data from the market. When real estate supply and demand are in equilibrium, however, it is common for rents and expenses to inflate at similar rates.

When operating expenses are calculated as a percentage of gross operating income, effective rental income, or potential rental income, keep the percentage constant unless there is data indicating that expenses are inflating faster than income. The increase in rental income will increase the expenses. If rents are declining, it is not appropriate to calculate expenses as a percentage of income.

In certain situations, overall expenses may increase as a percentage of income, even though expenses generally are not inflating faster than income. For example, for many new properties, expenses may actually grow as a percentage of income. In the first years, maintenance expenses and related expense items may be low because the property is new. After a few years of operation, these maintenance expenses grow to a normal level.

There may be situations in which the tenants pay or reimburse most of the operating expenses or the increases in the operating expenses. Be aware of any special lease clauses or contractual arrangements that may affect the inflation of expenses, and make your calculations accordingly.

NET OPERATING INCOME

Net operating income is a number resulting from the input of other data and does not need to be specifically inflated or decreased. If, however, inflation is the same for rents, other income, and expenses and the vacancy rate will remain constant, for quick evaluations you can simply inflate the net operating income after the first year and disregard income and expenses.

INTEREST

Interest can increase or decrease with an adjustable rate mortgage. If interest rates are steadily increasing or decreasing, that can be taken into account. But predicting interest rates is more difficult than predicting inflation. So use your best judgment. Participation loans provide the lender with a share of either or both of the net operating income (NOI) and the sales proceeds. Calculating future participation payments requires you to project future NOI and sale proceeds first.

Keep in mind that the amount of interest paid each year may change, depending on the terms of the loan. For a loan with amortization payments of principal and interest, the ratio of interest paid to principal paid changes with each payment. With each payment, a little less interest and a little more principal is paid. Annual interest will decrease each year of the projection. To determine how much interest will be paid each year on a loan, refer to the loan documents and make the appropriate calculations (see Chapter 8). It is only with adjustable rate mortgages and participation loans that considerations for inflation are necessary.

COST RECOVERY

The amount of cost recovery (depreciation) results from the specific calculations you do to determine the annual depreciation and requires no inflation (see Chapter 9). In fact, with accelerated cost recovery, the amount of depreciation will decline each year. With straight line, it will be the same. And with each capital addition, the annual cost recovery amount will increase.

NONOPERATING EXPENSES

This is a catchall category for nonobjective expenses. You must analyze each expense to determine how to inflate or decrease it. Often these expenses occur only in one year, so an inflation factor is not necessary.

TAXABLE INCOME

This is a number resulting from the input of other data and does not need to be specifically inflated or deflated. The input data is usually complex enough that it is not possible to use an inflation rate on taxable income by itself.

ANNUAL DEBT SERVICE

For amortized loans and "interest-only" loans, this is a constant amount. For principal payment loans, the debt service will change yearly. Look at the provisions of the loan (see Chapters 8 and 13). For adjustable rate mortgages and participation loans, calculate the debt service based on the same data you use for calculating interest.

NONOPERATING OUTLAYS

This is another catchall category similar but not necessarily identical to nonoperating expenses. Treat it similarly.

CAPITAL ADDITIONS

Capital additions are scheduled for the years in the future when they will be needed. For instance, if a roof costing $225,000 is needed in three years, it is scheduled for the third year. Between now and then, however, the cost of the roof is likely to increase with inflation. The cost should be inflated at the same rate as other expenditures. Annual capital replacements also should be inflated at the inflation rate for other expenses (i.e., the cost of capital replacements will increase each year).

RESERVES

When a reserve fund is used, it will be deposited in a bank to earn interest. However, not every owner uses a reserve fund to cover future capital additions. A reserve fund is elective and therefore subjective. The interest earned does not belong in the income & expense statement because it is subjective and is not attributable to the real estate. Additionally, there is no category for nonoperating income. Therefore, there is no place in the forecast to put the interest earned on the reserve account. Essentially, a reserve account is just a convenience for the owner like any savings account.

You can simply inflate the reserve fund at the interest rate earned on the reserve fund bank account. That will accurately show what really happens with the sinking fund. But, if you do, the interest earned will not be included in the income tax analysis. As a result, you will have the benefit of interest income included in your analysis without any corresponding tax liability.

For these reasons, the interest income for the reserve account is not included in an after-tax analysis. Perhaps the best way to account for the missing interest is simply not to inflate the cost of the capital additions. These two calculations are not likely to cancel each other exactly, but in cases in which they will be close to canceling each other, ignoring both interest and inflation may be the easiest solution. In other cases, decreasing the inflation rate for the capital additions (to offset the interest earned but not included in the analysis) may be the best adjustment.

If the analysis is before tax, interest may be calculated for the reserve account, and the reserve fund may be treated as a sinking fund.

When a reserve fund is set up only for routine capital replacements, the annual amount put into it can be converted to a percentage of rental income (potential rental income, effective rental income, or gross operating income). If rents increase with inflation, the reserves also increase. If rents are not anticipated to increase with inflation, reserves should not be calculated as a percentage of rental income.

A reserve fund set up to cover a specific anticipated capital addition can be set up to be a percentage of rental income much the same way it is done for capital replacements. The only difference is that you may want to discontinue it in the years after the capital addition is made.

RESERVES TO ADDITIONS

This is the amount of money from the reserve account applied to capital additions. It is paid only when capital expenditures are made, and it does not require inflation. There is an assumption that capital additions are completely paid out of the reserve fund. If the cost of the capital additions is an amount higher than the reserves, the balance in the reserve account is reduced to zero.

CASH FLOWS AND TAX LIABILITY

The cash flows before tax and after tax and the tax liability are numbers resulting from the input of other data. It is not necessary to inflate these categories.

SALE PRICE

When the sale price is determined by a capitalization rate (cap rate), there is no need for inflation. Inflation is built into the NOI, which is used with the cap rate to calculate value. Usually, the same cap rate used for the purchase price is used to determine the sale price. Yet if there is a upward or downward trend in cap rates, it may be reasonable to increase or decrease the cap rate over the years of the projection.

If a sale price is specified without using a cap rate to calculate it, the purchase price (market value) can be inflated each year of the projection with the same inflation rate used for income. But if expenses are inflating faster than income, a downward adjustment in the inflation rate for the sale price is warranted.

There may be instances in which the property is to be sold after a certain period for a price determined in a contract (e.g., lease-option). In such cases, read the contract to determine the anticipated sale price. If the contractual buyer has an election but no legal obligation to purchase, and a sale price lower than the one set in the contract is expected, then you should inflate or decrease the sale price based on market data.

RESERVE FUND

The reserve fund will grow each year as deposits are made into it. As the money is used to fund capital improvements, the balance will drop or perhaps go to zero. The reserve fund amount is a resultant number that does not require inflation.

LOAN BALANCES

The loan balances stay the same for "interest-only" loans. They decrease for most other types of loans as the loans are repaid. For negative amortization loans, the balances can increase. The loan balances are a result of financial calculations based on the provisions of the loans (see Chapter 23). They do not require inflation.

COST OF SALE

The cost of sale is usually expressed as a percentage of the sale price. Thus, it needs no inflation. If it is expressed as a specific amount, that amount should be inflated at the same rate as other expenses.

SALE PROCEEDS AND TAX LIABILITY ON SALE

The sale proceeds before tax, the sale proceeds after tax, and the tax liability on sale are numbers resulting from the input of other data. It is not necessary to inflate these categories.

SUMMARY

The failure to make predictions regarding the trends of income and expenses does not make the projections "conservative" ones. To the contrary, such methodology may generate erroneous financial information that otherwise would have been more accurate. Inflation factors determined by market data are not necessarily correct, but they are more likely to be more accurate than inflation factors determined without market research. And they are likely to be more accurate than using no inflation factors at all.

Always keep in mind that "inflation factor" as it is used in this chapter can also mean "decline factor" in a declining real estate market. Do your market research.

CHAPTER 37

INITIAL INVESTMENT

EQUITY

To acquire property, you must usually pay something. Assuming that you obtain a mortgage to finance your purchase, you pay a down payment. The down payment becomes your equity in the property: the difference between the purchase price and the amount of the mortgage. Your down payment is your investment in the property.

Because cash flow in the first year and the years after are compared, in effect, to this initial investment, the initial investment takes an added significance. So it is important to refine it for greater accuracy. Seldom is the down payment the total initial investment in a property. The costs of acquisition add to the initial investment.

INITIAL INVESTMENT FOR A PROPERTY PURCHASED

One of the additional costs of acquisition is the cost of obtaining financing: loan fees. Commonly, loan fees are 1 to 3 percent of the loan amount, sometimes higher. They are normally calculated separately from other acquisition costs.

All other costs are generally grouped into the category of "acquisition costs." One cost is for due diligence. Fees for attorneys, appraisers, real estate consultants, engineers, surveyors, accountants, employees, travel, and so on must be paid to adequately investigate the property. Closing costs can sometimes be a significant additional cost too.

If deferred maintenance on the property is left uncured by the seller as part of the purchase agreement, the cost of curing can increase the initial investment of the buyer if the curing is done before or soon after the purchase is closed. Likewise, capital additions made immediately or soon after the closing increase the initial investment. Any cost paid initially will add to the initial investment. All of these costs taken together with the down payment compose the initial investment also known as the "investment base."

It is convenient to make a rough estimate of the normal costs of acquisition by using a percentage of the sale price. Each investor has an investment style that is reflected in the acquisition costs. For instance, an institutional investor with very thorough and bureaucratic acquisition procedures will be likely to have higher acquisition costs than a small investor with streamlined acquisition procedures. The percentage used to estimate acquisition costs should reflect the investor's style.

For Maplewood Apartments (see Appendix I), 1 percent of the purchase price ($64,320) is used to estimate the acquisition costs in addition to loan fees. Loan fees are 1½ percent of the loan amount ($71,775), and the equity (down payment) is $1,647,000. The total initial investment is $1,783,095.

Purchase price	$ 6,432,000
−Mortgage balances	(4,785,000)
Equity	1,647,000
+Loan points	71,775
+Cost of acquisition	64,320
Initial investment (investment base)	1,783,095

Ultimately, a case can be made to attribute a portion of all general costs and business expenses including overhead to the initial investment as an acquisition cost. Whether you do this will depend on your role in the transaction, ownership, and asset management. Generally, only the direct costs incurred for the acquisition of the specific property are included.

Customarily, many of the rates of return and ratios are based on the investor's equity in the property (see Chapter 40). The equity is the difference between the purchase price and the mortgage balance. The equity, however, is not an accurate representation of the investor's investment in the property. It does not represent the entire initial investment. Greater accuracy in calculating rates of return requires a more accurately calculated initial investment.

BROKERAGE ARRANGEMENTS

Brokerage arrangements sometimes require close scrutiny. Brokers normally represent the seller. The "listing" broker signs a listing contract with the seller and has a legal duty to represent the seller. Usually a broker from a different brokerage firm works with the buyer. This broker is an agent of the listing broker and a subagent of the seller. Both brokers represent the seller. The seller pays the listing broker a commission that the listing broker splits with the other broker. This arrangement does not add to the acquisition costs of the buyer.

A less common arrangement is one in which the broker working with the buyer agrees to represent the buyer. Nonetheless, the buyer insists that this broker be paid by the seller. This arrangement does not add to the acquisition costs of the buyer either because the seller directly pays the broker working with the buyer.

Another less common arrangement is one in which the broker working with the buyer agrees to represent the buyer, and the buyer agrees to pay this broker. This broker becomes a "buyer's broker." Now, because the listing broker does not have to split the commission with anyone, the seller usually pays the listing broker only one-half of the commission. If the normal commission is 4 percent, theoretically the purchase price is 2 percent less with this arrangement and the down payment is reduced by that amount. But this arrangement increases the cost of acquisition for the buyer by 2 percent (assuming the buyer's broker agreement states a 2 percent commission) because the buyer must pay the buyer's broker. Nonetheless, the buyer's total initial investment does not change, in effect. Although the price of the property is 2 percent less and that amount also reduces the down payment, the buyer must pay the amount to the buyer's broker. With this arrangement, the loan amount may be slightly distorted because the purchase price is 2 percent less. Thus, the corresponding equity may be slightly different.

Another way to handle the buyer's broker situation is not to lower the purchase price. Instead, the seller gives the buyer a 2 percent discount off the purchase price and off the down payment because the buyer is paying the buyer's broker. (The seller would otherwise have to pay the buyer's broker as a subagent.) Because the purchase price stays the same, the buyer can obtain a loan based on the full purchase price instead of a loan based on a purchase price that's 2 percent less. Although this arrangement adds to the buyer's acquisition costs because the buyer must pay the buyer's broker, it does not add to the buyer's initial investment.

Regardless of how the brokerage arrangements work, the initial investment is essentially the same for the buyer in these examples. Yet you must be able to analyze the less common brokerage arrangements to avoid confusion when calculating the initial investment.

INITIAL INVESTMENT FOR AN OWNED PROPERTY

The initial investment also takes on a special importance for comparing a property already owned to a potential property to be acquired. This comparison arises any time you are tying to decide whether to continue to own the property you already have or to sell it and buy the other property. How do you calculate your theoretical initial investment—as of today—in the property you have already owned for a few years? The "investment base" concept taught by the Commercial Investment Real Estate Institute provides you with a rational way to do so.

To calculate a rate of return, you must know the investment amount. The investment base is the amount that must be given up after tax to get the investment. Today your investment base in the property you already own is what you are giving up after tax to continue to own the property. Were you to sell the property today, the total of what you will get for the property (after tax) is the sale proceeds after tax. Therefore, the anticipated sale proceeds after tax is your *current* investment base in the property you own. Once you have calculated an investment base for your property today, you can project the future cash flows for your property and make a net present value (NPV) or an internal rate of return (IRR) analysis. Then you can compare the continued investment in the property you own to the other investment opportunity.

A good example is to take Maplewood Apartments (see Appendix I) at the end of Year 3. The after-tax sale proceeds are $1,964,036. If you wanted to do a five-year projection of Maplewood Apartments at that time to compare with another investment opportunity, you would forecast Years 4 through 8. You would use $1,964,036 as your initial investment (investment base) for the NPV and IRR calculations.

EXCHANGES

The investment base concept as applied to a property already owned can be used to evaluate a real estate exchange opportunity. Your investment base in your current property is the anticipated sale proceeds after tax. Your investment base in the new property (the property for which you are exchanging) is your investment base for your current property plus any cash added or minus any cash received. Once you have determined the investment base for the new property, you can project the future cash flows and calculate a NPV or IRR.

BASIS

Do not confuse the concept of investment base (used for calculating investing returns) with the income taxation concept of *basis*. They are not the same. *Basis* is an essential concept in tax analysis and is an important consideration in tax-deferred exchanges. Tax-deferred exchanging is beyond the scope of this book.

SUMMARY

An accurate analysis requires a more finely tuned method of calculating the initial investment than just computing the equity. By including all the direct acquisition costs as part of the initial investment, you will calculate more realistic rates of return.

CHAPTER 38

PROJECTIONS

Once you make assumptions, decide on inflation factors, and calculate your initial investment, you are ready to make a future projection of your pro forma analysis beyond the first year. The first thing to keep in mind is that you are predicting the future. That can never be done with precision, even for the first year. The longer your projection, the more likely it is to be inaccurate.

The character of the tenancy it likely to dictate the length and accuracy of the projection. A 20-year projection, on a sale and leaseback, with a credit tenant, on a fixed rent, with the tenant paying all the expenses, for a 20-year lease term is going to be reasonably accurate, except for the sale proceeds. On the other hand, a five-year projection on an office building filled with tenants on three-year leases in an unstable market is going to be inaccurate.

The length of the projection is also determined by the anticipated holding period. The anticipated holding period is influenced by the tax laws and other factors. If you anticipate holding the property for five years, a five-year projection is useful. And if you plan to own for 20 years a building that has short-term leases in an unstable market, it may not make any sense to extend your projection more than five years. But long holding periods usually mandate long projections. High inflation tends to create shorter lease terms, shorter holding periods, and shorter projections for many types of properties.

Capital expenditures may require a longer projection than you had anticipated making. For instance, suppose you normally do 5-year projections but usually hold for 10 years. In the seventh year, a major capital improvement is planned (e.g., complete exterior and roof rehabilitation). You may want to extend your projection to seven years or more to see the effect of the rehab on the performance of the property.

Another reason to do a longer projection is to determine an advantageous selling point (i.e., the year the IRR is the highest). The ultimate use of projections is to compare one property to another. To make the comparison accurate, it is best to use the same length projection for each property. You should consider all of these factors in choosing a projection length. Once the length is set—and it may be difficult for different types of properties—it should be used consistently for all similar properties considered unless there is a compelling reason to do otherwise.

WHAT TO INCLUDE

You will notice that the "forecast" projection format places together the income & expense statement and the income tax analysis even though they are separate analyses. You will also notice that the four analyses (income & tax expense statement, income tax analysis, cash flow analysis, and sale proceeds analysis) can be easily arranged to provide a five-year projection on one page in normal-size type (see Appendices I–IV). Smaller type or condensed typefaces allow additional years on one page. Some line entries are backed up by schedules. In some cases, you may want to expand the analysis format to include such schedules or summaries of such schedules. For instance, for Crossroads Plaza Shopping Center (see Appendix III), you can show the schedule for other income rather than the line entry for other income:

Potential rental income
−Vacancy & credit loss
Effective rental income
+Reimbursements:
    CAM
    Real estate taxes
    Insurance
Gross operating income
−Operating expenses
    Net operating income

Were you to have a participating first loan and a second loan, you might want to include a schedule for interest:

Net operating Income
−Interest
    Loan 1 interest
    Participation payments
    Loan 2 interest
−Cost recovery
−Non-operating expenses
    Taxable income

The corresponding schedule for debt service is

Net operating income
−Debt service
    Loan 1 debt service
    Participation payments
    Loan 2 debt service
−Nonoperating outlays
−Capital additions
−Reserves
+Reserves to additions
    Cash flow before tax

Such schedules can be included when space permits and when they clarify how the numbers are calculated. Such schedules can always be printed on a separate page as back-up information.

To show multiple IRRs assuming the property will be sold each year of the holding period, you must create a series of projections with the first being one year, the second being two years, the third being three years, and so on. These can be arranged together in a format that shows this complex analysis as being just one projection in which there is a sale assumed at the end of each year. That is how the projections for Maplewood Apartments, Ridgeline Office Tower, Crossroads Plaza, and Four-Plex have been done in Appendices I, II, III, and IV.

The goal is to include as much on one page as possible. Those who review projections like to make comparisons. The more information on one page, the easier it is to compare to other information on the page or to other pro formas. The forecast is the primary summary of all the calculations. It should include as much information as possible. All other pages are back-up data for the forecast.

WHAT NOT TO INCLUDE

You can conveniently delete all tax considerations on the pro forma forecast by deleting the following line entries:

1. All line entries after net operating income in the top section of the forecast.
2. All line entries after cash flow before tax in the middle section of the forecast.
3. All line entries after sale proceeds before tax in the lower section of the forecast.

In fact, your spreadsheet program can make all the tax calculations, and such calculations will not affect the before-tax calculations. That allows you to use the same spreadsheet program for both before-tax and after-tax calculations. For a before-tax analysis, you print the forecast *less* the line entries indicated above. In other words, you simply make a format change when you print the forecast. The forecast for Crossroads Plaza in Appendix III is a before-tax forecast.

Other lines entries must be deleted with caution. For instance, you can delete the line entry for debt service for a property purchased for cash. There is no loan. This might not be a good idea, however, because most properties are purchased with financing. It is perhaps a better practice to include the debt service line entry with a zero. It will help remind reviewers of the forecast that the property has no financing. On the other hand, if no reserves are to be made during the operation of the property, the following line entries can be left out of the forecast: reserves, reserves to additions, and reserve fund. No one will miss them unless they need to be reminded that no reserves will be made.

NET PRESENT VALUE AND INTERNAL RATE OF RETURN

What is the objective of a projection? It is to provide an annual "bottom line" figure. The bottom line figures that are useful for the most sophisticated investment analysis are the cash flow before tax (CFBT), the cash flow after tax (CFAT), the sale proceeds before tax (SPBT), and the sale proceeds after tax (SPAT). These are the numbers you use to calculate a net present value (NPV) and an internal rate of return (IRR). See Chapter 42. The NPV and IRR analyses include the following for a five-year projection:

Year	Before Tax	Year	After Tax
0	Initial Investment	0	Initial Investment
1	CFBT	1	CFAT
2	CFBT	2	CFAT
3	CFBT	3	CFAT
4	CFBT	4	CFAT
5	CFBT + SPBT	5	CFAT + SPAT

The bottom line requirements of the analysis determine the format of the projections. For instance, if you are doing a before-tax analysis, you will not include those line entries that result from tax calculations.

The forecast examples in Appendices I, II, and III include only an IRR analysis. You can include an NPV analysis or any other indicator that you find useful (see Chapter 40). Most indicators, however, are based on only the first year of ownership. It might be more appropriate to include them on another page.

FORMAT

Do not make any additions or omissions that alter the integrity or readability of the format. A knowledgeable real estate professional can read a forecast in the standard format and understand in a matter of seconds how the property will perform. If you change the format, same person may take hours to reach the same understanding.

SUMMARY

The forecast is the summary of all the data and calculations made in the investment analysis. Although the tax analysis can be conveniently deleted without affecting the before-tax calculations, other deletions or additions should be made with caution. No change that fundamentally alters the format should be made. Schedules should be provided on separate pages when appropriate to back up the information included in the forecast.

Although most real estate professionals use the terms *forecast* and *projections* interchangably as they are used in this book, sometimes it is appropriate to differenciate between them. When real estate investment analysis is part of a securities offering, you must use these terms carefully and correctly to comply with securities statutes, rules, regulations, and customs.

PART 7

MEASUREMENTS

With the operation of the property projected over an anticipated holding period, you have the numbers to measure investment performance in a sophisticated way. This part of the book starts with some simple calculations that provide a rate of return or some other useful indicator of performance. Then the fundamentals of discounted cash flow analysis are thoroughly covered. Finally, the more complex measurements of net present value and internal rate of return are applied.

Chapters

39. Capitalization Rate
40. Indicators
41. Discounted Cash Flow Analysis
42. Net Present Value, and Internal Rate of Return.

CHAPTER 39

CAPITALIZATION RATE

Need an appraisal? Need a simple rate of return? Need an easy way to determine income? The capitalization rate (cap rate) provides these for you. The ratio of the net operating income (NOI) to the value, or sale price, of a property is the cap rate. It is expressed as follows:

$$R = I \div V$$

R = Rate of return (cap rate)

I = Income (NOI)

V = Value (sale price)

By the miracle of algebra, if you rearrange the original equation, you get two additional equations:

$$I = R \times V$$
$$V = I \div R$$

Each of these equations provides you with a useful tool for analyzing investment real estate. For instance, suppose you know of a small office building that recently sold for $1,700,000. You also know from surveying the market that the cap rate for that type of building is 8.9 percent. With that information, you can estimate the NOI:

$$0.089 \times \$1,700,000 = \$151,300$$

Thus, it's likely that the NOI of the office building is about $151,300.

In another case, suppose you know of a shopping mall that was purchased recently for $45,500,000 and that its NOI is $3,503,500. You can calculate the cap rate for the transaction:

$$\$3,503,500 \div 45,500,000 = 0.077$$

Thus, the cap rate for the transaction is 7.7 percent.

Finally, suppose you know that the NOI on an apartment project is $620,500. After surveying the market, you determine that the cap rate for that type of apartment project is 8.1 percent. You can make a calculation that estimates the value of the apartment project:

$$\$620,500 \div 0.081 = \$7,660,500$$

Thus, the value of the apartment project is $7,660,500.

Keep in mind that the cap rate is inversely related to the sale price: as the cap rate goes up, the sale price goes down. And a lower cap rate means a higher price. You can see that the math side of this cap rate business is simple. But there is more to know. These are the first questions you must ask: What NOI? What cap rate? What value?

NET OPERATING INCOME (NOI)

Buyers look to the future when buying property. What the buyer believes about the future is what motivates him or her to invest in the property. In many cases the buyer looks to the past for information to predict the future. Last year's income and expense statement is often the starting point for estimating what the income and expenses will be in the next year. But seldom does anyone believe that the income and expenses in the next year will be identical to those for the last year.

Sellers also look to the future when selling property. With inflation, rents are likely to be higher each year, and higher income may mean a higher sale price.

A year is a good period to use when considering income and expenses. In a year, a property will go through its complete cycle of expenses including one-time annual expenses such as insurance premiums and property taxes. Indeed, a year is commonly accepted as the most reasonable unit of time on which to base useful calculations. Therefore, the income and expenses estimated for the next year are considered by both the buyer and the seller to be a determinant of the sale price.

Naturally, the buyer and seller perceive the future differently. The buyer claims that expenses are likely to grow while income will stagnate. The seller claims that expenses will be about the same, but rents will go up substantially. These claims provide the ingredients for much negotiation. But the parties understand that everyone's attention is focused on the next year of operation.

Consequently, the next year's pro forma income and expense statement generates the NOI to be used for the cap rate calculation.

MARKET CAPITALIZATION RATE (CAP RATE)

The transactions in the real estate market generate cap rates. If you can obtain the sale price and the pro forma income and expense statement for each transaction, you can calculate the cap rates. This is what appraisers try to do.

An alternative method is to talk with commercial investment brokers and other real estate professionals who are continually playing a part in negotiations and transactions. They usually have an opinion, often accurate, regarding what current cap rates are. A real estate professional who specializes in shopping centers is apt to have a more accurate opinion of cap rates regarding shopping centers than a professional who doesn't specialize. A survey of such professionals may yield an accurate notion of the appropriate cap rate to use in your calculations.

VALUE (SALE PRICE)

The sale price ultimately determines the value of a property. Your review of the public records at the county recorder's office will yield information on sale prices. Contacting the buyers, sellers, brokers, accountants, attorneys, and so forth involved in the transactions may provide you with more detailed information and enable you to extract cap rates.

Estimating value is necessary for a multitude of analyses. Not only appraisers need to make this type of estimate. It is handy to be able to make such an estimate based on the NOI and a cap rate.

OBJECTIVITY

The pro forma income and expense statement used to calculate the NOI and the cap rate must be estimated objectively. Nonoperating expenses and capital improvements must be deleted from the expenses prior to the calculations. Likewise, management-intensive nonrental income must be deleted. And pro formas that reflect an advocacy point of view (the prospective of either the seller or buyer) may distort calculations.

Unfortunately, even sophisticated real estate professionals sometime use unobjective pro formas. There is also room for reasonable disagreement. Thus, the seller may sell the property at a different cap rate than the cap rate on which the buyer buys the property. Suppose an apartment building sells for $4,700,000 after a long and labored negotiation. The seller had forecast the NOI to be $399,500. The buyer had forecast the NOI to be $385,400. What is the market cap rate? The seller thought it was 8.5 percent, and the buyer thought it was 8.2 percent.

This example shows that the cap rate cannot be completely accurate. Perhaps the seller made a mistake, or perhaps the buyer made a mistake. Perhaps there was just reasonable disagreement concerning income and expenses. In any event, there was not a meeting of the minds regarding the appropriate cap rate, and certainly each party considered market cap rates while negotiating.

The only way to ensure uniformity in the calculation of cap rates when doing market research is to reconstruct the pro forma according to objective standards. A market survey can effectively estimate income. The prior year's expenses (obtained from sellers or buyers) provide a good start on estimating expenses. Such expenses have to be adjusted for the future, the next year, in an objective manner. Once income and expenses are estimated, management-intensive nonrental income items are removed, and nonoperating expenses and capital improvements are deleted, an objective NOI can be determined.

RESERVES

When researching cap rates and adjusting pro formas, do you use reserves as an expense? This is a question with different correct answers. Brokers, buyers, and sellers generally don't. Appraisers and financial institutions usually do. Perhaps the most important consideration for you is to be consistent in what you do.

If reserves are to be a part of the NOI calculation, they are usually replacement reserves for the annual capital replacements. For example, an apartment complex replaces small numbers of appliances and carpets each year. One usually estimates a reserve for these replacements using a nominal percentage.

Replacement reserves do not cover large, one-time capital improvements such as replacing roofs. If roofs need to be replaced soon, the cost is likely to be subtracted from the value of the property before the buyer makes an offer. If the roofs are anticipated to need replacement in about 10 years, the cost is likely to be ignored by the buyer in preparing a pro forma for valuation purposes.

Deferred maintenance can be considered as a large capital item. The buyer normally demands that the deferred maintenance be cured before closing by the seller or that a downward adjustment in the sale price be made.

STATISTICS

One way to check on the accuracy of your NOI calculation is to compare it to statistics. Various organizations publish operating statistics for different types of properties.

Shopping centers: Urban Land Institute (ULI) and International Council of Shopping Centers (ICSC)

Office buildings: Building Owners and Managers Association (BOMA) and Institute of Real Estate Management (IREM)

Apartments: Institute of Real Estate Management (IREM)

If your calculations are not within a reasonable range suggested by the statistics, it could mean a problem with the property or with your research.

RISK

The cap rate is an investment rate of return much like an interest rate earned on a savings account. Like any rate of return, it goes up and down with perceived risk.

For instance, two office buildings of identical construction quality and appeal may have different cap rates due to different locations. The one with the better location may have a lower cap rate because it is perceived as being less risky. The one with the obscure location may have a higher cap rate because it is perceived as being riskier. In this case, investors perceive that a better location provides more assurance that the property will be reliable in producing the projected income.

The potential for inflated expenses is also a consideration. Individually metered units (e.g., electricity and heat) are less risky than a central system supplied by the landlord. Charging common area maintenance (CAM) expenses directly to tenants, or passing on most expenses (net lease) directly to tenants, is safer than paying them out of the rent. In these cases, investors perceive that the pass-through expenses provide assurance that the property will be more reliable in generating income because a portion of the expenses is paid by tenants.

RISK EXAMPLE

Take two apartment properties, a 100-unit project (95,500 square feet) with an NOI of $410,000 and a 175-unit project (142,200 square feet) with an NOI of $410,000. The first is a prime property in a good neighborhood. The second is an old property in a declining neighborhood. They both have the same NOI. Are they worth the same to you? You are likely to be willing to pay more for the prime property. As a result, the prime property has a lower cap rate.

Assume that the market cap rate for prime apartments is 8.0 percent and the market cap rate for old apartments is 9.5 percent. That sets the value of the 100-unit apartment project at $5,125,000 ($54 per SF and $51,250 per unit). The value of the old 175-unit apartment project is $4,315,800 ($30 per SF and $24,660 per unit). This is quite a difference for two properties with the same NOI, but that's not unusual.

Investors perceive a risk that the old property will decline further. Who knows what problems the old property will experience with excess maintenance, unexpected capital improvements, difficult tenants, and the like? It's just safer to buy the prime property.

GEOGRAPHY

Cap rates differ between geographical locations. For instance, the cap rate for a prime 400-unit apartment building might be 8.6 percent in Atlanta and 7.9 percent in Los Angeles. In this case, national investors perceive the chances of the property generating the projected income will be better in Los Angeles.

VACANCY

When the vacancy rate rises for a type of property, investors perceive that type of property as having more risk, and cap rates go up accordingly. For example, when office buildings are in excess supply, a high vacancy rate will exist in the local market. That tends to raise the local cap rate for office buildings. Even an office building that is completely leased is likely to be affected because one wonders how long high occupancy can be maintained in a market with low occupancy.

DESIGN QUALITIES

Investors perceive that a property with high-quality construction will require less maintenance. Granite endures better than Masonite. Less maintenance means higher income. So the cap rate is lower. A superior design and other desirable features encourage reliable income because the building attracts better tenants. Such a building has a lower cap rate. Properties lacking these desirable qualities realize a higher cap rate.

TERMS

Different transactions terms result in different cap rates. An all-cash purchase brings a high cap rate because the purchaser takes all the risk of owning the property. Seller-provided financing brings a lower cap rate for the transaction because the seller retains an interest (mortgage) in the property, leaving the purchaser with less risk. This is just a different way of saying that an all-cash purchase brings a lower price; if you want seller financing, you usually pay a higher price.

SUPPLY AND DEMAND

There are always niches where supply and demand are out of equilibrium. High demand and low supply act to depress cap rates. For instance, there are usually fewer regional malls for sale than the many institutional purchasers waiting to buy them. Thus, such properties have lower cap rates than the more numerous, smaller shopping centers.

In contrast, in many places small residential properties (e.g., four-plexes) experience great demand and have lower cap rates than larger apartment projects. Almost everyone with savings to invest can afford a small residential property.

Popularity has much to do with supply and demand. One year Minneapolis and Memphis might be hot cities for real estate, and the national popularity depresses the local cap rates. Every national investor wants to get in on the action. Then these cities fall out of favor, for economic reasons or whatever, and local cap rates start to rise. Other cities become the popular hot spots. Sometimes it is difficult to determine the rationale for what's hot and what's not.

Popularity affects property types too. Shopping centers, office buildings, apartment buildings, and other income properties have different cap rates. Usually properties with long-term leases have lower cap rates because the future NOI seems more secure. When there is an oversupply of one type of property, however, cap rates for that type of property may be unusually high regardless of long-term leases.

OTHER FACTORS

Any characteristic of the property or its environment that adversely affects the reliability of the NOI will tend to raise the cap rate.

A MULTITUDE OF CAP RATES

Multiple cap rates exist for every type of property. For instance, for an office building there may be several cap rates, one for primary property, another for average property. One for Cleveland, another for Orlando. One for a large project, and another for a small one. You have to fit the cap rate to the property to ensure accuracy.

CAP RATE SURVEYS

Many organizations sponsor and publish cap rate surveys. Because most do the surveys poorly without proper controls to ensure accuracy, they are not accurate. If you rely on a survey to get cap rate information, make sure you evaluate the methodology used to acquire the cap rate data.

One reliable national survey is the *National Real Estate Index* published by the Liquidity Fund in Emeryville, California. It offers cap rates quarterly for institutional properties in more than 30 major cities.

Although cap rates change slowly in normal circumstances, they can change quickly during times of economic trauma. A publisher compiling statistics for a quarterly cap rate survey distributes such statistics long after the end of the quarter. Some of those statistics come from the beginning of the quarter being reported. You may have to use those statistics two months after they have been published. Accordingly, the cap rate information you are using from a quarterly survey might be as much as seven months old. In times of rapid change, such a survey may provide you with stale information.

PERPETUITY

Although the cap rate is calculated based on the next year of operation, investors assume the property will continue to yield the same annual return *forever.* Thus, in theory, the cap rate exhibits a long-term characteristic.

HISTORY

Generally, real estate cap rates move in synchronization with long-term rates of return, such as those offered by corporate bonds. Many institutional investors see prime real estate as an alternative investment to corporate bonds. Nonetheless, be aware that real estate cap rates occasionally move out of synchronization with such long-term rates of return.

CHAPTER 40

INDICATORS

Real estate professionals routinely use a number of rates of return and ratios. This chapter defines each with both its dividend and divisor and then applies it using the Maplewood Apartments analysis from Appendix I. Most of these indicators are not accurate measures of how a property will perform financially. Nevertheless, you can use some of them to screen properties with good investment potential from properties with no potential.

CAPITALIZATION RATE

Chapter 39 considers in detail the capitalization rate (cap rate). Appraisers customarily use this rate of return for appraising income property. It's the ratio between the net operating income (NOI) and the value and is also known as the "overall rate" or the "free-and-clear rate."

NOI ÷ Value

Maplewood Apartments: $566,041 ÷ $6,432,000 = 8.8%

The cap rate is the rate of return on the property for the first year, assuming the property is purchased for cash. Like all rates of return based on only the first year of ownership, the cap rate is assumed to be perpetual. That is, the net operating income (NOI) shall continue unchanged forever. Or, if the NOI does not continue forever, the purchase price (value)—no more, no less—shall be returned in a lump sum as soon as the yearly cash flows cease (i.e., on sale). Since the cap rate doesn't take into account any of the details of ownership, it cannot be considered a revealing rate of return except in its customary use for valuation. For instance, if a loan exists, it does not take into account the effect of debt service on the performance of the property.

EQUITY DIVIDEND RATE

This rate of return attempts to be more accurate than the cap rate for properties with loans. It is the cash flow before tax (CFBT) for the first year divided by the equity. It is also known as the "cash throw-off rate." Investors use it because it provides a yield that takes into account how much cash remains after the debt service is paid.

CFBT ÷ Equity

Maplewood Apartments: $26,153 ÷ $1,647,000 = 1.58%

If the CFBT is defined simply as the NOI less the debt service, then the ratio may be different:

Maplewood Apartments: $51,505 ÷ $1,647,000 = 3.12%

Moreover, if you define equity as the initial investment, then the ratio may be different:

Maplewood Apartments: $26,153 ÷ $1,783,095 = 1.46%

Essentially, the equity dividend rate includes the effect of the debt service on the investment. But it does not include the effect of annual income taxation on the performance of the property, nor does it consider equity buildup. The equity dividend rate of return provides a more subjective analysis than the cap rate but has most of the same limitations.

CASH ON CASH

Many investors use the cash on cash rate of return. It takes the cash invested in the property and compares it with the cash flow after tax (CFAT) for the first year. This is simply an after-tax version of the equity dividend rate.

CFAT ÷ Equity

Maplewood Apartments: $26,153 ÷ $1,647,000 = 1.58%

In the case of Maplewood Apartments, the cash on cash is the same as the equity dividend rate because there is no tax liability. While someone desiring to receive regular cash flow from a property might use this indicator routinely, this rate of return does not take into account equity buildup.

Many use cash on cash as a before-tax rate of return. When used that way, it is identical to the equity dividend rate above.

EQUITY RETURN RATE

When you add the equity buildup to the after-tax cash flow, it makes this rate of return potentially the highest (particularly in times of real estate appreciation). Those who desire to show a large yield use this rate of return.

Loan amount	$4,785,000
−Loan balance end of Year 1	(4,759,763)
Principal paydown	25,237
Value end of Year 1	6,689,578
−Purchase price	(6,432,000)
Equity increase	257,578
Equity buildup	$25,237 + $257,578 = $282,815
(CFAT + Equity buildup) ÷ Equity	
Maplewood Apartments:	($26,153 + $282,815) ÷ $1,647,000 =18.7%

Equity buildup can include both the increase in equity due to the reduction of principal as the loan is paid and the increase due to the appreciated value of the property. It is calculated above with both. Although this rate of return takes into account additional data, it is calculated only for the first year and is only a partial picture of the investment performance. It does not consider the effect of income taxation (on sale) on equity buildup, and the cost of sale is also ignored.

NET PRESENT VALUE AND INTERNAL RATE OF RETURN

Net present value (NPV) and internal rate of return (IRR) are valuable analytic devices that are covered in detail in Chapter 42. They are an application of discounted cash flow analysis. They have the advantage of being based on the projected future multiyear operating performance of the property and on an anticipated sale in the future. By including either

CFBT or the CBAT for every year of the holding period, more than just the first year of operation can be covered. The IRR is also known as the "equity yield rate."

Maplewood Apartments: NPV = $63,396

IRR = 12.8%

The NPV and IRR above analyze a five-year holding period based on the CFBT. Unlike the other rates of return above, the NPV and the IRR include a return "on and a return of" the investment amount. Virtually every financial institution and sophisticated investor uses NPV and IRR to evaluate property.

PROFITABILITY INDEX

The total present value of the before-tax cash flows for the holding period divided by the equity investment calculate this ratio. It makes NPV analysis more useful and is used by sophisticated analysts who find NPV analysis more useful than IRR analysis.

Total present value ÷ Equity

Maplewood Apartments:

$1,846,491 ÷ $1,783,095 = 1.035%

The discount rate used for this total PV calculation was 12%. (Chapter 42 covers NPV analysis.)

PAYBACK PERIOD

The indicator shows how quickly an initial investment in a property will be paid back (before-tax analysis).

Investment base ÷ Cash flows

Maplewood Apartments: $1,783,095 ÷ $26,153

+ 47,780

+ 54,373

+ 93,665

+ 117,993

+ 2,854,766

= 5 years

Because the analysis stops at the end of the payback period and does not take into consideration anything beyond the end of the payback period, few find it useful. In the case of Maplewood Apartments, this is not a factor because the property does not repay the initial investment until the sale at the end of the holding period.

BREAK-EVEN ANALYSIS

The break-even analysis, sometimes used by lenders, shows how susceptible the property is to a decline in rental income. The higher the ratio, the more susceptible the property is to adverse fluctuations.

(Operating expenses + Debt service) ÷ Gross operating income
Maplewood Apartments:
($398,712 + $514,041) ÷ $964,753 = 94.6%

This ratio is also known as the "default ratio" because it shows how close the debt service is to the property's ability to pay it.

UNDERWRITING ANALYSIS

This is a more sophisticated version of the break-even analysis:

((Gross operating income × 82%) − Operating expenses)
    ÷ Annual loan constant
Maplewood Apartments:
$964,753 × 0.82 = $791,097 − $398,712 = 392,385
$392,385 ÷ 0.107532 = $3,649,006

As is indicated, this conservative analysis shows you that the maximum loan allowable for a 30-year loan at 10¼ percent on Maplewood Apartments is $3,649,006. The information to determine the loan constant was taken from the Maplewood Apartments forecast in Appendix I. (See Chapter 41 for a method of calculating the loan constant.) In actual practice, however, to determine what loan constant to use, you take 75 percent of the remaining economic life of the property to set the term. Then take 125 percent of the interest rate offered by comparable length Treasury bonds to set the interest rate. For underwriting purposes, a lender will most likely subtract operating expenses that include a reserve for replacements. The 82 percent of the gross operating income, the 75 percent of the remaining economic life, and the 125 percent of the Treasury bond rate may be subject to small variations. The operating expenses for different types of properties vary greatly. This formula will work for a broad range of properties with little alteration. To make this analysis work effectively, however, the economic life must be estimated accurately.

GROSS RENT MULTIPLIER

Unsophisticated investors like this ratio because it's easy to calculate. It is the purchase price divided by the potential rental income for the first year.

Purchase price ÷ Potential rental income

Maplewood Apartments: $6,432,000 ÷ $1,014,096 = 6.3%

This indicator does not take into account operating expense ratios, which often fluctuate, and it is based only on the first year of operation.

GROSS (NET) INCOME MULTIPLIER

Similar to the gross rent multiplier, you can calculate this ratio four different ways:

1. Purchase price ÷ Potential rental income (same as gross rent multiplier)
2. Purchase price ÷ Effective rental income
3. Purchase price ÷ Gross operating income
4. Purchase price ÷ Net operating income

If you use this multiplier, you will have to define it or name it more specifically (e.g., effective rental income multiplier).

VACANCY RATE

You use this rate for calculating the vacancy & credit loss. A vacancy rate obtained from market research gives you a rate you can use in a forecast.

Vacancy & credit loss ÷ Potential rental income

Maplewood Apartments: $60,846 ÷ $1,014,093 = 6%

The Institute of Real Estate Management (IREM) makes the divisor gross possible income (Potential rental income + Other income) rather than just potential rental income alone for its statistical publications.

OPERATING RATIO

You can use the operating ratio to consider how efficiently the property is performing. It is the ratio between the operating expenses and the gross operating income. Many investors use this ratio to identify properties that have high operating expenses.

Operating expenses ÷ Gross operating income

Maplewood Apartments: $398,712 ÷ $964,753 = 41.3%

Many find that this ratio is quite handy. Unfortunately, much confusion exists as to whether the divisor is potential rental income, effective rental income, or gross operating income. It should not be considered a substitute for more careful analysis.

LOAN TO VALUE RATIO

This is the ratio between the loan made on a property and the appraised value of the property. Lenders use this as part of their underwriting criteria. The loan to value ratio determines the upper limit on the amount that they will loan on the property (e.g., 75 percent).

Loan amount ÷ Property value

Maplewood Apartments: $4,785,000 ÷ $6,432,000 = 74.4%

Lenders use this ratio to attempt to make sure that if the market declines and they must foreclose on the property, the property will not be worth less than the balance due on the loan. Lenders apply another ratio, too: the debt coverage ratio.

DEBT COVERAGE RATIO

This is the ratio between the annual debt service and the net operating income (NOI). Lenders use this also as part of their underwriting criteria. The debt coverage ratio determines the upper limit on the amount that they will loan on the property.

NOI ÷ Annual debt service

Maplewood Apartments: $566,041 ÷ $514,536 = 1.1%

A lender worries that the property be able to pay the debt service. Theoretically, lenders don't make loans to people but to properties. They look to the property to pay back the loan. Otherwise, the loan would have to be considered a type of personal loan. So the first concern is that the property—the NOI—be able to cover the loan payments. But just covering the loan payments usually isn't quite enough. A lender likes to see a margin of safety; that is, a lender likes to see an NOI larger than the debt service. The question is, how much larger? The required debt coverage ratio shows you.

Take a property with an NOI of $227,010. The lender proposes to make a loan at 10 percent with monthly payments amortized over 25 years. The lender requires a debt coverage ratio of 1.15. That means that the NOI has to be 1.15 times the debt service, or 115 percent of the debt service. How do you figure the size of the loan available for this property? You must use a financial calculator. Here's the calculation using the minimodel (see Chapter 41):

$227,010 ÷ 1.15 = $197,400 ÷ 12 = $16,450
available for each monthly loan payment

FV =
PMT = (16450)
PV = ?   PV = 1810277
I   = 10 ÷ 12
N   = 25 × 12

It calculates that $16,450 at 10 percent interest over 25 years pays off a loan of $1,810,277.

Keep in mind that a loan must usually satisfy the underwriting requirements for *both* the loan to value ratio and the debt coverage ratio.

SUMMARY

There is a problem using these indicators. The only objective indicators are the capitalization rate (cap rate), the gross rent multiplier, the gross income multiplier, the vacancy rate, and the operating ratio. They are based on an objective analysis of how the property performs. They are the same for any investor, at least in theory. On the other hand, the other indicators are based on subjective analysis. They take into account the details of ownership (e.g., debt service), which vary from investor to investor. Therefore, they differ for each investor. Unfortunately, many investors treat these subjective indicators as if they were objective.

For example, someone tells you that the property offers a 5 percent cash on cash return. How is that possible? It is not possible. The property cannot offer a 5 percent cash on cash return except to a specific investor. Perhaps the person is telling you that the property offers a 5 percent cash on cash return to the "typical investor." If so, you must decide whether the details of ownership of the typical investor fit you. If they do, the 5 percent cash on cash return may be accurate. If they don't, the 5 percent cash on cash return is incorrect.

There is another problem using these rates of indicator. Note that all the rates of return are based on the first year of operation except the NPV and IRR. This means that the first year must be representative of the yearly operation of the property. If it is not, the rates of return may be misleading. For instance, suppose that a substantial nonoperating outlay or capital addition exists in the first year but not in succeeding years. If either the cash flow before tax or cash flow after tax is the dividend or a portion of the dividend, then the resulting rate of return will be misleading. Thus, you may have to calculate a special cash flow before tax or cash flow after tax to have the rates of return make sense; that is, you will have to calculate cash flow before tax or cash flow after tax without considering such line entries as nonoperating outlays and capital additions.

These two problems lead you in the direction of redefining certain categories for the purpose of making these indicators more objective. For instance, if you redefine cash flow before tax to be simply NOI less debt service and do not consider nonoperating outlays, capital additions, and reserves, then any indicator that includes cash flow before tax will be objective for all investors who buy the property with identical financing (same loan amount, same interest rate, same term). Unfortunately, having two definitions for cash flow before tax (or any other line entry) leads to confusion.

In indicators that use the equity as the divisor, the equity has customarily been defined as the difference between the purchase price and the loan (or loans). If your goal is to attempt objectivity, this may be acceptable. If your goal is to provide an accurate analysis for yourself, however, you should use the initial investment (investment base) as the divisor instead of the equity.

Because analysis, definitions, and categories vary from one group of real estate professionals to another, using these indicators may lead to confusion. Indeed, confusion abounds! Nonetheless, it usually makes sense to use these indicators in a subjective way. That is, you can use them to compare the investment opportunities available to you so long as you calculate them and apply them consistently. Only when you compare your rates of return to someone else's rates of return, or your rates of return to some self-proclaimed standard does the confusion start.

Because most of the indicators have serious deficiencies, the application of discounted cash flow analysis to real estate financial analysis has proven very useful. Calculations of NPV and IRR provide a more rational evaluation of how the property will perform.

Perhaps you can best use the indicators in this chapter as a filter. By using these easy-to-calculate devices, you can filter out unacceptable properties without having to do a full analysis on each, and you can save your energy for doing comprehensive analysis on the properties that are better prospects for meeting your investment goals.

CHAPTER 41

DISCOUNTED CASH FLOW ANALYSIS

Discounted cash flow analysis is useful in analyzing the results of your forecasts and in making useful calculations regarding loans and other financial arrangements. The next chapter covers net present value and internal rate of return. But first, in this chapter, you can review the basics. Keep in mind that an annuity is a recurring periodic payment, always the same amount. (The book shows negative numbers in parentheses.)

MINIMODEL

In bygone days, investors used compound interest tables to make the complicated calculations required by discounted cash flow analysis. Today, financial calculators and computers are widely available to do these calculations quickly and easily. Every financial calculator and every program are a little different, and you must spend some time learning how to use them. But each is based on a general financial model. This book labels the general financial model the "minimodel." The minimodel has its required inputs and provides the appropriate outputs. This minimodel is quite simple and is represented by five symbols:

N   I   PV   PMT   FV

For most calculations, you will need three inputs. If you can supply three inputs, the financial calculator (or computer) will give you an output. For instance, if you can supply n, i, and PV, the calculator will calculate PMT for you. Sometimes the biggest problem is figuring out where to input the information you have. That's easy up to a point.

n = Periods

Periods can be years, quarters, months, or even days. Periods represent the time element in the time value of money. When you think about it, it's pretty difficult to confuse periods with the other numbers required for the minimodel.

i = Rate of return

A rate of return can be an interest rate, a yield, a discount rate, or even a compound growth rate. You can express it as a percentage in conversation and as a decimal in calculations. When you think about it, it's pretty difficult to confuse a rate of return with the other numbers required for the minimodel.

PMT = Payment

A payment for a financial calculator must be a periodic payment. That is, it must be a recurring payment made at regular intervals, and each recurring payment must be the same amount. It might be an amortized loan payment, an annuity, or a sinking fund payment. When you think about it, it's pretty difficult to confuse payments with the other numbers required for the minimodel.

That leaves PV and FV. These are sometimes easy to get confused. They are especially easy to get confused when the FV in one part of your calculations must be used as a PV in a later calculation. But generally, these concepts can be kept straight.

PV = Present value (the value today)

FV = Future value (the value at a certain time in the future)

The PV usually represents an amount at the beginning of the financial arrangement being analyzed (beginning of the periods), and the FV usually represents an amount at the end of the financial arrangement being analyzed (at the end of the periods). For instance, the amount of money loaned is the PV. After a few payments are made, the principal is reduced. What is left is a remaining balance. The FV represents the remaining balance on the loan (after the few payments have been made).

This minimodel will be used in the following form throughout this book:

FV =
PMT =
PV =
I =
N =

These symbols represent the keys on your financial calculator. If you can provide the input for just three of the five possible inputs, the calculator will give you an output from one of the two remaining symbols (keys). You need just three of five to make a calculation.

There are two additional rules for using this minimodel. First, the periods (n) must be coordinated with i and PMT. If n represents months, i must represent interest per month or yield per month, and the PMT must be a monthly payment. Second, on many financial calculators, the direction of cash flow must be designated by a positive number (no + sign required) or a negative number (must have a − sign). A borrower, for example, would show PV as a positive number because it is the loan amount coming into pocket. The PMTs (loan payments) made would be shown as negative numbers because they are going out of pocket. Thus, the rule is that PV can never be the same sign as PMT or FV. This is .called the "sign convention" and indicates the direction of cash flow from the point of view of one of the parties to a financial arrangement. If you change the above example to the point of view of the lender, the PV will be negative (the loan amount flows out of pocket), but the PMTs will be positive (the loan payments flow into pocket). It is just the opposite of the borrower.

Before you start with the basics, try the minimodel to calculate an amortized monthly loan payment. The loan is $33,000,000 at 10½ percent interest amortized over 25 years.

$$FV \ =$$
$$PMT = (?)$$
$$PV \ = 33000000$$
$$I \ \ = 10.5 \div 12$$
$$N \ \ = 25 \times 12$$

Your financial calculator will probably convert the interest to a decimal automatically. Notice, however, that you have to convert the interest rate to a monthly rate, because the PMT is monthly. Likewise, you have to convert the periods to months, because the PMTs are monthly. Some calculators will do these conversions too. To calculate the monthly amortization payment, you use the PMT output (i.e., you push the PMT key):

$$PMT = (311,579.96)$$

Thus, the monthly payment is $311,579.96. The minimodel works this way, and your financial calculator works this way too.

T-CHART

To avoid getting confused while doing discounted cash flow analysis calculations, you may find it helpful to chart the cash flows on a T-chart. The initial cash flow (PV) is at period 0; the payments (PMT) correspond to the numbered periods 1 through 300; and the FV, when required to be calculated, is at the last period. The T-chart for the calculation above looks like this:

0	33,000,000
1	(?)
↓	↓
300	(?)

PMT = **(311,579.96)**

i = 10.5%

Any time you have difficulty understanding how to analyze a financial arrangement, you should immediately put the cash flows in a T-chart. It's another device, like the minimodel, that will provide a helpful perspective.

COMPOUNDING

To understand discounted cash flow analysis, you have to start with the fundamentals. This type of analysis is based on compounding. Compounding means earning interest on interest. First, look at simple interest. If you invest $10,000 at 8 percent simple interest for five years with principal and interest due and payable at the end of the fifth year, here's what you get:

$$\$10,000 \times 0.08 \quad = \$ \quad 800$$
$$\$ \quad 800 \times 5 \quad = \$ \ 4,000$$
$$\$10,000 + \$4,000 = \$14,000$$

You receive $14,000 at the end of five years. But change the simple interest to compound interest, and you will receive a different amount at the end of five years:

Year		
1	$10,000 × 0.08 = $ 800	$10,000 + $ 800 = $10,800
2	$10,800 × 0.08 = $ 864	$10,800 + $ 864 = $11,664
3	$11,664 × 0.08 = $ 933	$11,664 + $ 933 = $12,597
4	$12,597 × 0.08 = $1,008	$12,597 + $1,008 = $13,605
5	$13,605 × 0.08 = $1,088	$13,605 + $1,088 = $14,693

Thus, with compound interest you would receive $14,693, or $693 more than you would with simple interest.

Can this be worked in reverse? That is, if you were to be given $14,693 at the end of five years for an investment earning interest at the rate of 8 percent compounded, could you calculate how much you would have to invest today just to get that amount? Sure! It might take you longer to work it backwards, but it's just math. And once you devised algebraic formulas to work it forward and backward, it would be quick and easy. Discounted cash flow analysis is based on doing these easy compounding calculations both forward and backward. Fortunately, you don't have to worry about the alegbra, because your financial calculator does all the work. Use the minimodel to calculate this investment arrangement backwards:

$$FV = 14693$$
$$PMT =$$
$$PV = (?)$$
$$I = 8$$
$$N = 5$$

With the above inputs, you can calculate what amount will give you $14,693 in five years at 8 percent interest compounded:

$$PV = (10,000)$$

With discounted cash flow analysis, you can do six calculations that are useful in normal financial arrangements. They are done below using the minimodel. Although using compound interest tables is redundant—and therefore, this book includes no such tables—the book gives the proper column in the compound interest tables for each of the six calculations.

FUTURE VALUE OF A LUMP SUM

The first calculation is determining the "future value of a lump sum." You invest $20,000 in a certificate of deposit (CD) at 9 percent compounded annually. What is your CD worth at the end of five years?

FV = ?   FV = 30772
PMT =
PV = (20000)
I   = 9
N   = 5

On the T-chart it looks like this:

0	(20,000)
1	0
2	0
3	0
4	0
5	?

i   = 9%

FV = **30,772**

Use the Amount of One at Compound Interest column in the compound interest tables.

FUTURE VALUE OF AN ORDINARY ANNUITY

The second calculation is the "future value of an ordinary annuity." Assume that you will deposit $3,000 every year for five years into an account bearing 8 percent interest. At the end of five years, how much will be in the account?

FV = ?   FV = 17599
PMT = (3000)
PV =
I   = 8
N   = 5

It looks like this on a T-chart:

0	0
1	(3,000)
2	(3,000)
3	(3,000) i = 8%
4	(3,000)
5	(3,000) + ? FV = **17,599**

Use the Accumulation of One per Period column in the compound interest tables.

SINKING FUND PAYMENT

The third calculation is the "sinking fund payment." Assume that you need $50,000 at the end of five years. You can deposit funds in a savings account to earn 7 percent. What annual payments will it take to accumulate $50,000 at the end of five years?

```
FV  = 50000
PMT = (?)            PMT = (8694)
PV  =
I   = 7
N   = 5
```

The T-chart shows this:

0	0
1	(?) PMT = **(8,694)**
2	(?)
3	(?) i = 7%
4	(?)
5	(?) + 50,000

This is also known as "ordinary annuity required for a future value." Use the Sinking Fund Factor column in the compound interest tables.

PRESENT VALUE OF A LUMP SUM

The fourth calculation is the "present value of a lump sum." If you will be paid $100,000 at the end of five years and you can invest money today at a safe rate (e.g., savings account) of 7 percent, what is that $100,000 worth to you now, if it were paid to you today?

$$FV = 100000$$
$$PMT =$$
$$PV = (?) \qquad PV = (71298)$$
$$I = 7$$
$$N = 5$$

The T-chart shows the cash flows:

0	(?)
1	0
2	0
3	0
4	0
5	100,000

PV = (71,298)

i   = 7%

This is also known as the "reversion." Use the Present Value, Reversion of One column in the compound interest tables.

PRESENT VALUE OF AN ORDINARY ANNUITY

The fifth calculation is the "present value of an ordinary annuity." You desire to take five years off to explore the Amazon rain forest and want an income of $60,000 per year. How much will an annuity of $60,000 per year cost if the insurance company offers a yield of 4 percent?

$$FV =$$
$$PMT = 60000$$
$$PV = (?) \qquad PV = (267109)$$
$$I = 4$$
$$N = 5$$

Here is the T-chart:

0	(?)
1	60,000
2	60,000
3	60,000
4	60,000
5	60,000

PV = (267,109)

i   = 4%

Use the Present Value Ordinary Annuity column in the compound interest tables.

PAYMENTS REQUIRED TO AMORTIZE A LUMP SUM

The sixth calculation is the "payments required to amortize a lump sum." The lender offers to loan you $200,000 at 9 percent interest amortized over 25 years with monthly payments to buy a house. What are your loan payments?

$$
\begin{aligned}
FV &= \\
PMT &= (?) \qquad\qquad PMT = 1678) \\
PV &= 200000 \\
I &= 9 \div 12 \\
N &= 25 \times 12
\end{aligned}
$$

The T-chart looks like this:

0	200,000
1	(?)
↓	↓
300	(?)

PMT = (1,687)

i   = 9%

Use the Installment to Amortize One column in the compound interest tables.

The preceding six uses of discounted cash flow analysis have practical applications in many different financial calculations. Some special applications follow.

CALCULATING LOAN BALANCES

The amount of a loan equals the present value of its loan payments at the interest rate of the loan. For instance, a $12,000,000 loan at 11½ percent interest amortized over 30 years has a loan payment of $118,834.97 per month. If you calculate the PV of the 300 monthly loan payments at 11½ percent, you will calculate the loan amount:

$$FV \ =$$
$$PMT = (118834.97)$$
$$PV \ = (?) \qquad\qquad PV = 12000000$$
$$I \ \ = 11.5 \div 12$$
$$N \ \ = 30 \times 12$$

Once payments have been made on the loan, the balance due on it is always the present value of the remaining payments at the loan interest rate. For instance, suppose 12 payments have been made on the above loan. The loan balance is

$$FV \ =$$
$$PMT = (118834.97)$$
$$PV \ = ? \qquad\qquad PV = 11951475$$
$$I \ \ = 11.5 \div 12$$
$$N \ \ = 360 - 12$$

On the T-chart it looks like this:

0	?
1	(118,834.97)
↓	↓
348	(118,834.97)

PV = **11,951,475**

i = 11.5%

INTEREST PAID

Most financial calculators will provide you with an automatic means of calculating the interest paid for one amortized payment or for a number of amortized payments. There is also a simple but more burdensome way to figure it. Subtract the remaining balance from the beginning balance to calculate the principal paid. Then subtract the principal paid from the total of the payments to calculate the interest paid. In the above example for the 12 payments made, the calculations follow:

Beginning balance	= $12,000,000
−Remaining balance	= $11,951,475
Principal paid	= $ 48,525
Loan payment = $118,834 × 12	= $ 1,426,008
−Principal paid	= $ 48,525
Interest paid	= $ 1,377,483

IN REVERSE

Most discounted cash flow analyses can be done in reverse; that is, you can solve for an unknown. In the loan example above, if you have the loan amount, the loan payment, and the number of payments, you can calculate the interest rate:

```
FV  =
PMT = (118834.97)
PV  = 12000000
I   = ? ÷ 12              I = 11.5
N   = 30 × 12
```

This gets back to the basic use of the minimodel. If you can find three inputs, you can get an output.

LOAN CONSTANT

The loan constant comes from the compound interest tables. For instance, the loan constant for a 15-year loan is 0.131474 in the 10 percent annual compound interest table (i.e., for a loan at 10 percent with annual payments). You can calculate the constant using your financial calculator. Simply calculate the loan payment for a loan of $1 for 15 years at 10 percent:

```
FV  =
PMT = (?)                 PMT = 0.13147
PV  = 1
I   = 1
N   = 15
```

The loan constant can also be calculated by dividing the debt service by the loan amount. For example, a $100,000 loan at 10 percent interest amortized over 15 years has a yearly payment of $13,147. The loan constant is $13,147 ÷ 100,000 = 0.13147. These calculations come in handy sometimes when you need a loan constant but do not have access to the tables.

PRESENT VALUE OF IRREGULAR CASH FLOWS

Suppose you are analyzing a property you plan to hold for three years. Your forecast shows that the after-tax cash flows are as follows:

Year	Cash Flows
1	$28,200
2	29,750
3	33,150 + 990,850 = 1,024,000

The extra cash flow in the third year is the sale proceeds or "reversion," and it is added to the third year's cash flow. Suppose you want to know the maximum initial investment (Down payment + Loan points + Acquisition costs) you can have in the property and get the 14 percent rate of return you expect to get from real estate investments. These cash flows cannot be analyzed using the PMT function in the minimodel because they are not identical cash flows. They are different amounts. So the only way you can solve this analysis is to break it up into three parts:

Part I: PV of $28,200 for one year at 14 percent

```
FV  = 28200
PMT =
PV  = (?)              PV = (24736)
I   = 14%
N   = 1
```

Part 2: PV of $29,750 for two years at 14 percent

```
FV  = 29750
PMT =
PV  = (?)           PV = (22891)
I   = 14%
N   = 1
```

Part 3: PV of $1,024,000 for three years at 14 percent

```
FV  = $1024000
PMT =
PV  = (?)           PV = (691170)
I   = 14%
N   = 3
```

Total PV = (738,797)

By dividing the calculations into three parts and adding together the results of your discounted cash flow analysis calculations, you have calculated the highest amount your investment base can be in this investment and still achieve the 14 percent yield. In other words, if your investment base is $738,797 for this investment, you will get a 14 percent rate of return. You have calculated the total present value of the cash flows. Fortunately, your financial calculator or computer program makes it easier to calculate the total present value by using the NPV function, which is covered in the next chapter.

ORDINARY ANNUITY AND ANNUITY DUE

Most discounted cash flow calculations are based on "payments-in-arrears" or "end-of-period" payments. This method calculates an "ordinary annuity." You can make the calculations another way, which is more appropriate to some financial circumstances, based on "payments-in-advance" or "beginning-of-period" payments. This method calculates an "annuity due." Beginning-of-period discounted cash flow calculations are relevant only to annuity calculations (i.e., future value of an annuity, sinking fund payment, present value of an annuity, and payments required to amortize a lump sum). Although this more specialized use of discounted cash flow analysis is beyond the scope of this book, it is relevant to know that discounted cash flow analysis has this additional flexibility. Your financial calculator has a BEGIN/END switch that allows you to switch back and forth. It is also handy to know that you should keep your financial calculator switched to END unless you switch it to BEGIN specifically to make a beginning-of-period calculation. You must make most discounted cash flow analysis calculations in the END mode.

SUMMARY

In the next chapter, you will be better able to understand the process of calculating net present values (NPV) and internal rates of return (IRR) based on your review of elementary discounted cash flow analysis in this chapter. These techniques of discounted cash flow analysis will provide you with a way to analyze investment opportunities using more than just the property's first year of operation. But, additionally, you can use many of the calculations in this chapter to assist you in computing the forecast.

CHAPTER 42

NET PRESENT VALUE AND INTERNAL RATE OF RETURN

In Chapter 41, the payments considered for discounted cash flow analysis are annuity payments. In other words, they are payments that are recurring, periodic, and identical, such as loan payments. They are *regular* cash flows.

NET PRESENT VALUE

What about *irregular* cash flows? What do you do when the cash flows are not identical in an investment or financial arrangement? You treat each cash flow separately. For instance, if you want to know the present value (PV) of the following irregular cash flows from a real estate investment, assuming you will earn a 9 percent interest rate (discount rate), you must treat each cash flow as if it were a lump sum. Keep in mind that you add the reversion (the sale proceeds from the sale of the property) to the fifth year's cash flow.

0	(?)	PV = **1,066,713**
1	35,210	
2	41,350	
3	69,160	i = 9%
4	31,820	
5	37,440 + 1,383,730	

First, you determine the present value of $35,210 at one year in the future at 9 percent; that's $32,302. Next you determine the present value of $41,350 at two years in the future at 9 percent; that's $34,803. And

$69,160 at three years equals $53,404; and $31,820 at four years equals $22,542; and, finally, $1,421,170 at five years equals $923,662. You have calculated the PV of each cash flow individually as if it were a lump sum. Now, when you add the PVs together, you get a total PV, which is the PV of the irregular cash flow.

$$\$32,302 + \$34,803 + \$53,404 + \$22,542 + \$923,662$$
$$= \$1,066,713$$

Fortunately, your financial calculator will do this automatically for you when you use the NPV function.

Suppose you invest $1,003,500 to purchase the real estate investment above. The NPV function will subtract the initial investment (the first cash flow at Year 0) to provide you a net present value (NPV).

$$\$1,066,713 - \$1,003,500 = \$63,213 = NPV$$

Thus, the NPV at a 9 percent discount rate for this real estate investment is $63,213.

DISCOUNT RATES

When you calculate an NPV, you must use a yield (interest rate). This is designated a "discount rate." For instance, when you calculate the present value of the remaining loan payments to determine the balance on an amortized loan, you use the interest rate of the loan. When the loan was originally made, the interest rate (yield) was put into an agreement, a promissory note. You determine the balance on that loan according to the interest rate specified in the note.

What is the yield (discount rate) when you are doing calculations not defined by an agreement? You use different yields for different purposes:

Risk-free rate: The rate of return offered by a highly liquid investment essentially free of the risk of default (e.g., short-term federal security). This is an objective rate.

Safe rate: The rate of return offered by a liquid investment safe from the risk of default (e.g., FDIC insured savings account). This is an objective rate.

Reinvestment rate: The rate of return offered by a real estate investment that is readily available (e.g., an average income property offering an average real estate rate of return). This rate often has a minimum investment amount as a condition (e.g., the average initial investment amount required for the average income property). This is a subjective rate. It relies on the ability, knowledge, and experience of the investor to establish the type of average real estate investments readily available to the investor.

Opportunity cost of capital: The rate of return offered by the best alternative investment of comparable risk, size, and duration to the investment opportunity being evaluated. This is a subjective rate. It relies on the ability, knowledge, experience, and ambition of the investor. This rate is usually higher than the reinvestment rate, but it could be the same.

For NPV analysis, you use the opportunity cost of capital, or "opportunity rate." The opportunity cost of capital is the yield that you can reasonably hope to get in a similar investment. For instance, if you invest in shopping centers and get yields of 12 percent to 15 percent, then the minimum discount rate you will want to use in a NPV analysis is 12 percent.

USES OF NPV

The PV analysis shows you how much you will have to invest to get the specified irregular cash flows and achieve your yield (discount rate). The NPV analysis shows you the additional amount (the "net" amount) you will get after you have achieved your yield. You desire to purchase the property represented by the cash flow above and achieve a 13 percent yield. You do a PV analysis using a discount rate of 13 percent. Use the NPV function in your financial calculator:

0	(?)	PV = **902,343**
1	35,210	
2	41,350	
3	69,160	i = 13%
4	31,820	
5	37,440 + 1,383,730	

The PV is $902,343. This shows you that you can make an initial investment in this property of $902,343 and get a 13 percent yield.

Use the flow model (similar to the minimodel) for an easy way to envision this calculation. The symbols correspond to those on most financial calculators:

$$CF\ 0 =$$
$$CF\ 1 =$$
$$CF\ 2 =$$
$$CF\ 3 =$$
$$CF\ 4 =$$
$$CF\ 5 =$$
$$I\quad =$$

For the flow model, all the inputs are made except CF 0 for the calculation of PV. Or all the inputs are made except i for the calculation of the internal rate of return (IRR). All inputs including both the CF 0 and i inputs are used for NPV calculations. Here's how the flow model looks for the PV calculation of the cash flows above:

CF 0 = (?)   PV = 902343
CF 1 = 35210
CF 2 = 41350
CF 3 = 69160
CF 4 = 31820
CF 5 = 37440 + 1383730
I   = 13

Again, this calculation tells you that you can make an initial investment of $902,343 in this property and get a 13 percent yield.

But what if you can buy this property with only an initial investment of $900,000? The NPV calculation is done as follows:

CF 0 = (? - 900000)   NPV = 2034
CF 1 = 35210
CF 2 = 41350
CF 3 = 69160
CF 4 = 31820
CF 5 = 37440 + 1383730
I   = 13

In this case, you subtract the initial investment from the PV to give you NPV. The NPV is $2,034. With the NPV analysis, if you calculate a positive number for NPV, you have achieved your yield (discount rate). If you calculate a negative number, you have not achieved your yield.

The NPV analysis can be used to choose between real estate investment opportunities. Assume you are making a choice between investing in Maplewood Apartments (Appendix I) or Crossroads Plaza Shopping Center (Appendix III) and your opportunity rate is 12 percent:

Maplewood Apartments

CF 0 = (? − 1783095) = (?)   NPV = 63396
CF 1 = 26153
CF 2 = 47780
CF 3 = 54373
CF 4 = 93665
CF 5 = 117993 + 2854766
I   = 12

The NPV at a 12 percent discount rate for investing in Maplewood Apartments for five years (CFBT) is $63,396.

Crossroads Plaza

CF 0 = (? − 1303140) = (?)   NPV = 95912
CF 1 = 19942
CF 2 = 40465
CF 3 = 53739
CF 4 = 69301
CF 5 = 85052 + 2147299
I   = 12

The NPV at a 12 percent discount rate for investing in Crossroads Plaza for five years (CFBT) is $95,912. What does this show you? It indicates that each investment will provide a rate of return of at least 12 percent, or each NPV would have been negative.

On further inspection, you see that with a smaller investment of $1,303,140, Crossroads Plaza returned 12 percent plus $95,912, while

Maplewood Apartments with a larger investment of $1,783,095 returned only $63,396 plus 12 percent. Since the initial investments are not the same however, it's not obvious without further inspection which investment offers the better return. You can make the meaning of the NPV analysis quicker to perceive by calculating the profitability index. Instead of subtracting the initial investment from the total PV, you divide the total PV by the initial investment. The profitability indexes follow:

| Maplewood Apartments: | $1,846,491 ÷ $1,783,095 = 1.035 |
| Crossroads Plaza: | $1,399,052 ÷ $1,303,140 = 1.073 |

The profitability index provides you with a dollar-per-dollar return for the dollars returned over the 12 percent discount rate. For Maplewood Apartments, every $1 returns $1.03. For Crossroads Plaza, every $1 returns $1.07. One way to look at this is that Maplewood Apartments gives you a 12 percent return plus a bonus amount of 3.5 percent while Crossroads Plaza gives a 12 percent return plus a bonus amount of 7.3 percent. With the profitability index, you can easily see with a quick glance that Crossroads Plaza offers a more profitable investment.

Although NPV analysis and the profitability index are helpful analytic devices, do ordinary people understand returns on investment in a different way? Is it easier to understand an investment in Crossroads Plaza by showing that it has a rate of return of 13.7 percent or by showing it has an NPV of $95,912 at a discount rate of 12 percent? Does showing that it has a profitability index of 1.073 make understanding easier? In contrast, you can compare the IRR of 13.7 percent for Crossroads Plaza directly to other investment yields.

INTERNAL RATE OF RETURN

The IRR procedure also analyzes irregular cash flows. It starts with an initial investment and then determines at what discount rate (yield) the total PV of the cash flows equals the initial investment. Keep in mind the definition of IRR: *The discount rate at which the PV of the cash flows equals the initial investment.* Another definition is *the discount rate that results in an NPV of 0.*

Suppose that the original investment example (for NPV above) requires an initial investment of $850,000. What is the IRR? The T-chart looks like this:

0	(850,000)
1	35,210
2	41,350
3	69,160
4	31,820
5	37,440 + 1,383,730

$i = ?$

To determine the correct discount rate (the IRR), you must calculate total PV by trial and error using different discount rates. You will try to bracket the correct discount rate by using a trial discount rate that is lower and then one that is higher. Once you have the correct discount rate bracketed, you will increase the lower one a little and decrease the higher one a little. Finally, after many trials and errors, you find the discount rate that results in an NPV of 0. Such a discount rate is the IRR. Of course, the IRR function on your financial calculator does this trial and error calculation for you automatically, so you don't have to go through the process. Just use the flow model:

```
CF 0 = (850000)
CF 1 = 35210
CF 2 = 41350
CF 3 = 69160
CF 4 = 31820
CF 5 = 37440 + 1383730
I   = ?                    I = 14.4%
```

What does the IRR tell you? It gives you the yield on your investment for an irregular cash flow. In the above example, the IRR is 14.4 percent. That means that this real estate investment compares to investing in a savings account bearing 14.4 percent or a corporate bond bearing 14.4 percent. The IRR computes a rate of return for a multiyear projection. It is a discounted cash flow technique for measuring the rate of return from a series of cash flows that are dissimilar. It takes into account the yearly cash flows from a real estate project as well as the cash flow resulting from the sale. Year 0 is the initial investment. Years 1–5 are the annual cash flows. And the additional number in Year 5 is the reversion (sale proceeds), which must be added to the operating cash flow for Year 5. You must use a financial calculator or a computer program to calculate the IRR. Because a programmed routine of trial error calculates the IRR, it usually takes a calculator or a computer a little longer than other calculations.

The IRR has been criticized on the following technical grounds:

1. It is mathematically possible that there is more than one answer to the IRR calculation. This happens sometimes with multiple negative cash flows. Every sign change increases the risk that multiple IRRs may result for the same cash flows. But this is rare. Negative cash flows do not necessarily mean that there will be multiple IRRs. If there are multiple IRRs for a series of cash flows, many calculators and computer programs are programmed to give you an error message. If there are no negative cash flows, there is no problem.

2. The IRR assumes that you reinvest the cash flows at a rate of return equal to the IRR. Critics say that in most cases this is not practical so the IRR is not correct. In the above example, if the investor cannot reinvest the cash flows at 14.4 percent, the rate of return will be less than 14.4 percent. This is an important consideration. The essential ideas to consider are the same as those regarding discount rates. If the IRR is comparable to the opportunity cost of capital (i.e., if the opportunity cost of capital is about 14½ percent) and you can reinvest the positive cash flows at such a rate, then the IRR is correct. If the IRR is above the opportunity cost of capital, then the IRR is incorrect. Or, if you cannot reinvest at the opportunity rate, the IRR is incorrect.

3. It doesn't make sense to discount negative cash flows at the IRR. The funds to cover the future outlay (negative cash flow) can seldom be invested at the IRR. Realistically, such funds can be invested only at a safe rate (e.g., savings account).

4. The IRR doesn't take into account the size differences (initial investment sizes) between investment opportunities. For instance, if you have $3,000,000 to invest and you invest $2,850,000 in an apartment project at an IRR of 12 percent, can you take the remaining $150,000 and invest it to make 12 percent in a comparable investment? Probably not. You will probably invest the excess $150,000 at a safe rate. But if you find an apartment project requiring a $3,000,000 investment for an IRR of 12 percent, all your funds can be invested at the higher rate.

If you use the IRR in a situation in which it is accurate, you can compare the IRR directly to a savings account yield, a bond yield, or other investment yields. Moreover, the IRR is a good comparative measurement. If two properties are equal in most respects except that one has an IRR of 14.4 percent and the other has an IRR of 11.7 percent, you will want to choose the one with the highest yield. Since making money (getting a yield) is an important part of making an investment, the IRR is a comparative device that is very important.

Either cash flows before tax (CFBT) or cash flows after tax (CFAT) may be used to calculate the IRR. Using the former gives you a before-tax IRR (yield not taking into account the effects of income taxation), and using the latter gives you an after-tax IRR (a yield that takes everything into account).

ALTERED IRRs

There have been a number of attempts to cure the deficiencies of the IRR by altering it. The results include a Modified IRR (MIRR), Adjusted IRR (AIRR), and a Financial Management Rate of Return (FMRR). Although an extended treatment of these goes beyond the scope of this book, the ideas are presented here to show you that these more complex techniques may be appropriate to use for some analysis situations.

MIRR or AIRR

The Modified IRR or the Adjusted IRR have been advocated in various configurations. For one method, you discount all negative cash flows back to the time of the initial investment. You compound all positive cash flows forward to the end of the last year of the holding period. You do the discounting and compounding at the opportunity cost of capital. This results in an initial investment (modified by any discounted negative cash flows) and only one cash flow, which comes at the end of the investment. This eliminates the multisolution problem.

Another version compounds all cash flows forward at either a safe rate or a reinvestment rate rather than at the opportunity rate. This results in an initial investment and only one cash flow, which comes at the end of the investment. This eliminates the problem caused by the assumption that all cash flows are reinvested at the IRR and also eliminates the multi-solution problem. There are other variations of MIRR and AIRR too.

FMRR

The Financial Management Rate of Return is more elaborate yet. It requires that only after-tax discount rates be used (e.g., an after-tax safe rate). You use the safe rate for reinvesting cash flows until you accumulate a large enough sum to make an investment at the reinvestment rate. (In other words, to use the reinvestment rate, you must have a minimum investment amount.) You discount all negative cash flows back to the prior positive cash flow at the safe rate. You discount all remaining negative cash flows back to the initial investment at the safe rate. You compound all positive cash flows forward at either the safe rate or the reinvestment rate. This results in an initial investment (modified by any discounted negative cash flows) and only one cash flow, which comes at the end of the investment. The FMRR attempts to cure all the problems of the IRR analysis. It is flexible enough to analyze mixed portfolios (real estate and non-real estate) too.

The biggest drawback of these concepts may be their complexity. Complexity is not necessarily a drawback for the analyst who makes these calculations regularly and can understand them. Complexity may be a drawback in situations in which the concepts are difficult to understand for ordinary people involved in the decision-making process. But a real estate investment analysis computer program can be programmed to calculate these special IRRs automatically. (For further reading consult the investment real estate books in the Bibliography.)

SUMMARY

Intelligent scholars and practitioners continually debate whether NPV or IRR analysis is better for analyzing real estate. It seems apparent that each real estate analyst will develop a style. Your style will include your choice of discounted cash flow analysis techniques. And either NPV or IRR will foster more rational decisions than using the rates of return based on only the first year of operation (outlined in Chapter 40). Many prefer using the IRR, probably because ordinary people understand a rate of return more easily. Not everyone is a real estate analyst, but many nonanalysts may have to understand the results of the analysis. Yet the deficiencies of the IRR are real ones. If you use the IRR, you must be ready to switch to NPV analysis in situations in which the IRR may be misleading. Those situations were outlined in this chapter.

The altered IRRs may be unduly complex—regardless of automatic computation in computer programs—for simple comparisons of real estate investment opportunities in situations in which an IRR analysis is adequate. When the IRR may be misleading or in portfolio analysis, the altered IRRs may provide a more rational analysis.

PART 8

OTHER CONSIDERATIONS IN REAL ESTATE ANALYSIS

There are important considerations beyond the collection of basic data and the analytical calculations that attempt to provide a reliable assessment of potential financial performance. These considerations are beyond the scope of this book, but they are covered here, albeit superficially, to put real estate investment analysis in perspective. In one sense, these considerations are warnings that give you a sense of the limitations of financial analysis. In another sense, they are invitations to broaden the scope of your perspective, both in general and in regard to specific properties, people, and transactions.

Chapters

CHAPTER 43

FEASIBILITY ANALYSIS

Many people talk about real estate feasibility and about feasibility studies, but there is confusion as to what they are talking about. An investment analysis examines the financial feasibility of a property. Is it a feasibility study? A demographic profile provides information on the current population of an area. Is it a feasibility study? A rental survey indicates the current rents for specific types of real property. Is it a feasibility study? There are additional questions: When do you need a feasibility study? Who does feasibility studies? What type of properties require feasibility studies?

A feasibility study analyzes the performance of an investment property in its total economic environment.

An investment analysis is an important component of a feasibility study. In creating an investment analysis, you should be careful to substantiate all the information used. For instance, you do an informal rental survey to help determine what current and future rents will be used in the pro forma financial reports being created. But substantiating the inputs needed to calculate pro forma reports cannot be considered a thorough analysis of the local economic environment. You need something more.

MARKET STUDY

A *market study* can contribute valuable knowledge about the economic environment. A market study analyzes the demographic and economic conditions that affect the supply and demand for a specific type of real estate (e.g., office buildings). It may also include cultural, political, social, and other factors.

MARKETABILITY STUDY

A *marketability study* analyzes the capability of a specific property to be absorbed; that is, it predicts how the property will be sold or rented under current and future market conditions. Unlike a market study, which focuses on the economic conditions for a type of property, a marketability study goes a step further and concentrates on a particular property at a particular location. An absorption rate, which predicts how fast units will be sold or space will be rented, and at what price, is one of the conclusions of this type of analysis.

Suppose your marketability study shows that the city will use an additional 35,000 SF of office space each year in the foreseeable future. Currently, there are 15,000 SF vacant with only one other office building of 20,000 SF currently under construction. That office building will become available for occupancy about the same time as your project. You propose to build a 50,000-SF office building over an 18-month construction period. Eighteen months from now, presumably, the city will need another 52,500 SF of office space, which the existing inventory will reduce to 37,500 SF. The marketability study shows that you are likely to get 80 percent of the office rental market due to your superior location. Thus, you can expect to fill about 30,000 SF of your building on completion and to fill the remainder in the first year after completion (80% × 35,000 SF = 28,000 SF, more than enough to fill your building). Of course, that assumes that no one builds a third office building that will compete with yours. The marketability study will also provide you with the highest rental rate you can expect to get and stay competitive. Additionally, a marketability study can provide you with some marketing strategies that will enhance the success of your building.

FEASIBILITY STUDY

A *feasibility study* takes the market study and the marketability study, which offer a rich supply of economic information, and combines them with an investment analysis, which offers the detailed financial calculations for a specific property. Thus, the investment analysis rests on a well-researched foundation. The investment analysis shows you what your rate of return will be assuming your property is occupied at the stated occupancy rate and at the projected rent. The feasibility study tells you, in addition, whether the stated occupancy rate is achievable and sustainable and whether the market will support the projected rent.

Properties to be developed need feasibility studies. Sometimes a developer will contract a real estate consultant or another real estate professional for a feasibility study. Sometimes a developer will do a feasibility study in-house. When done in-house, sometimes a feasibility study is thorough and put into a formal report, and sometimes it's informal. Sometimes it is not done at all. Unlike appraisals that are always required by lenders, feasibility studies are required inconsistently and are thus not always done. Perhaps that was one of the contributing causes of the savings and loan debacle of the 80s.

It is less obvious that existing properties need feasibility studies. If you are going to develop a property, you will want to know whether the local economy will support that property and make it financially successful. If you are going to acquire a property, you will want to know whether the local economy will *continue* to support that property and make it financially successful. If you are making a decision as to whether to sell or to continue to hold a property, you will want the same information too.

Suppose you are considering buying a successful three-year-old 80,000 SF office building that is 93 percent occupied in a small city. Occupancy is high in the city, but there is no shortage of space this year. Ground has been broken for a new 75,000-SF office building nearby. If a market study were to show that this city can absorb only 15,000 additional square feet of office space per year, the new building will be providing a five-year supply of office space when it is finished one year from now. This is important information for the current owner of the 80,000-SF office building as well as for you, the potential buyer. The oversupply of space is likely to have a detrimental effect on the performance of every office building in the market area.

What else can feasibility studies do? They can test the marketability of various components of your real estate project. For instance, suppose you want to know what additional rent you can command by including a living room fireplace in each unit in your new apartment building. A marketability study can predict the cost effectiveness of such a component. Or it can predict which components will sell (or rent) the best. These studies can be simple and inexpensive or elaborate and expensive.

Feasibility studies can be used to market retail space. Retail chains usually do their own market and marketability studies before they make a decision to lease space in a new location. But many potential retail tenants are not so sophisticated. A feasibility study that shows them the predicted level of sales for different types of retail stores may be helpful to them in making a decision.

HIGHEST AND BEST USE STUDY

An extension of the feasibility study idea is the *highest and best use study*. It is a series of feasibility studies on different types of development projects to determine which will achieve the highest value for a specific site. For example, a highest and best use study will show you whether to build an office building or a shopping center on a parcel of commercially zoned land. Or whether a rezoning should be sought to build an apartment project.

BUSINESS PLAN

Another variation on the feasibility study is the *business plan*, a feasibility study for an underperforming property. One important component of this type of study is an analysis of what can be done to make the property perform better. A rehabilitation (rehab) may be required at considerable expense. The business plan predicts the cost-effectiveness of such a rehab. Changes in the use of the property must always be explored. When a potential change is fanciful, additional feasibility work may not be appropriate. But where significant market demand supports a potential change, the feasibility of such a change should be thoroughly investigated. Thus, the business plan becomes similar to a highest and best use study. For instance, perhaps an unsuccessful old shopping center can be demolished and replaced with successful new multiple office buildings.

MORE ON FEASIBILITY STUDIES

Who does feasibility studies? Real estate consultants, some appraisers, some commercial brokers, some property managers, and some accountants have the background and technical skills to do these studies. To do them well takes hands-on, grass-roots, field work. You have to talk with the people in the community who are involved in the real estate market. It's difficult to do these studies in the abstract. Extensive local inspection and investigation are required.

Because feasibility studies are traditionally provided to clients for a noncontingent fee, they cost at least as much as an income property appraisal and often more. And the cost must be paid whether the transaction is completed or whether the development goes ahead. Since lenders do not always require them, they are not always done.

Market studies, marketability studies, and feasibility studies are outside the subject matter of this book, but they are becoming a required element of real estate analysis. As real estate ownership becomes institutionalized (i.e., as more property is owned by pension funds, insurance companies, national syndications, etc.), the information required for development, transactions, and asset management increases. Institutional owners often act as fiduciaries when developing, acquiring, or managing real estate assets. Being a fiduciary requires one to act as a "prudent" person. What prudent person wouldn't want complete information on the property and the local economy in which it operates? Perhaps some day there will be no separate market studies, marketability studies, and investment analyses. The feasibility study will become the standard.

SENSITIVITY ANALYSIS

The sensitivity analysis is an extension of the investment analysis. A mathematical sensitivity study is a "what-if" analysis. It gives the reader the choice of varying one or more of the inputs that go into an investment analysis. For instance, the sensitivity studies for Maplewood Apartments (see Appendix I) show the effect that changes in certain input have on a specific output. The first table shows how differences in the potential rental income and the vacancy rate affect the net operating income. The second table shows the effect that changes in the net operating income and the capitalization rate have on the value. In each of the tables created there are 17 choices for one input and at least 9 choices for the other. This results in over 150 choices in each table.

For instance, in the net operating income sensitivity table (Appendix I), the pro forma NOI $566,041 (pro forma potential rental income and 6 percent vacancy) is in the middle of the table. If you believe that potential rental income will be 2 percent more and that the vacancy will be only 4 percent, the table shows you that the NOI will be $605,794.

A sensitivity table can be created for any resultant or bottom-line calculation. It shows how the bottom line changes when the inputs change. In the sales price sensitivity table (Appendix I), the pro forma sale price of $6,432,287 (pro forma NOI and an 8.8 percent cap rate) is in the center of the table. Suppose you believe the NOI will be $605,794 as you derived from the NOI sensitivity table above. You also believe that a cap rate of 9 percent is more representative of the market. To use the sale price sensitivity table, you first have to compute the percentage change in the NOI ($605,794 ÷ $566,041 = 1.07 − 1 = 0.07, a 7 percent increase). Then look at the sale price sensitivity table in the 9 percent cap rate column. A 6 percent increase in NOI yields a sale price of $6,666,708. An 8 percent increase in NOI yields a sale price of $6,792,495. Thus, a 7 percent increase in NOI will yield a sale price half way between: $6,729,601 ($6,792,495 − $6,666,708 = $125,787 ÷ 2 = $62,893 + $6,666,708 = $6,729,601). Thus, you have used the sensitivity tables to make your own predictions without reworking the forecast.

Any reader of the sensitivity studies who does not agree with the assumptions of the pro forma can make choices based on different assumptions and find the corresponding result in the tables. Thus, the tables offer results for different points of view. In addition, the tables show how sensitive the results are to changes in the inputs.

Although the sensitivity tables in Appendix I look complex, once you set them up in the abstract, the computer does all the work for the specific analysis. They are merely mathematical sensitivity tables using easy-to-understand math to make the calculations. But another type of sensitivity analysis that involves statistical calculations exists. Some call it a "risk analysis simulation," and it uses the Monte Carlo "routine" (i.e., Monte Carlo risk simulation model). This complex statistical analysis calculates the probability that certain results will occur. Since part of the input for the model is subjective, the probability calculated is only as accurate as the subjective input. The Monte Carlo analysis goes beyond the scope of this book, but it is mentioned to show that there are additional methods available to refine your investment analysis.

APPRAISAL

Some real estate studies should not be confused with feasibility studies. Income property *appraisals* include many of the elements of an investment analysis or a feasibility study. But an appraisal focuses specifically on determining the value of a property. Appraisals adhere to a traditional format that emphasizes this strict focus on determining value. The appraisal format includes the income approach, the cost approach, and the sales comparison approach. Not only is the format different, but the information sought is often different too.

COST-BENEFIT ANALYSIS

Certain studies done for or by public agencies are similar to feasibility studies but specialized in their scope. A *cost-benefit analysis* compares the cost of creating an improvement to those benefits that will be created by the improvement. Often some of the benefits are nonmonetary, but a monetary value has to be assigned to such benefits. This kind of analysis, therefore, goes beyond determining purely economic benefits and is of use primarily to public agencies and other bureaucracies.

LAND UTILIZATION STUDY

A *land utilization study* contemplates the highest and best use of a parcel of land but in the context of all the parcels in a given area or community. The considerations of markets and financial feasibility are not included or are given little weight. Public agencies use this study primarily as a planning device.

ENVIRONMENTAL IMPACT STUDY

The law in some states requires an environmental impact study before real estate development or rehabilitation can be commenced. This is not an economic study, although it may have economic implications. Rather, it is an analysis of the impact the proposed use will have on its environment.

SUMMARY

Feasibility studies take the financial analysis of a property one step further than investment analysis and provide a foundation of economic and market data that can increase the accuracy. Although feasibility studies are beyond the scope of this book, it is appropriate to see how they compare to investment analyses.

CHAPTER 44

RISK

One of the elements of real estate knowledge conspicuously missing from this book is a discussion of risk. Why? This is not a book on investing in real estate. It is simply a book on making sophisticated calculations. But certain risk concepts directly relate to doing analysis. So this chapter will treat three concepts of risk relevant to making calculations.

HIGHER RETURN, HIGHER RISK

The higher the rate of return, the riskier the investment. Why is this true? Many knowledgeable people make investments, including real estate investments, and the more risk they take, the more reward they seek. The market works reasonably efficiently. Therefore, high rates of return go hand-in-hand with high risk.

What does this mean to you? An uncommonly high rate of return could be a warning. Perhaps a risk exists that you have not perceived yet. Or an uncommonly high rate of return could also mean an opportunity. Perhaps the risk that others have perceived does not really exist or does not exist for you (e.g., an unusual property management problem that falls within your special expertise). Maybe the more practical meaning is that a high rate of return without a corresponding degree of obvious risk is your signal to investigate further. Dig in a little more deeply to accumulate more information on the property, on the local economy, and even on local politics. The relationship between risk and rate of return does sometimes get out of synchronization. That may provide you with an opportunity to make an especially good real estate investment. Or it may trap you in a disappointing investment.

An uncommonly high rate of return may uncover a mistake in the calculations. You can usually ferret out such mistakes without difficulty and easily correct them. More elusive is a mistake in the data supporting the calculations. You can detect such mistakes only by a review of the research that provided the underlying data.

Even more insidious is nonobjective data; that is, someone has provided data slanted toward creating a higher rate of return. For instance, research may show that the rents for office buildings fall in a range of $9.45 to $13.71 per SF per year while operating expenses fall in a range of $4.73 to $6.19 per SF per year. Were someone to provide you data that estimated rents at $13.71 and estimated expenses at $4.73, that would not necessarily be a mistake. It would certainly be misleading, however, and an uncommonly high rate of return would likely be the result. So, if an uncommonly high rate of return does not reflect a commensurate degree of risk, double-check the data, your assumptions, and your calculations.

LEVERAGE

Be aware that high leverage creates risk: financial risk. As an analyst, you can often create uncommonly high rates of return just by manipulating the leverage in a real estate investment. Since one of the attractions of real estate investments is the customary leverage readily available (e.g., 75 percent loans), manipulating leverage is a normal activity for investors.

A stable and secure property in a stable and secure local economy can be made into a risky investment by leverage. Suppose an apartment building has a net operating income (NOI) of $250,000 with 5 percent vacancy; and if you finance this apartment at 95 percent of value, it will have a breakeven cash flow and a very high internal rate of return (IRR) over a five-year holding period. With 95 percent financing and a high IRR, there is no NOI cushion. If rents do decrease, you will have to invest more money in this apartment investment to avoid foreclosure. If you finance the apartment at 75 percent of value, there would be enough excess NOI to cushion substantial downturns in the local economy that lead to lower rents; yet the initial investment would be five times more and the IRR much lower.

What is the additional risk for the smaller initial investment? There are at least two risks here. And different investors may perceive such risks differently. First, the investor may have to put more money at risk to keep this investment operating and to pay the loan payments. Second, the investor may lose the property through foreclosure to the lender if additional money to invest is not available.

For example, assume that the apartment above has a gross operating income of $500,000, expenses amounting to 50 percent of gross operating income, a 95 percent loan, and a break-even cash flow. Suppose gross operating income decreases 10 percent ($50,000) in an unforeseen market downturn. Gross operating income will be $450,000. If the amount of the expenses remains the same (as a percentage) and the vacancy rate doesn't change, the new NOI will be $225,000 ($25,000 less). Now the property has a negative cash flow of $25,000 per year, or $2,083 per month. For a wealthy investor, only additional funds will be put at risk. There will be no risk of losing the real estate. However, if the investor is a limited partnership with 15 limited partners, there may be a more adverse situation. Assuming that the partnership reserve fund contains inadequate funds, each of the limited partners will have to make a further investment in the property to keep it operating and to avoid foreclosure. Getting money from the limited partners may not be practical or possible for many reasons. If the limited partners do not make the additional investment in the property, the lender will foreclose, and the property will be lost. That is a significant risk.

Thus, higher leverage can create additional risk. And the financial structure itself (without considering the underlying business risk of the operating the property) causes the risk. In the example above, the unforeseen 10 percent decline in rents would not affect the operation of the property itself, nor would it have a devastating effect on the investor with the 75 percent loan. When manipulating the leverage in your analyses, you must be careful to keep the risks in mind.

RISK AND RETURN

The closer you get to zero for the initial investment, the less correlation you will find between risk and rate of return. Suppose you are investing in the following property. The NOI is $600,000 for five years on a sale and leaseback. You can purchase the property for $6,214,100 (9.65 percent cap rate). You can get a loan for up to $6,214,100 at 9 percent amortized over 30 years. At the end of five years, the lease term ends, the rent can be increased, and the NOI will jump 10 percent to $660,000. If the cap rate of 9.65 percent remains the same, the value of the property at the end of five years will be $6,839,378.

If you do a simplistic before-tax analysis for this investment assuming initial investments of 0 percent, $1, and 1, 2, 5, 10, and 25 percent, you get the following IRRs:

Initial investment = 0%

0	(0)	
1	$600,000 − $600,000 = 0	
2	$600,000 − $600,000 = 0	IRR = ∞
3	$600,000 − $600,000 = 0	
4	$600,000 − $600,000 = 0	
5	$600,000 − $600,000 = 0 + $6,839,378 − $5,958,091	
	= $881,287	

Initial investment = $1

0	(1)	
1	$600,000 − $600,000 = 0	
2	$600,000 − $600,000 = 0	IRR = 1,445%
3	$600,000 − $600,000 = 0	
4	$600,000 − $600,000 = 0	
5	$600,000 − $600,000 = 0 + $6,839,378 − $5,958,091	
	= $881,287	

Initial investment = 1%

0	($62,141)	
1	$600,000 − $594,000 = $6,000	
2	$600,000 − $594,000 = $6,000	IRR = 76.6%
3	$600,000 − $594,000 = $6,000	
4	$600,000 − $594,000 = $6,000	
5	$600,000 − $594,000 = $6,000 + $6,839,378 − $5,898,506	
	= $946,872	

Initial investment = 2%

0	($124,282)
1	$600,000 − $588,000 = $12,000
2	$600,000 − $588,000 = $12,000 IRR = 56.8%
3	$600,000 − $588,000 = $12,000
4	$600,000 − $588,000 = $12,000
5	$600,000 − $588,000 = $12,000 + $6,839,378
	− $5,838,925 = $1,012,453

Initial investment = 5%

0	($310,705)
1	$600,000 − $570,000 = $30,000
2	$600,000 − $570,000 = $30,000 IRR = 36.7%
3	$600,000 − $570,000 = $30,000
4	$600,000 − $570,000 = $30,000
5	$600,000 − $570,000 = $30,000 + $6,839,378
	− $5,660,183 = $1,209,195

Initial investment = 10%

0	($621,410)
1	$600,000 − $540,000 = $60,000
2	$600,000 − $540,000 = $60,000 IRR = 26%
3	$600,000 − $540,000 = $60,000
4	$600,000 − $540,000 = $60,000
5	$600,000 − $540,000 = $60,000 + $6,839,378
	− $5,362,278 = $1,537,100

Initial investment = 25%

0	($1,553,525)
1	$600,000 − $450,000 = $150,000
2	$600,000 − $450,000 = $150,000 IRR = 17.1%
3	$600,000 − $450,000 = $150,000
4	$600,000 − $450,000 = $150,000
5	$600,000 − $450,000 = $150,000 + $6,839,378
	− $4,468,565 = $2,520,813

Note: The loan balances at the end of the fifth year vary according to the amount of the loan required.

The IRRs go from 17.1 percent for a 25 percent initial investment to 1,445 percent for a $1 initial investment and on to infinity for a 0 percent initial investment.

Look at the difference in the cash flows between a 5 percent initial investment ($2,500/month) and a 1 percent initial investment ($500/month). There is only $2,000/month difference on a property purchased for $6,214,100. Yet the IRRs are 36.7 percent and 76.6 percent, respectively. Is the 1 percent initial investment really twice as risky as the 5 percent initial investment? Probably not for most investors. These examples show that the closer you get to an initial investment of zero, the less correlation between risk and return.

Why is there less correlation? Is the risk misleading, or is the return misleading? Your common sense indicates that the return is misleading. The IRR goes up steeply once you have reduced the initial investment to a small amount. Keep in mind this important concept when doing analysis on high leverage investments. The IRR may no longer be meaningful for investments with small down payments. And extreme reductions in the initial investment to increase the IRR may be an exercise in self-deception.

CHAPTER 45

PSYCHOLOGY

This book offers you 44 chapters of numbers crunching. In this last chapter, it is appropriate to acknowledge that real estate is more than doing the numbers. Psychology is a major component of every real estate decision and transaction, an enduring fact that is worth keeping in mind.

POINT OF VIEW

Much as been written already about the points of view that various parties have regarding the real estate investment and about the potential for a biased point of view to distort the numbers. This is an important psychological concept to remember.

THE FUTURE

The process of creating the forecast brings you a broad range of data to be analyzed. The amount of data is large and requires complex calculations. Once you make the calculations, you will tend to believe that you have "the answer." When you can refine your data more by combining your investment analysis with a market study and a marketability study, your confidence in the answer will grow even higher. But there is a sobering thought to keep in mind: No matter how refined your data becomes for your forecast, you are still attempting to predict the future. You cannot predict the future. In other words, you don't have the answer. The pro forma calculations are just a best effort, nothing more. Don't get carried away and lose your perspective.

PEOPLE

The financial facts and projections for the property are only a part of the total picture. Real estate does not exist in a vacuum, nor is it an animate object. Real estate is inert and meaningless until human beings own, operate, and use it. Thus, the "people" aspects of any real estate project predominate. The people aspects encompass the habits, abilities, and aspirations of a long chain of people including owners, lessees, customers of lessees, and property managers, all seeking a separate package of benefits from the real estate. The people aspects are difficult, often impossible, to quantify.

It is people who make transactions, not numbers. Each real estate transaction involves many people. The psychological milieu is more than any computer can analyze. Each person looks for benefits. Each person influences another person or persons in the transaction. Thus, the financial aspects of an investment or transaction are only a part of the reality.

Why would someone in Philadelphia invest in a rental house in Denver offering an IRR of 8 percent when she could get double that on a similar rental house at home? Her son is going to college in Denver, using one room and renting the other rooms to students.

Why would a national syndicator turn down the opportunity to buy a "pride of ownership" apartment project with a high IRR? Incoming jets fly over the property on their way to the airport 12 miles north. For the 30 percent of the time that the wind blows in a certain direction, the planes fly over about 4,000 feet above ground. The staff property manager believes that the noise from such air traffic will adversely affect occupancy some day. No one else on the staff can argue against such "expertise." Market vacancy is 6 percent, and the project vacancy is 3 percent.

Why would someone in New York City own an office building in San Diego generating about the same IRR as one close to home? He wants to make a tax deductible visit to the property a few times each winter.

These situations have little to do with the financial analysis, the real numbers. Yet they are not unusual situations. People have their motives. And the people part of real estate transactions and operations usually requires the most attention. Don't get swept away by your own clever financial analysis. Keep people in mind.

ANALYSIS PARALYSIS

One who gets carried away with the numbers in real estate is said to have "analysis paralysis." What does this mean? There are a number of possibilities. First, it might mean that the analysis requires the collection of so much data for each property that *every* property is shown to have some imperfection that disqualifies it. Second, it might mean that the analysis requires so much data that it is virtually impossible to collect enough data in the normal course of business to complete the analysis. In either case, no one will make a decision because the analysis is unsatisfactory. Third, it might mean that one party is so enamored by his or her own analysis that he or she refuses to be realistic about other aspects of the transaction. As a result, nothing happens. Whatever it might mean, analysis paralysis can have a deadly effect on the conduct of real estate business. Don't get caught up in it.

CONFIDENCE

Having warned you about potentially adverse psychology, it is only proper to make a case for the psychological benefit that sound financial analysis delivers. Everyone making a real estate investment wants to be sure how the income property will perform. Even though it is impossible to predict the future, most people feel comfortable making some basic assumptions about the future. If the analysis shows them how the property will perform if their basic assumptions become true, they will develop confidence in the information that is generated. If the information is relevant to some proposed action to be taken, they will develop the confidence to make a decision. The information must not only include the investor's basic assumptions but must be complete too. No questions can be left unanswered.

The financial analysis outlined in this book attempts to provide you with a scheme of analysis that generates enough information to create the confidence to act. Such confidence is an important psychological element of successful real estate decisions. Indeed, those who play professional roles in the income real estate business are psychologically lost without the confidence generated by sound financial analysis.

PART 9

SUMMARY

This book covers many of the major concerns of creating real estate pro forma financial reports and utilizing them for investment analysis. The first 27 chapters correspond to the 27 individual line entries in the pro forma forecast. This format makes it easy to use this book as a reference as well as a sensibly focused and readable book on the analysis process. Likewise, the first 27 chapters can be correlated to the line entries on a computer spreadsheet program.

The book presents real estate analysis as it has traditionally been practiced by many sophisticated real estate investors. One troubling aspect of traditional real estate analysis, however, may need revision. In fact, many investors have been using a revised approach for a long time. That is, the concept of an *adjusted* net operating income needs to be developed. It is misleading to relegate capital expenditures such as tenant improvements (TIs) and capital replacements (e.g., refrigerators) to the cash flow analysis. They are more like operating expenses than capital improvements, and the treatment given them by the Tax Code (amortization or cost recovery) may not be relevant to the determination of NOI.

If an office building averages $90,000 in TIs per year, why should that be considered anything except an operating expense (except by the IRS)? Likewise, if an apartment project averages $55,000 per year for appliance and carpeting replacement, why should that be considered anything but an operating expense (except by the IRS)?

In order to maintain the integrity of the taxable income analysis, the traditional calculation of net operating income (NOI) is important to retain. But an adjusted NOI can additionally be calculated. Here's how it might look:

Adjusted Net Operating Income

Net Operating Income
-Capital Improvements
-Tenant Improvements
-Replacements
-Leasing Commissions
Adjusted Net Operating Income

The adjusted NOI (ANOI) could be used with a capitalization rate to determine value. This is not a new idea. Some investors have used this concept for many years, particularly financial institutions. And, when the real estate markets are depressed, many potential investors become very sensitive to cash flow. At such times various versions of the ANOI become popular. But, when the real estate markets boom again, some of those investors revert to the traditional method of calculating NOI. (Inflation will take care any analysis deficiencies. Right?) Unfortunately, there is some evidence that depressed real estate markets can be mitigated by a more realistic approach to real estate analysis (e.g., the depressed market caused by the savings & loan debacle). Thus, it is worth considering that the ANOI concept should permanently replace NOI for evaluating income property.

Keep in mind that one of the reasons that these expenditures traditionally have not been used in the calculation of NOI is that they are often irregular from year to year. One way to smooth out the annual fluctuations is to use reserve accounts:

Adjusted Net Operating Income

Net Operating Income
-Reserve for Capital Improvements
-Reserve for Tenant Improvements
-Reserve for Replacements
-Reserve for Leasing Commissions
Adjusted Net Operating Income

By properly estimating the annual reserve amounts to cover these expenditures over a multiyear projection, a sum can be calculated that reasonably reflects the reality of the property's operation.

The four reserve line entries suggested above may not be the only non-operating expenditures worth considering for inclusion in the calculation of ANOI. They are examples. Perhaps the following is a better format:

Adjusted Net Operating Income

Net Operating Income

−Scheduled Reserves

Adjusted Net Operating Income

As the income real estate investment business matures over future years (following in the wake of the securities industry) and as real estate investment is institutionalized (the pension funds already own most of the securities and are now investing in real estate), the concept of ANOI should develop into an industry standard. A capitalized NOI is a convenient valuation and screening device for real estate analysis. A capitalized ANOI is more realistic.

There are some problems in calculating the reserves so as to be objective. For instance, how can you be objective about capital replacements? Many property managers can accurately estimate how long appliances, carpeting, and other replaceables will last on the average. You simply divide the number of years into the amount of replaceables to get an annual estimate. But what happens when the property manager tells you that refrigerators last nine years on the average, the apartment complex is eight years old, and no refrigerators have been replaced yet? Do you show them all being replaced in the ninth year, or do you simply schedule the replacements as you normally would? Is there an objective method for determining a reserve for replacements?

Tenant improvements (TIs) are more difficult to estimate. In a building that is not new, some suites need minor TIs for new tenants or for old tenants re-leasing and some suites need major TIs. You can tell from the leases when tenants will move out or re-lease, but which will they do? If space becomes vacant, how long will it remain vacant before being leased? Even if you ascertain the answers to these questions, how long is the period over which you average these TIs? Five years? Ten years? Twenty years? Is there an objective method for determining a reserve for TIs?

Leasing commissions present the same problem as TIs. Will you pay a full commission for a new tenant or a partial commission for an old tenant re-leasing? Or, perhaps, no commission will be paid for some new tenants and for some old tenants re-leasing. Over what period do you average the leasing commissions? Is there an objective method for determining a reserve for leasing commissions?

Perhaps capital improvements are the most difficult problem to handle objectively. If a roof lasts 15 years, what is the reserve amount if the roof is five years old? Such a reserve estimate requires you to choose a holding period. Presumably if the holding period is five years, no reserve is required. If the holding period is 10 years, a reserve is required (one-tenth of the new roof cost each year). If the holding period is 15 years, a reserve is required, but the reserve amount is smaller (one-fifteenth of the roof cost each year). Or, is it? Would you need a reserve after the tenth year? So, the question is: How long is the holding period for the purposes of objectivity? Another question is what items can reasonably be expected to be replaced? It doesn't make sense to consider the replacement of every component in the building. Rather, it is just the components that will need to be replaced during the holding period that are of concern to investors. Is there an objective method for determining a reserve for capital improvements?

Keep in mind, the purpose is not to do these estimates for the IRS. That is done in the taxable income analysis. The purpose is not to do these estimates to satisfy some obscure accounting rules. That is done by accountants in presenting a broad view of the property's operation to the owner. The purpose is not to estimate reserves for a specific owner. That is done in the cash flow analysis and is not necessarily the same. The information goal here is a simple and narrow one: What is the expected return from the property for every owner? How will the property perform for every owner? What is an objective cash flow that can be capitalized to establish an objective value for the property? Obviously, capital improvements, TIs, replacements, and leasing commissions do diminish the cash flow of most income properties. If there is to be objectivity, some objective standards have to be set.

The real estate profession will have to work out objective standards for estimating reserves for capital improvements, TIs, replacements, and leasing commissions before the use of the ANOI will be widely accepted for the purpose of capitalization. The starting point will be the general acceptance for the length of an objective holding period. But additional standards will have to achieve wide acceptance, too, before a capitalized ANOI will become a standard measurement of value.

This book provides information on analysis as it is commonly practiced today. Analysis changes very slowly over the years (except tax analysis in a tax change year). This summary advocates a change that has already begun to emerge. Real estate investment analysis is unique and is not the same as financial analysis for other areas of business endeavor. Real estate investment analysis is ultimately common sense combined with financial knowledge applied to the measurement of real estate investment opportunities. Analysis techniques must follow their own logic and should not be distorted by the provisions of the Tax Code or other artificial considerations.

APPENDIX I

MAPLEWOOD APARTMENTS

Pro Forma Income & Expense Statement

Potential rental income		$1,014,096
− Vacancy & credit loss		(60,846)
Effective rental income		953,250
+ Other income		11,503
Gross operating income		964,753
	Management fee	40,592
	Other administrative	43,234
	Supplies	–0–
	Heating fuel	–0–
	Electricity	13,439
	Water and sewer	14,335
	Gas	27,392
	Building services	8,350
	Other operating	1,015
	Security	–0–
	Grounds maintenance	20,975
	Maintenance and repairs	66,262
	Painting and decorating	42,531
	Real estate taxes	65,749
	Other tax fees and permits	225
	Insurance	15,100
	Recreation and amenities	16,643
	Other payroll	22,870
− Operating expenses		(398,712)
Net operating income (NOI)		$ 566,041

Assumptions

Purchase price	$6,432,000
− Mortgage balances	(4,785,000)
Equity	1,647,000
+ Loan points	71,775
+ Cost of acquisition	64,320
Initial investment (investment base)	1,783,095

Assumptions (*concluded*)

Loan 1 amount	4,785,000
Loan 1 interest rate	10.25%
Loan 1 amortization periods	360
Purchase capitalization rate	8.8%
Income inflation rate	4%
Vacancy & credit loss rate	6%
Expenses inflation rate	4%
Future capital additions	Yearly Data
Percent of income for reserves	2.5%
Percentage cost of sale	5%
Capitalization rate for sale price	8.8%

Tax Analysis Assumptions

Type of investor	Passive
Capital gain tax rate	34%
Ordinary income tax rate	34%

Forecast

	Pro Forma	Year 1	Year 2	Year 3	Year 4	Year 5
Potential rental income	$1,014,096	$1,014,096	$1,054,660	$1,096,846	$1,140,720	$1,186,349
− Vacancy & credit loss	(60,846)	(60,846)	(63,280)	(65,811)	(68,443)	(71,181)
Effective rental income	953,250	953,250	991,380	1,031,035	1,072,277	1,115,168
+ Other income	11,503	11,503	11,963	12,442	12,939	13,457
Gross operating income	964,753	964,753	1,003,343	1,043,477	1,085,216	1,128,625
− Operating expenses	(398,712)	(398,712)	(414,660)	(431,247)	(448,497)	(466,437)
Net operating income	566,041	566,041	588,683	612,230	636,719	662,188
− Interest		(489,299)	(486,586)	(483,584)	(480,257)	(476,572)
− Cost recovery		(185,258)	(185,926)	(189,488)	(190,156)	(190,825)
− Nonoperating expenses		(2,393)	(2,393)	(2,393)	(2,393)	(2,393)
Taxable income		−0−	−0−	−0−	−0−	−0−
Net operating income		$ 566,041	$ 588,683	$ 612,230	$ 636,719	$ 662,188
− Debt service		(514,536)	(514,536)	(514,536)	(514,536)	(514,536)
− Nonoperating outlays		−0−	−0−	−0−	−0−	−0−
− Capital additions		(4,680)	(4,680)	(85,680)	(4,680)	(4,680)
− Reserves		(25,352)	(26,366)	(27,421)	(28,518)	(29,659)
+ Reserves to additions		4,680	4,680	69,780	4,680	4,680
Cash flow before tax		26,153	47,780	54,373	93,665	117,993
− Tax liability		−0−	−0−	−0−	−0−	−0−
Cash flow after tax		26,153	47,780	54,373	93,665	117,993
Sale price	$6,432,000	$6,689,578	$6,957,161	$7,235,448	$7,524,866	$7,825,860
+ Reserve fund		20,672	42,359	−0−	23,838	48,817
− Loan balances	(4,785,000)	(4,759,763)	(4,731,813)	(4,700,861)	(4,666,582)	(4,628,618)
− Cost of sale		(334,479)	(347,858)	(361,772)	(376,243)	(391,293)
Sale proceeds before tax		1,616,009	1,919,849	2,172,814	2,505,879	2,854,766
− Tax liability on sale		47,917	(71,634)	(176,129)	(321,217)	(479,956)
Sale proceeds after tax		1,663,926	1,848,216	1,996,686	2,184,662	2,374,810
Capitalization rate	8.8%	8.8%	8.8%	8.8%	8.8%	8.8%
IRR before tax		− 7.9%	5.8%	9.0%	11.5%	12.8%
IRR after tax		− 5.2%	3.9%	6.1%	8.0%	9.1%

Sale Proceeds After Tax Analysis

	Year 1	Year 2	Year 3	Year 4	Year 5
Acquisition basis	$6,496,320	$6,496,320	$6,496,320	$6,496,320	$6,496,320
+ Capital additions	4,680	9,360	95,040	99,720	104,400
– Cost recovery	(185,258)	(371,184)	(560,672)	(750,829)	(941,654)
Adjusted basis	6,315,742	6,134,496	6,030,688	5,845,211	5,659,066
Sale price	$6,689,578	$6,957,161	$7,235,448	$7,524,866	$7,825,860
– Cost of sale	(334,479)	(347,858)	(361,772)	(376,243)	(391,293)
– Adjusted basis	(6,315,742)	(6,134,496)	(6,030,688)	(5,845,211)	(5,659,066)
– Suspended losses	(110,908)	(197,130)	(260,364)	(296,451)	(304,052)
– Recapture of cost recovery	–0–	–0–	–0–	–0–	–0–
Capital gain	(71,551)	277,677	582,623	1,006,960	1,471,449
× Capital gain tax rate	34%	34%	34%	34%	34%
Tax on capital gain (savings)	(24,327)	94,410	198,092	342,366	500,293
Recapture of cost recovery	–0–	–0–	–0–	–0–	–0–
– Unamortized expenditures	($69,383)	($66,990)	($64,598)	($62,205)	($59,813)
Ordinary income on sale	(69,383)	(66,990)	(64,598)	(62,205)	(59,813)
× Ordinary income tax rate	34%	34%	34%	34%	34%
Tax on ordinary income (savings)	(23,590)	(22,777)	(21,963)	(21,150)	(20,336)
Sale price	$6,689,578	$6,957,161	$7,235,448	$7,524,866	$7,825,860
+ Reserve fund	20,672	42,359	–0–	23,838	48,817
– Loan balances	(4,759,763)	(4,731,813)	(4,700,861)	(4,666,582)	(4,628,618)
– Cost of sale	(334,479)	(347,858)	(361,772)	(376,243)	(391,293)
Sale proceeds before tax	1,616,009	1,919,849	2,172,814	2,505,879	2,854,766
– Tax on capital gain	24,327	(94,410)	(198,092)	(342,366)	(500,293)
– Tax on ordinary income	23,590	22,777	21,963	21,150	20,336
Sale proceeds after tax	1,663,926	1,848,216	1,996,686	2,184,662	2,374,810

Cost Recovery Schedule

	Cost	Year 1	Year 2	Year 3	Year 4	Year 5
Real improvements	$5,010,500	$178,946	$178,946	$178,946	$178,946	$178,946
Personal property	39,500	5,643	5,643	5,643	5,643	5,643
Capital replacements Y1	4,680	669	669	669	669	669
Capital replacements Y2	4,680		669	669	669	669
Capital replacements Y3	4,680			669	669	669
Capital replacements Y4	4,680				669	669
Capital replacements Y5	4,680					669
Capital addition Y3	81,000			2,893	2,893	2,893
Total yearly cost recovery		$185,258	$185,926	$189,488	$190,156	$190,825

309

Comparative Statistics

	Property	City
Units	100	6,216
Projects	1	38
Average units per project	100	163
Percent of gross possible income		
Income		
Gross possible rental income	98.9%	98.7%
− Vacancies and rent loss	5.9%	5.1%
Total rents collected	92.9%	93.1%
+ Miscellaneous income	1.1%	1.3%
Gross possible income	100.0%	100.0%
Total collections	94.1%	94.9%
Expenses		
Administrative	8.2%	9.0%
Operating	6.3%	6.1%
Maintenance	12.7%	6.8%
Tax and insurance	7.9%	6.2%
Service	1.6%	.3%
Other payroll	2.2%	2.9%
Total	38.9%	34.7%
Net operating income	55.2%	60.1%

Net Operating Income Sensitivity Analysis

Pro Forma

$1,014,096	Potential rental income (PRI)	
(60,846)	− Vacancy and credit loss	6%
953,250	Effective rental income	
11,503	+ Other income	
964,753	Gross operating income	
(398,712)	− Operating expenses	
566,041	Net operating income (NOI)	

Sensitivity Analysis—Net Operating Income—Variables are vacancy and potential rental income

Vacancy PRI	11%	10%	9%	8%	7%	6%	5%	4%	3%	2%	1%
Minus 16%	370,929	379,448	387,966	396,484	405,003	413,521	422,040	430,558	439,076	447,595	456,113
Minus 14%	388,980	397,701	406,423	415,144	423,865	432,586	441,307	450,029	458,750	467,471	476,192
Minus 12%	407,031	415,955	424,879	433,803	442,727	451,651	460,575	469,499	478,423	487,347	496,271
Minus 10%	425,082	434,209	443,336	452,462	461,589	470,716	479,843	488,970	498,097	507,224	516,351
Minus 8%	443,133	452,462	461,792	471,122	480,452	489,781	499,111	508,441	517,770	527,100	536,430
Minus 6%	461,184	470,716	480,249	489,781	499,314	508,846	518,379	527,911	537,444	546,976	556,509
Minus 4%	479,235	488,970	498,705	508,441	518,176	527,911	537,647	547,382	557,117	566,853	576,588
Minus 2%	497,286	507,224	517,162	527,100	537,038	546,976	556,914	566,853	576,791	586,729	596,667
Pro forma	515,336	525,477	535,618	545,759	555,900	566,041	576,182	586,323	596,464	606,605	616,746
Plus 2%	533,387	543,731	554,075	564,419	574,762	585,106	595,450	605,794	616,138	626,481	636,825
Plus 4%	551,438	561,985	572,531	583,078	593,625	604,171	614,718	625,264	635,811	646,358	656,904
Plus 6%	569,489	580,239	590,988	601,737	612,487	623,236	633,986	644,735	655,485	666,234	676,983
Plus 8%	587,540	598,492	609,445	620,397	631,349	642,301	653,253	664,206	675,158	686,110	697,062
Plus 10%	605,591	616,746	627,901	639,056	650,211	661,366	672,521	683,676	694,831	705,986	717,142
Plus 12%	623,642	635,000	646,358	657,716	669,073	680,431	691,789	703,147	714,505	725,863	737,221
Plus 14%	641,693	653,253	664,814	676,375	687,936	699,496	711,057	722,618	734,178	745,739	757,300
Plus 16%	659,744	671,507	683,271	695,034	706,798	718,561	730,325	742,088	753,852	765,615	777,379

Sale Price Sensitivity Analysis

$	566,041		Net operating income (NOI) Year 1
	8.8%		Divided by capitalization rate for sale price (cap rate)
	6,432,000		Sale price—Purchase price (beginning of Year 1)

Sensitivity Analysis—Sale Price—Variables are net operating income and capitalization rate

Cap rate NOI	9.6%	9.4%	9.2%	9.0%	8.8%	8.6%	8.4%	8.2%	8.0%
Minus 16%	4,952,861	5,058,241	5,168,203	5,283,052	5,403,121	5,528,775	5,660,412	5,798,471	5,943,433
Minus 14%	5,070,786	5,178,675	5,291,255	5,408,839	5,531,767	5,660,412	5,795,184	5,936,530	6,084,943
Minus 12%	5,188,711	5,299,109	5,414,308	5,534,625	5,660,412	5,792,050	5,929,956	6,074,589	6,226,454
Minus 10%	5,306,637	5,419,544	5,537,360	5,660,412	5,789,058	5,923,687	6,064,728	6,212,648	6,367,964
Minus 8%	5,424,562	5,539,978	5,660,412	5,786,199	5,917,704	6,055,325	6,199,499	6,350,707	6,509,474
Minus 6%	5,542,487	5,660,412	5,783,465	5,911,986	6,046,350	6,186,962	6,334,271	6,488,765	6,650,985
Minus 4%	5,660,412	5,780,847	5,906,517	6,037,773	6,174,995	6,318,600	6,469,043	6,626,824	6,792,495
Minus 2%	5,778,338	5,901,281	6,029,570	6,163,560	6,303,641	6,450,237	6,603,814	6,764,883	6,934,005
Pro forma	5,896,263	6,021,715	6,152,622	6,289,347	6,432,287	6,581,875	6,738,586	6,902,942	7,075,516
Plus 2%	6,014,188	6,142,150	6,275,675	6,415,134	6,560,933	6,713,512	6,873,358	7,041,001	7,217,026
Plus 4%	6,132,113	6,262,584	6,398,727	6,540,921	6,689,578	6,845,150	7,008,130	7,179,060	7,358,536
Plus 6%	6,250,039	6,383,018	6,521,780	6,666,708	6,818,224	6,976,787	7,142,901	7,317,118	7,500,046
Plus 8%	6,367,964	6,503,453	6,644,832	6,792,495	6,946,870	7,108,425	7,277,673	7,455,177	7,641,557
Plus 10%	6,485,889	6,623,887	6,767,884	6,918,282	7,075,516	7,240,062	7,412,445	7,593,236	7,783,067
Plus 12%	6,603,814	6,744,321	6,890,937	7,044,069	7,204,161	7,371,700	7,547,217	7,731,295	7,924,577
Plus 14%	6,721,740	6,864,755	7,013,989	7,169,856	7,332,807	7,503,337	7,681,988	7,869,354	8,066,088
Plus 16%	6,839,665	6,985,190	7,137,042	7,295,643	7,461,453	7,634,975	7,816,760	8,007,413	8,207,598

APPENDIX II

RIDGELINE OFFICE TOWER

Pro Forma Income & Expense Statement

Potential rental income		$ 763,971
− Vacancy and credit loss		(30,559)
Effective rental income		733,412
+ Other income		4,881
Gross operating income		738,293
	Utilities	88,279
	Janitorial/maintenance & repair	74,473
	Admin/other payroll	33,116
	Insurance/services	51,672
	Real estate taxes	65,279
	Other tax/fee/permits	6,167
− Operating expenses		(318,986)
Net operating income (NOI)		419,307

Assumptions

Purchase price	4,875,000
− Mortgage balances	(3,656,000)
Equity	1,219,000
+ Loan points	36,560
+ Costs of acquisition	48,750
Initial investment (investment base)	1,304,310
Loan 1 amount	3,656,000
Loan 1 interest rate	9.500%
Loan 1 amortization periods	360
Purchase capitalization rate	8.6%
Income inflation rate	Yearly data
Vacancy & credit loss rate	4%
Expenses inflation rate	4%
Future capital additions	Yearly data
Percent of income for reserves	5.0%
Percentage cost of sale	4%
Capitalization rate for sale price	8.6%

Tax Analysis Assumptions

Type of investor	Passive
Capital gain tax rate	34%
Ordinary income tax rate	34%

Forecast

	Pro Forma	Year 1	Year 2	Year 3	Year 4	Year 5
Potential rental income	$ 763,971	$ 763,971	$ 793,497	$ 819,451	$ 849,893	$ 876,493
− Vacancy & credit loss	(30,559)	(30,559)	(31,740)	(32,778)	(33,996)	(35,060)
Effective rental income	733,412	733,412	761,757	786,673	815,897	841,433
+ Other income	4,881	4,881	5,047	5,220	5,400	5,587
Gross operating income	738,293	738,293	766,804	791,893	821,297	847,020
− Operating expenses	(318,986)	(318,986)	(331,745)	(345,015)	(358,816)	(373,169)
Net operating income	419,307	419,307	435,059	446,878	462,481	473,852
− Interest		(346,354)	(344,119)	(341,661)	(338,958)	(335,985)
− Cost recovery		(126,818)	(131,192)	(132,151)	(132,704)	(132,966)
− Nonoperating expenses		(2,473)	(7,615)	(7,615)	(12,726)	(13,121)
Taxable income		—0—	—0—	—0—	—0—	—0—
Net operating income		$ 419,307	$ 435,059	$ 446,878	$ 462,481	$ 473,852
− Debt service		(368,892)	(368,892)	(368,892)	(368,892)	(368,892)
− Nonoperating outlays		(4,086)	(30,856)	0	(30,607)	(2,150)
− Capital additions		(10,930)	(139,979)	(30,658)	(17,700)	(8,409)
− Reserves		(38,199)	(39,675)	(40,973)	(42,495)	(43,825)
+ Reserves to additions		10,930	66,943	30,658	17,700	8,409
Cash flow before tax		8,131	(77,400)	37,013	20,488	58,985
− Tax liability		—0—	—0—	—0—	—0—	—0—
Cash flow after tax		8,131	(77,400)	37,013	20,488	58,985
Sale price	$4,875,000	$5,058,822	$5,196,252	$5,377,691	$5,509,904	$5,663,777
+ Reserve fund		27,269	—0—	10,315	35,109	70,525
− Loan balances	(3,656,000)	(3,633,462)	(3,608,689)	(3,581,458)	(3,551,524)	(3,518,617)
− Cost of sale		(202,353)	(207,850)	(215,108)	(220,396)	(226,551)
Sale proceeds before tax		1,250,276	1,379,713	1,591,440	1,773,093	1,989,133
− Tax liability on sale		15,607	(2,086)	(86,657)	(155,385)	(248,894)
Sale proceeds after tax		1,265,883	1,377,628	1,504,783	1,617,708	1,740,240
Capitalization rate	8.6%	8.6%	8.6%	8.6%	8.6%	8.6%
IRR before tax		−3.5%	0.2%	6.0%	7.7%	9.2%
IRR after tax		−2.3%	0.2%	4.1%	5.3%	6.4%

Sale Proceeds After Tax Analysis

	Year 1	Year 2	Year 3	Year 4	Year 5
Acquisition basis	$4,923,750	$4,923,750	$4,923,750	$4,923,750	$4,923,750
+ Capital additions	10,930	150,909	181,567	199,267	207,676
− Cost recovery	(126,818)	(258,011)	(390,161)	(522,865)	(655,831)
Adjusted basis	4,807,862	4,816,648	4,715,156	4,600,152	4,475,595
Sale price	$5,058,822	$5,196,252	$5,377,691	$5,509,904	$5,663,777
− Cost of sale	(202,353)	(207,850)	(215,108)	(220,396)	(226,551)
− Adjusted basis	(4,807,862)	(4,816,648)	(4,715,156)	(4,600,152)	(4,475,595)
− Suspended losses	(56,338)	(104,205)	(138,754)	(160,659)	(168,880)
− Recapture of cost recovery	–0–	–0–	–0–	–0–	–0–
Capital gain	(7,731)	67,549	308,674	528,697	792,751
× Capital gain tax rate	34%	34%	34%	34%	34%
Tax on capital gain (savings)	(2,628)	22,967	104,949	179,757	269,535
Recapture of cost recovery	–0–	–0–	–0–	–0–	–0–
− Unamortized expenditures	($38,173)	($61,415)	($53,800)	($71,681)	($60,711)
Ordinary income on sale	(38,173)	(61,415)	(53,800)	(71,681)	(60,711)
× Ordinary income tax rate	34%	34%	34%	34%	34%
Tax on ordinary income (savings)	(12,979)	(20,881)	(18,292)	(24,372)	(20,642)
Sale price	$5,058,822	$5,196,252	$5,377,691	$5,509,904	$5,663,777
+ Reserve fund	27,269	–0–	10,315	35,109	70,525
− Loan balances	(3,633,462)	(3,608,689)	(3,581,458)	(3,551,524)	(3,518,617)
− Cost of sale	(202,353)	(207,850)	(215,108)	(220,396)	(226,551)
Sale proceeds before tax	1,250,276	1,379,713	1,591,440	1,773,093	1,989,133
− Tax on capital gain	2,628	(22,967)	(104,949)	(179,757)	(269,535)
− Tax on ordinary income	12,979	20,881	18,292	24,372	20,642
Sale proceeds after tax	1,265,883	1,377,628	1,504,783	1,617,708	1,740,240

Cost Recovery Schedule

	Cost	Year 1	Year 2	Year 3	Year 4	Year 5
Real improvements	$4,047,250	$126,477	$126,477	$126,477	$126,477	$126,477
Personal property	–0–	–0–	–0–	–0–	–0–	–0–
Tenant improvements Y1	10,930	342	342	342	342	342
Tenant improvements Y2	139,979		4,374	4,374	4,374	4,374
Tenant improvements Y3	30,658			958	958	958
Tenant improvements Y4	17,700				553	553
Tenant improvements Y5	8,409					263
Total yearly cost recovery		$126,818	$131,192	$132,151	$132,704	$132,966

Lease Schedule

	Year 1	Year 2	Year 3	Year 4	Year 5	Year 6
1. Transland Insurance	$154,037	$156,335	$158,632	$160,993	$163,354	$165,778
Vacancy	–0–	–0–	–0–	–0–	–0–	–0–
2. IBC	144,962	156,510	162,285	168,059	173,954	179,728
Vacancy	–0–	–0–	–0–	–0–	–0–	–0–
3. Bledsoe & Gatmier	70,304	73,108	76,294	82,524	84,988	88,358
Vacancy	–0–	–0–	19,838	20,631	–0–	–0–
4. Travel Time	15,165	15,769	16,396	16,411	16,425	17,076
Vacancy	–0–	–0–	–0–	–0–	–0–	–0–
5. James R. Luddington, CPA	21,285	22,028	22,764	23,507	23,856	24,376
Vacancy	–0–	–0–	–0–	–0–	5,973	–0–
6. Harvest Sales	168,532	175,151	178,333	185,462	192,844	200,482
Vacancy	–0–	–0–	–0–	–0–	–0–	–0–
7. Future Stock	158,579	162,555	171,426	178,279	185,375	192,717
Vacancy	–0–	82,470	–0–	–0–	–0–	–0–
8. Vacant Space	31,107	32,041	33,320	34,659	35,697	37,107
Vacancy	7,776	–0–	–0–	8,749	–0–	–0–
Total potential rental income	$763,971	$793,497	$819,451	$849,893	$876,493	$905,624
Total vacancy & credit loss	$ 7,776	$ 82,470	$ 19,838	$ 29,380	$ 5,973	–0–
Percent vacancy & credit loss	1%	10%	2%	3%	1%	0%

APPENDIX III

CROSSROADS PLAZA SHOPPING CENTER

Pro Forma Income & Expense Statement

Potential rental income		$ 475,794
− Vacancy and credit loss		(14,274)
Effective rental income		461,520
+ Other income		110,577
Gross operating income		572,097
	Building maintenance	8,947
	Common areas	46,893
	Utilities	3,192
	Office area services	−0−
	Advertising and promotion	4,312
	Real estate taxes	51,783
	Insurance	11,901
	Administration	28,715
	Property management	22,299
− Operating expenses		(178,042)
Net operating income (NOI)		$ 394,055

Assumptions

Purchase price	$4,696,000
− Mortgage balances	(3,522,000)
Equity	1,174,000
+ Loan points	70,440
+ Cost of acquisition	58,700
Initial investment (investment base)	1,303,140
Loan 1 amount	3,522,000
Loan 1 interest rate	9.500%
Loan 1 amortization periods	360
Purchase capitalization rate	8.4%
Income inflation rate	Yearly Data
Vacancy and credit loss rate	3%

Assumptions *(concluded)*

Expenses inflation rate	4%
Future capital additions	Yearly Data
Percent of income for reserves	1.0%
Percentage cost of sale	4%
Capitalization rate for sale price	8.4%

Forecast

	Pro Forma	Year 1	Year 2	Year 3	Year 4	Year 5
Potential rental income	$ 475,794	$ 475,794	$ 501,012	$ 518,387	$ 537,077	$ 557,162
– Vacancy and credit loss	(14,274)	(14,274)	(15,030)	(15,552)	(16,112)	(16,715)
Effective rental income	461,520	461,520	485,982	502,835	520,965	540,447
+ Other income	110,577	110,577	115,001	119,601	124,385	129,360
Gross operating income	572,097	572,097	600,983	622,436	645,350	669,807
– Operating expenses	(178,042)	(178,042)	(185,164)	(192,570)	(200,273)	(208,284)
Net operating income	394,055	394,055	415,819	429,866	445,077	461,523
– Debt service		(355,368)	(355,368)	(355,368)	(355,368)	(355,368)
– Nonoperating outlays		(14,400)	(14,976)	(15,575)	(16,198)	(16,845)
– Capital additions		–0–	–0–	–0–	–0–	–0–
– Reserves		(4,758)	(5,010)	(5,184)	(5,371)	(5,572)
+ Reserves to additions		–0–	–0–	–0–	–0–	–0–
Cash flow before tax		19,529	40,465	53,739	68,140	83,739
Sale price	$4,696,000	$4,950,226	$5,117,454	$5,298,532	$5,494,324	$5,713,717
+ Reserve fund		4,758	9,768	14,952	20,323	25,894
– Loan balances	(3,522,000)	(3,500,294)	(3,476,434)	(3,450,206)	(3,421,374)	(3,389,679)
– Cost of sale		(198,009)	(204,698)	(211,941)	(219,773)	(228,549)
Sale proceeds before tax		1,256,681	1,446,090	1,651,336	1,873,499	2,121,383
Capitalization rate	8.4%	8.4%	8.4%	8.4%	8.4%	8.4%
IRR before tax		-2.1%	7.6%	10.8%	12.4%	13.4%

Lease Schedule

	Year 1	Year 2	Year 3	Year 4	Year 5	Year 6
1. Market Fair	$249,545	$259,527	$269,908	$280,704	$291,932	$303,610
Vacancy	–0–	–0–	–0–	–0–	–0–	–0–
2. Christie's Cleaners	21,835	21,835	21,835	21,835	22,363	23,225
Vacancy	–0–	–0–	–0–	–0–	–0–	–0–
3. Primavera	15,332	15,332	15,332	15,332	15,349	15,963
Vacancy	–0–	–0–	–0–	–0–	–0–	–0–
4. Fallbrook's	11,938	12,568	13,071	13,594	14,137	14,703
Vacancy	–0–	–0–	–0–	–0–	–0–	–0–
5. Screen Scene	16,540	17,202	17,890	18,605	19,349	20,123
Vacancy	–0–	–0–	–0–	–0–	–0–	–0–
6. Electronic Emporium	23,167	31,623	31,716	32,890	34,205	35,573
Vacancy	–0–	2,634	–0–	–0–	–0–	–0–
7. Trimart	92,514	96,215	100,064	104,066	108,229	112,558
Vacancy	–0–	–0–	–0–	–0–	–0–	–0–
8. Yorkshire Table	44,922	46,711	48,571	50,051	51,598	53,661
Vacancy	–0–	–0–	–0–	–0–	–0–	–0–
Total potential rental income	$475,794	$501,012	$518,387	$537,077	$557,162	$579,416
Total vacancy & credit loss	–0–	$ 2,634	–0–	–0–	–0–	–0–
Percent vacancy & credit loss	0%	1%	0%	0%	0%	0%

APPENDIX IV

FOUR-PLEX

Pro Forma (APOD)

Potential rental income		$ 30,816
– Vacancy & credit loss		(1,541)
Effective rental income		29,275
+ Other income		–0–
Gross operating income		29,275
	Real estate taxes	2,090
	Personal property taxes	140
	Property insurance	581
	Offsite management	2,342
	Payroll–On-site personnel	–0–
	Expenses/benefits	–0–
	Taxes/worker's comp.	–0–
	Repairs and maintenance	902
	Utilities	880
	Accounting and legal	320
	RE leasing commissions	–0–
	Adv/licenses/permits	275
	Supplies	706
	Miscellaneous	1,296
	Contract services	1,020
– Operating expenses		(10,552)
Net operating income (NOI)		$ 18,723

Assumptions

Purchase price	$191,250
– Mortgage balances	(153,000)
Equity	38,250
+ Loan points	2,295
+ Cost of acquisition	478
Initial investment (investment base)	41,023
Loan 1 amount	153,000
Loan 1 interest rate	9.500%
Loan 1 amortization periods	360

Assumptions *(concluded)*

Purchase capitalization rate	9.8%
Income inflation rate	4%
Vacancy & credit loss rate	5%
Expenses inflation rate	4%
Future capital additions	Yearly Data
Percent of income for reserves	1.0%
Percentage cost of sale	6%
Capitalization rate for sale price	9.8%

Tax Analysis Assumptions

Type of investor	Active
Capital gain tax rate	28%
Ordinary income tax rate	28%

Forecast

	Pro Forma	Year 1	Year 2	Year 3	Year 4	Year 5
Potential rental income	$30,816	$30,816	$32,049	$33,331	$34,664	$36,050
– Vacancy & credit loss	(1,541)	(1,541)	(1,602)	(1,667)	(1,733)	(1,803)
Effective rental income	29,275	29,275	30,446	31,664	32,931	34,248
+ Other income	–0–	–0–	–0–	–0–	–0–	–0–
Gross operating income	29,275	29,275	30,446	31,664	32,931	34,248
– Operating expenses	(10,552)	(10,552)	(10,974)	(11,413)	(11,870)	(12,344)
Net operating income	18,723	18,723	19,472	20,251	21,061	21,903
– Interest		(14,494)	(14,402)	(14,300)	(14,188)	(14,064)
– Cost recovery		(6,038)	(6,038)	(6,038)	(6,038)	(6,038)
– Nonoperating expenses		(77)	(77)	(77)	(77)	(77)
Taxable income		(1,885)	(1,044)	(163)	759	1,725
Net operating income		$18,723	$19,472	$20,251	$21,061	$21,903
– Debt service		(15,432)	(15,432)	(15,432)	(15,432)	(15,432)
– Nonoperating outlays		–0–	–0–	–0–	–0–	–0–
– Capital additions		–0–	–0–	–0–	–0–	–0–
– Reserves		(308)	(320)	(333)	(347)	(361)
+ Reserves to additions		–0–	–0–	–0–	–0–	–0–
Cash flow before tax		2,983	3,720	4,486	5,282	6,111
– Tax liability		528	292	46	(213)	(483)
Cash flow after tax		3,511	4,012	4,531	5,070	5,628
Sale price	$191,250	$198,695	$206,643	$214,909	$223,505	$232,445
+ Reserve fund		308	629	962	1,309	1,669
– Loan balances	(153,000)	(152,062)	(151,032)	(149,900)	(148,656)	(147,288)
– Cost of sale		(11,922)	(12,399)	(12,895)	(13,410)	(13,947)
Sale proceeds before tax		35,020	43,841	53,076	62,747	72,880
– Tax liability on sale		184	(3,620)	(7,507)	(11,482)	(15,547)
Sale proceeds after tax		35,204	40,221	45,569	51,266	57,333
Capitalization rate	9.8%	9.8%	9.8%	9.8%	9.8%	9.8%
IRR before tax		– 7.4%	11.4%	17.2%	19.6%	20.6%
IRR after tax		– 5.6%	8.2%	12.9%	15.2%	16.4%

Sale Proceeds After Tax Analysis

	Year 1	Year 2	Year 3	Year 4	Year 5
Acquisition basis	$191,250	$191,250	$191,250	$191,250	$191,250
+ Capital additions	–0–	–0–	–0–	–0–	–0–
– Cost recovery	(6,038)	(12,075)	(18,113)	(24,150)	(30,188)
Adjusted basis	185,213	179,175	173,138	167,100	161,063
Sale price	$198,695	$206,643	$214,909	$223,505	$232,445
– Cost of sale	(11,922)	(12,399)	(12,895)	(13,410)	(13,947)
– Adjusted basis	(185,213)	(179,175)	(173,138)	(167,100)	(161,063)
– Suspended losses	–0–	–0–	–0–	–0–	–0–
– Recapture of cost recovery	–0–	–0–	–0–	–0–	–0–
Capital gain	1,561	15,069	28,877	42,995	57,436
× Capital gain tax rate	28%	28%	28%	28%	28%
Tax on capital gain (savings)	437	4,219	8,085	12,039	16,082
Recapture of cost recovery	–0–	–0–	–0–	–0–	–0–
– Unamortized expenditures	($2,219)	($2,142)	($2,066)	($1,989)	($1,913)
Ordinary income on sale	(2,219)	(2,142)	(2,066)	(1,989)	(1,913)
× Ordinary income tax rate	28%	28%	28%	28%	28%
Tax on ordinary income (savings)	(621)	(600)	(578)	(557)	(536)
Sale price	$198,695	$206,643	$214,909	$223,505	$232,445
+ Reserve fund	308	629	962	1,309	1,669
– Loan balances	(152,062)	(151,032)	(149,900)	(148,656)	(147,288)
– Cost of sale	(11,922)	(12,399)	(12,895)	(13,410)	(13,947)
Sale proceeds before tax	35,020	43,841	53,076	62,747	72,880
– Tax on capital gain	(437)	(4,219)	(8,085)	(12,039)	(16,082)
– Tax on ordinary income	621	600	578	557	536
Sale proceeds after tax	35,204	40,221	45,569	51,266	57,333

Cost Recovery Schedule

	Cost	Year 1	Year 2	Year 3	Year 4	Year 5
Real improvements	$157,850	$5,638	$5,638	$5,638	$5,638	$5,638
Personal property	2,800	400	400	400	400	400
Total yearly cost recovery		6,038	6,038	6,038	6,038	6,038

BIBLIOGRAPHY

Appraisal

Appraisal of Real Estate, 9th ed. Chicago: Appraisal Institute, 1987.

Development

Miles, Mike E.; Emil E. Malizia; Marc A. Weiss; Gayle L. Berens; and Ginger Travis. *Real Estate Development*. Washington, D.C.: Urban Land Institute, 1991.

Economics

Rothschild, Michael. *Bionomics*. New York: Henry Holt, 1990.

Sullivan, Arthur M. *Urban Economics*. Homewood, Ill.: Richard D. Irwin, 1990.

Feasibility

Barrett, G. Vincent, and John P. Blair. *How to Conduct & Analyze Real Estate Market & Feasibility Studies*, 2nd ed. New York: Van Nostrand Reinhold, 1988.

Carn, Neil; Joseph Rabianski; Ronald Racster; and Maury Seldin. *Real Estate Market Analysis*. Englewood Cliffs, N.J.: Prentice Hall, 1988.

Roca, Ruben A., ed. *Market Research for Shopping Centers*. New York: International Council of Shopping Centers, 1988.

Seldin, Maury, and James H. Boykin, eds. *Real Estate Analysis*. Homewood, Ill.: Richard D. Irwin, 1990.

General

Gettel, Ronald E. *Real Estate Guidelines and Rules of Thumb.* New York: McGraw-Hill, 1976.

Investment and Taxation

Messner, Stephen D.; Victor L. Lyon; Robert L. Ward; and Charles Freedenberg. *Real Estate Investment and Taxation,* 4th ed. Englewood Cliffs, N.J.: Prentice Hall, 1991.

Investment Real Estate

Greer, Gaylon E. and Michael D. Farrell. *Investment Analysis for Real Estate Decisions,* 2nd ed. Chicago: Longman Financial Services, 1988.

Plattner, Robert H. *Real Estate Investment Analysis and Management.* Columbus, Ohio: Merrill, 1988.

Pyhrr, Stephen A.; James R. Cooper; Larry E. Wofford; Steven D. Kapplin; and Paul D. Lapides. *Real Estate Investment Strategy, Analysis, Decisions,* 2nd ed. New York: John Wiley & Sons, 1989.

Wiedemer, John P. *Real Estate Investment,* 4th ed. Englewood Cliffs, N.J.: Prentice Hall, 1989.

Corporate Real Estate

Nourse, Hugh O. *Managerial Real Estate.* Englewood Cliffs, N.J.: Prentice Hall, 1990.

Property Management

Downs, James C. *Principles of Real Estate Management.* Chicago: Institute of Real Estate Management, 1980.

Tax

Levine, Mark Lee. *Real Estate Transactions Tax Planning and Consequences.* St. Paul, Minn.: West, 1991.

Robinson, Gerald J. *Federal Income Taxation of Real Estate,* 5th ed. New York: Warren Gorham & Lamont, 1988.

Underwriting

Britton, James A., Jr., and Lewis O. Kerwood. *Financing Income-Producing Real Estate*. New York: McGraw-Hill, 1977.

Natale, Robert A. *Property Specific Commercial Mortgage Underwriting*. Scottsdale, Ariz.: Todd, 1992.

GLOSSARY

abatement The abatement of rent for a certain period offered to a potential tenant to induce the tenant to lease space.

absorption study An analysis of the appropriate market to determine how much additional space (square feet) or how many additional units (residential) the market will demand within a defined time period.

accelerated cost recovery The uneven amortization of the cost of a capital addition with the initial amortization payments being in excess of straight line cost recovery.

acquisition The purchase of an income property.

active investor An investor eligible (under the Tax Code) to apply current income property losses against non–real estate income.

adjustable rate mortgage A mortgage for which the interest rate adjusts periodically based on a published yield index.

adjusted basis The original basis of the property (at purchase) adjusted for cost recovery (decrease) and capital additions (increase).

adjusted internal rate of return A modified version of the internal rate of return designed to make the IRR more accurate for a specific investor. See Chapter 42.

adjusted net operating income The net operating income adjusted to reflect the effect of regularly occurring non–operating expenditures. See Part 9 Book Summary.

AIRR See adjusted internal rate of return.

allocation The allocation of the cost (value) of the property between its component parts such as land, improvements, and personal property.

amortize The payments required to reduce an amount over multiple time periods.

anchor tenant A large tenant in a shopping center that creates a large volume of customer traffic.

Annual Property Operating Data A widely used income & expense statement form published by the Commercial Investment Real Estate Institute.

ANOI See adjusted net operating income.

annuity Even payments over multiple time periods.

APOD See Annual Property Operating Data.

balloon payment The balance due on the loan, if any, at the end of the loan term.

base rent The beginning rent or minimum rent before adjustment for inflation or for percentage rent.

basis A concept defined by the Tax Code used to calculate the capital gain or loss for an investment.

buy-out The cost to the owner of paying off a potential tenant's landlord in another building to release the potential tenant to become a new tenant in the owner's building.

CAMs See common area maintenance.

cap rate See capitalization rate.

capital additions The improvements or replacements required by the Tax Code to be amortized for purposes of tax deductibility. See Chapter 15.

capital gain The difference, generally, between the sale price of the property and the adjusted basis, as defined by the Tax Code.

capitalization rate The ratio between the net operating income and the value of the property. See Chapter 39.

carry-back loan A loan provided by the seller to the buyer to purchase the property, often a second loan.

cash flow after tax The annual amount of funds flowing into (or out of) an investor's pocket as a result of owning the property, after income tax has been paid or tax shelter has been applied. See Chapter 20.

cash flow before tax The annual amount of funds flowing into (or out of) an investor's pocket as a result of owning the property and calculated before income tax liability is considered. See Chapter 18.

CFAT See cash flow after tax.

CFBT See cash flow before tax.

common area maintenance The maintenance expense of the common areas of a shopping center or other building for which the landlord is reimbursed by the tenants.

compound interest table A series of tables, now made obsolete by financial calculators, giving the multiplication factors to be used in the calculations of discounted cash flow analysis.

concession   A concession (incentive) offered to a potential tenant to induce the tenant to lease space.

Consumer Price Indexes   The in multiple versions governmental publications of statistics regarding the rate of inflation.

contract services   The services necessary for the operation of an income property contracted with a subcontractor by a property manager on behalf of the landlord.

cost of sale   The real estate broker's commissions, closing costs, and other expenses incurred by the investor upon sale of the property. See Chapter 24.

cost recovery   The annual depreciation for improvements and personal property allowed by the Tax Code. See Chapter 9.

CPI   See Consumer Price Indexes.

credit loss   The loss to the landlord due to the nonpayment of rent by a tenant occupying space.

credit tenant   A large corporate tenant with excellent and verifiable credit.

debt coverage ratio   The ratio of the net operating income to the annual debt service.

deposits   The deposits made by tenants to secure the payment of rent.

depreciation   See cost recovery.

discounted cash flow analysis   Financial analysis that is based on compound yields. See Chapter 40.

discount rate   The market rate of return chosen for net present value analysis.

due diligence   The thorough investigation of a property and its market prior to a purchase.

effective rental income   The potential rental income less vacancy & credit loss. See Chapter 3.

economic life   The number of years an income property is anticipated to be usable without a major rehab.

end of year   The basis on which virtually all discounted cash flow analysis is done for real estate calculations.

equity   The difference between the value of the property and the loan balances on the loans secured by the property.

EOY   See end of year.

equity build-up   The increase in equity due to a reduction in the mortgage balances or an increase in the value of the property, or both.

feasibility study   A combination of a market study, a marketability study, and an investment analysis. See Chapter 43.

financial management rate of return A modified version of the internal rate of return designed to make the IRR more accurate for a specific investor. See Chapter 42.

FMRR See financial management rate of return.

forecast The pro forma estimate of the performance of an income property for one year or for multiple years.

free and clear rate See capitalization rate.

free rent A rent abatement (concession, incentive) offered to a potential tenant to induce the tenant to lease space.

gross operating income The potential rental income less vacancy & credit loss and plus other income. See Chapter 5.

Gross Possible Income The divisor (potential rental income + other income) used in the Institute of Real Estate Management statistical publications to determine income and expense percentages.

ground lease See land lease.

holding period The length of time an investor anticipates the property will be owned (from purchase to sale).

incentive The incentive (concession) offered to a potential tenant to induce the tenant to lease space.

initial investment The down payment, acquisition costs, loan points, and other costs, if any, of making an investment in an income property.

institutional investor A large financial institution investor such as an insurance company, a national syndicator, or a pension fund.

interest expense The annual amount of interest paid on a loan or loans. See Chapter 8.

internal rate of return A measurement of investment return for irregular cash flows. See Chapter 42.

investment base The initial investment for a property to be acquired, or the determination of the equivalent amount for a property already owned for the purposes of comparison to current investment opportunities.

investment grade A general standard of quality and acceptability for income properties used by institutional investors.

IRR See internal rate of return.

irregular cash flow A series of cash flows in which at least one of the cash flows is not the same as the others.

land lease A lease of the land only wherein the tenant has the responsibility of building and maintaining the improvements.

leasing commissions The contingent fees paid to licensed real estate brokers for finding tenants for an income property.

line entry The individual lines in the pro forma forecast. Note: some line entries are not input but rather are resultant numbers from the calculations on the forecast itself.

loan balances The unpaid balances on the real estate loans at the time of sale. See Chapter 23.

loan point A loan fee equal to 1 percent of the loan amount.

loan to value ratio The ratio of the loan amount to the appraised value of the property.

management fee The fee paid to a property manager.

management-intensive A term used to describe business activities that require a high level of management and are beyond the scope of normal property management.

marginal tax bracket The tax bracket in which each *additional* dollar of the investor's income is taxed.

market research The market surveys, economic statistical research, and other information gathering directed at establishing economic information about an appropriate market.

market survey A survey of the appropriate market to establish market rents or other economic or economic-related statistics.

market rents The rent that tenants will pay to occupy space or units usually verified by a market study.

minimodel The name this book gives to the financial model built into financial calculators.

MIRR See modified internal rate of return.

modified internal rate of return A modified version of the internal rate of return designed to make the IRR more accurate for a specific investor. See Chapter 42.

mortgage constant The ratio of the loan amortization payment to the amount of the loan.

negative cash flow A cash flow "loss" that must be covered by the investor.

negative yield A return on investment that yields less than the investment amount.

net operating income The potential rental income less vacancy & credit loss, plus other income, and less operating expenses. See Chapter 7.

net present value An analysis for measuring irregular cash flows. See Chapter 42.

NOI   See net operating income.

non–operating expenses   The tax deductible expenses which are not operating expenses. See Chapter 10.

non–operating outlays   The expenditures related to the property which are not operating expenses. See Chapter 14.

NPV   See net present value.

ordinary income   The income not resulting from capital gains.

overall rate   See capitalization rate.

paper expense (loss)   An amortized portion of an expense incurred in another year, deductible for tax purposes in the current year, that does not affect the cash flow for the current year.

participation loan   A loan in which the lender is paid a portion of the net operating income and sale proceeds as additional interest to the stated interest rate or a loan that gives a lender an equity interest.

participation payments   Those payments on a participation loan that are in addition to the debt service resulting from the stated interest rate.

passive investor   An investor not eligible (under the Tax Code) to apply current income property losses against non–real estate income.

percentage rent   The rent calculated as a percentage of a retail tenant's gross sales.

periodic payment   See annuity.

potential rental income   100 percent of the market rent for all the space rented 100 percent of the time. See Chapter 1.

pro forma   A forecast of the performance of an income property expressed in a written report in a customary format.

projection   See forecast.

property tax   The ad valorum tax levied on real estate by the county and other municipalities.

occupancy rate   The percentage occupancy of a building.

on-site   The property management personnel or other employees or agents of the owner located at the property.

operating expenses   The expenses necessary to the operation of the property regardless of ownership. See Chapter 6.

opportunity rate   A discount rate based the ability of the investor to reinvest money in the most favorable investment that is reasonably available to the investor. See Chapter 42.

opportunity cost of capital   The rate of return on the most favorable available alternative investment. See Chapter 42.

other income The non–management-intensive, non–rental income related to the operation of the property. See Chapter 4.

recapture The amount of cost recovery recaptured by the Tax Code upon sale due to the earlier election of accelerated cost recovery.

rehabilitation A substantial improvement to the existing improvements designed to maintain or increase the revenue of the property.

rehab See rehabilitation.

reimbursements The reimbursement to the landlord by the tenants of certain operating expenses.

reinvestment rate A discount rate based the ability of the investor to reinvest money in an investment that is readily available to the investor. See Chapter 42.

rent schedule A list of space or units showing the occupant (tenant), if any, and the rent being paid (by the tenant) or the market rent (for vacant space).

rent survey A market survey done to establish rent statistics.

repairs and maintenance The minor repairs and maintenance not considered to be capital additions.

replacements (capital replacements) The personal property or improvements expected to be replaced on an annually recurring basis.

reserves The funds subtracted from cash flow and placed in a reserve account to cover capital additions. See Chapter 16.

reserve fund The amount of unspent funds in the reserve account. See Chapter 22.

reserves to additions The funds in a reserve account which are used to pay for capital additions. See Chapter 17.

reversion An investment amount that reverts to the investor at the end of the investment.

taxable income That portion of income from a property which is taxable to a specific investor. See Chapter 11.

tax liability on sale The income tax paid or tax shelter applied as a result of the sale of the property. See Chapter 26.

tenant allowance A budget, usually funded by the landlord, to complete minimal tenant improvements.

tenant improvements The cost of materials and labor required to build a tenant's space within a building.

tenant mix The categorization of multiple tenants by type of service or type of retail sales.

TIs See tenant improvements.

safe rate A discount rate based on a low risk investment.

sale and leaseback The sale of a property by a credit tenant that maintains occupancy and leases the property from the new owner after the sale.

sale price The price for which the property is sold at the end of the investor's holding period. See Chapter 21.

sale proceeds after tax The cash flow into (or out of) an investor's pocket resulting from the sale of the property after the income tax is paid. See Chapter 27.

sale proceeds before tax The cash flow into (or out of) an investor's pocket resulting from the sale of the property before income taxation is considered. See Chapter 25.

sensitivity analysis A table showing how a resultant number will change due to changes in one or more variables.

sign convention The practice of labeling negative cash flows with a negative sign for calculator or computer input and output.

sinking fund The annuity required for a future value. See Chapter 41.

straight line cost recovery The even amortization of the cost of a capital addition.

suspended losses The income property income tax losses not allowed to be applied to current non–real estate income by the Tax Code but which offset gain upon the sale of the property.

T-chart A cash flow diagram also known as a T-account or a T-bar.

Tax Code The Internal Revenue Statutes of the United States.

tax liability The annual income tax due or the annual tax shelter applied resulting from a specific owner's investment in and operation of the property. See Chapter 19.

tax shelter The tax losses incurred in the ownership of income property that are permitted by the Tax Code to offset non–real estate income.

unamortized expenditures The remaining unamortized amount at sale of an expenditure required to be amortized under the Tax Code.

vacancy & credit loss The lost of rent due to lack of occupancy or nonpayment of rent. See Chapter 2.

vacancy rate The vacancy & credit loss expressed as a percentage of potential rental income.

INDEX